ANIMAL
TRACKS

ANIMAL TRACKS

Text by Miroslav Bouchner

BLITZ EDITIONS

Picture Acknowledgements

153 colour photographs by: M. Anděra (4), L. Bartoš (5), M. Blahout (1), M. Bouchner (10), J. Červený (2), J. Cibulka (1), P. Fišer (1), J. Formánek (4), M. Hain (1), Z. Humpál (1), L. Kunc (3), V. Motl (1), J. Motyčka (1), V. Novák (1), J. Pavlásek (1), P. Pavlík (65), P. Rödl (16), J. Ševčík (2), E. Studnička (17), F. Tvrz (1), J. Zumr (15)

175 b/w photographs by: L. Bartoš (4), M. Bouchner (88), J. Chlumský (3), J. Cibulka (2), J. Formánek (4), J. Hanzák (6), L. Kunc (1), V. Novák (26), P. Pavlík (2), P. Rödl (11), J. Ševčík (4), E. Studnička (11), J. Zumr (13)

425 line drawings and 46 colour illustrations by Miloš Váňa

Text by Miroslav Bouchner
Translated by Olga Kuthanová
Graphic design by Joska Skalník

Designed and produced by Aventinum Publishing House, Prague, Czech Republic
This English edition published 1999 by Blitz Editions, an imprint of Bookmart Ltd.
Registered Number 2372865
Trading as Bookmart Limited
Desford Road, Enderby, Leicester LE9 5AD

ISBN 1-85605-442-X
Printed in the Czech Republic by Polygrafia, a.s., Prague
3/07/11/51-03

Contents

Foreword

Animals reveal their presence in the wild in a variety of ways. If you are lucky, you can see and identify them by direct observation, but this is usually possible only when a species is present in large numbers in a locality or when the animals are not unduly shy. Have you ever wondered why you encounter different species of birds on your rambles but rarely come across a mammal? The reasons are relatively simple: there are far more species of birds than there are mammal species, birds have a wide range of distinctive vocal expressions, and they are mostly active during the day. On the other hand mammals are mostly active during the night or at twilight; during the day they are hidden in well-concealed hideouts. Like most birds, we are creatures of diurnal habits and that is why we do not often encounter mammals.

Many people out for a walk in woods or forests are disappointed when they do not catch a glimpse of a Red Deer or Roe Deer after being told there were plenty of both species in the area they visited. What they do not realize is that they would get a lot more out of their country walks if they noticed the many tracks and signs that animals leave behind them. These markings would tell them which mammals and birds had been in the area and also about the habits, behaviour, diet and rearing of the offspring of the animals — in short, about everything the animals had just been doing.

There are a great many such signs to watch out for, and only those who are in constant touch with nature, are patient and very observant, will be able to read them easily. Even quite insignificant signs can indicate the presence and even the behaviour of a given animal. You do not always need actual tracks — paw, hoof or toe prints. Often all that is required for identification are signs, such as an animal's dwelling place, feeding remains, feeding damage on fruits and seeds, farm crops and trees, food caches, droppings, meeting grounds and resting places, bird feathers shed during the moult, or the bodily or skeletal remains of animals that have died through natural causes or been killed. Tracks and signs can be found in whatever part of the world you live in. Although the natural environment is being increasingly destroyed by the inroads of civilization, there are still plenty of wild animals to be found there and many opportunities for tracking them.

The art of reading tracks and signs dates well back into our earliest history. As soon as early man began to hunt for food he had to learn the habits of his prey, for otherwise he would have never caught anything. We know from archaeological finds that prehistoric man was extraordinarily inventive and with the aid of primitive weapons and traps was able to capture and kill even such large strong animals as bears and mammoths. However, there is no need to go that far back in history. Even today there are still groups of people living in remote parts of the world, such as the Kalahari Desert, for whom hunting forms an important part of their way of life. The art of reading tracks and knowledge of animal habits is for them a question of life and death.

Originally, then, tracking was an inseparable part of hunting and it continues to figure, but to a lesser degree, in some forms of modern game management. Well-equipped hunters today may not even need to track at all. For example, tracking may well be superfluous on an organized hare hunt. The same applies to pheasant and partridge shoots, although on these the hunters need some knowledge of the birds' habits and whereabouts. On hunts for large game animals, however, one must be able to read tracks (unless, of course, the preferred form of hunting is sitting on a raised platform and waiting until the game comes within shooting range!). When hunting such animals, the hunter must be able to identify tracks and read all necessary information from them, he must know the pathways regularly treaded by the game, he must also be able to determine the presence of the animals by such signs as droppings, trampled vegetation, scrapes and feeding damage on trees and bushes, and he must likewise be able to pinpoint them by their calls. When the Red Deer rut begins in mid-September the roaring of the males (stags) can be heard from miles away. Experienced hunters are well versed in these roarings and can tell if the rutting stag is young or old, if he is looking for a mate or already has a harem, if his bellow is a challenge to wage battle, an angry threat to a troublesome antagonist, a command when he is herding hinds or a cry of weariness at the end of an exhausting rut. Some hunters can even locate by smell a concealed stag that is not making any sounds, for during the rut the stag has a pronounced musky odour. This ability also belongs to the art of tracking.

The art of reading tracks, however, is not limited to hunting. The modern gamekeeper observes principles that are very different from the habits of our ancestors. First and foremost he breeds and takes care of gamebirds and animals and only if circumstances permit does he also hunt. In the future, it will be increasingly important to breed and care and not hunt for wildlife because the numbers of some game animals are becoming seriously depleted. One of the cornerstones of wildlife management is knowledge of the numbers of game populations and the changes that occur in each population during the year. The winter census tells the gamekeeper how many animals there will be in the coming breeding season and so it is important that he can read tracks in freshly fallen snow. Tracks in snow also tell him what predators there are in his area, whether or not their number poses a threat to the other animals, whether poaching cats and dogs are roaming about or whether a human poacher is at work there.

Being able to read tracks and other signs is also important for foresters, farmers and fruit-growers. Many animals like feeding on cultivated plants. When they roam over a large territory or are of solitary habit the damage they do to crops passes unnoticed. However, when plant-eating animals occupy only a small territory and occur together in great numbers, the crop damage can be pronounced. The kind of feeding damage, the tracks on the ground, droppings and other signs aid in the identification of the culprit so making it easier for effective measures to be taken to prevent or at least lessen the damage.

Woodland animals may damage the bark of mature trees, or they may eat young seedlings, seeds and fruits. Fruit growers bemoan the nibbling of trees, emerging buds and ripening fruits. Even beehives are not immune to the visits of unwelcome creatures. They are often damaged, particularly in winter, by woodpeckers that peck at the hive with their beaks till they get at the hibernating bees, which they then eat. Small rodents cause great damage to cereals and root crops in storehouses. They may even eat into water pipes, electric cables and telephone wires. In order to prevent such damage it is necessary to know the originator. Thus, the seemingly ordinary knowledge of being able to read tracks and signs proves to be an important factor in economic terms, and a whole new branch of science has evolved to deal with the problem of the mechanical and chemical control of animal pests of all shapes and sizes. Some thermoplastic products now have rat and mice repellents added to them.

These are just a few examples of how the art of reading animal tracks can be usefully applied. The tracking of animals also has its place in the cultural and ethical sides of our life.

In today's overcrowded world more and more people are escaping from noisy, dusty and smoky cities to seek respite in wild places. Perhaps it is the excess of technology that is making us take an interest in living things, so that we want to know and understand more about nature than our predecessors did. Each walk in the countryside can be an exciting adventure if we know how to go about unveiling nature's secrets.

Wildlife Habitats

It is often assumed that wild animals move freely from place to place and that there are no boundaries to prevent them from doing so. To us birds represent the ideal of unfettered freedom because they can fly. They give one the impression that they have a life of complete independence, that today they are here but tomorrow they will be miles and miles away. However, by observing a specific bird for a length of time you will soon discover that you have been deceived. Every individual, pair or group of animals is confined fairly rigidly to a specific area with established boundaries within which it ranges and which it rarely leaves. This area, called the home range, includes an even smaller area called the territory. The territory is an area with which the animal is thoroughly acquainted; it knows where the best sources of food and water are, where there are places of concealment, and it marks out the boundaries in some way and tries to exclude other individuals of the same species from it.

Each territory is divided up into various parts which are used by the respective animal species for different purposes. A stag's territory must have a wallowing place and trees against which the animal can rub, but it does not need a dust-bath, which is a must for the daily hygiene of partridges. A shrike's territory must have a thorny shrub on which the bird can impale its prey as a food reserve whereas that of the Little Owl, which stores its food in tree cavities, must include trees suitable for the purpose. Essentially every territory must include places where the animal feeds or hunts food, places where it sleeps, where it has its dwelling place (a burrow, rock or tree cavity, dense thickets, nest and suchlike places) where it cleans and grooms itself, places where it puts its droppings, and places where it leaves the signs that mark its territorial rights. In general the Earth's surface is divided into milliards of small or large territories inhabited by various species of animals. Such territorial division enables better utilization of the whole environment and prevents competition between individuals of the same species.

Remember, however, that a given territory is not occupied just by one but many animal species. The Roe Deer buck defends his territory against another buck, the Kingfisher against another Kingfisher, the Pine Marten against another Pine Marten. However, the Roe Deer buck does not mind if he shares his territory with a Brown Hare, Pheasant, Woodcock, Common Shrew, Blue Tit or insects, just as the Kingfisher does not mind the presence of a Muskrat, Blackbird, Water Vole and other animals. But each territory must be large enough to feed and meet the needs of the respective individual, pair, family or band. The size of territories is thus not always the same. It is determined by the animal's size and population density, by its age and sex, by the kind of food it eats, by the carrying capacity and the configuration of the terrain, and by the season of the year. The Roe Deer buck selects and defends a territory large enough to provide him with sufficient food throughout the year. If he defends a territory that is too small then he would put himself in danger of going hungry because he would graze up and perhaps even destroy all the vegetation, which would not have time to grow again. This would interfere with the natural balance of the environment — there would be a discrepancy between the amount of food available and the amount consumed. The buck's very existence would thus be endangered.

The size of a territory of a particular species, however, is not always the same throughout the animal's entire range. A significant factor in this case is the carrying capacity of the particular habitat, in other words the amount of food available there. In fertile lowlands where good soil and climatic conditions ensure a lush growth of vegetation, the territory of a Brown Hare is much smaller than in the mountains where plant growth is poorer and where hares must forage for food over a far greater area. In general the territory of plant eaters (herbivores) is usually smaller than that of meat eaters (carnivores), which feed on the herbivores; but remember that a Fox in a mountainous region has a far larger home range than its relatives in the lowlands, which have a surplus of small rodents and other prey to feed on. If a gamekeeper cites the population density of game in a specific hunting ground or in a larger area then he is indirectly telling you the carrying capacity of that environment. In fertile lowlands the population density of hares is higher than in less fertile highlands where the density per unit of area decreases.

As yet there is little specific information about the size of the territories of individual animal species, the main reason for this being that observing an animal, unless it has been conspicuously marked by man, is extremely difficult and time consuming. An added difficulty is the habit of many mammals of being active only during the night. On the whole the territory of animals varies according to the size of the species. The territory of small rodents, such as voles and mice, is no larger than several square metres or several tens of square metres. The same is true in the case of certain species of lizards, frogs, and fish. A small fish, such as the Minnow, is content with a very small pool; the Common Vole feeds on plants only in the immediate vicinity of its burrow; but the Yellow-necked Mouse and shrews, which have a specialized diet, inhabit a territory of several hundred square metres. The territory of the Mute Swan covers about 1 km^2, that of the Roe Deer about 10 ha, that of the Red Deer is about 25 ha, and that of large carnivores many square kilometres — the Brown Bear's territory is 10 to 30 km^2 and the Tiger's is about 1,000 km^2 (the Tiger's is the largest territory known). The size of the defended territory also depends on the sex and age of the respective individual. As a rule the territory of females and young males is smaller than that of strong adult males.

Animals mark the boundaries of their territories in distinctive ways characteristic for each species. They use various marks or signs that are comprehensible to every other member of the same species and clearly indicate that crossing the boundary into alien territory means danger of attack. These signs may by visual, acoustic or olfactory (that is chemical), or they may occur in combination. Whereas we can easily perceive the visual and acoustic signs, we are at a disadvantage in respect of olfactory signs because we can distinguish only a fraction of the many natural odours.

Acoustic signs or sounds used by animals to mark their territories are extremely diverse and vary in pitch, intensity, modulation and interval. When they are produced by air passing over a system of membranes in the respiratory tract they are called vocal sounds. There are many other ways of producing sounds. For example, some snakes rub their scales together or shake specially adapted segments at the end of the tail to produce a rattling or buzzing sound; storks clap their beaks; hoofed animals thump the ground, and so on. Birds produce the most highly developed vocal sound signals — their songs — and these are what we admire the most. The melodious trills of warblers, the bubbling song of the Nightingale, and the grating cry of the Partridge are nothing more than signals informing other warblers, nightingales and partridges that the territory within the voice's range is occupied. The bird's song thus has a practical purpose and the explanation for it is simple. When he sings the male is also trying to attract a female to his territory; the song is definitely not for his or her pleasure and not in the least for our enjoyment.

Visual signs are very conspicuous and generally catch the attention of other animals besides those for which they are intended. They are widely understood and widely used. The same signal is often used by various species but may have a different meaning for each group of animals. For example, raised mouth corners and bared teeth are a threatening gesture in the Tiger, an expression of uncertainty in the Chimpanzee and a smile in Man. Visual signs are also extremely diverse: many animal species have striking colour markings on the body, which may be permanently or only temporarily visible; others posture in various ways or change the volume and shape of the body or its parts. For example, the face masks of some antelopes are a permanent characteristic, but the white patch on the rump of the Roe Deer and Red Deer is exposed only when danger threatens. Animals raise or flatten their hair, feathers, ears, inflate their bodies, and so on, all as means of visual communication.

On the whole, mammals mark their territory with scent signs. The Badger, for instance, has a special sac-like scent gland above the anal opening that produces a musky odour with which it marks important objects throughout its territory. This it does by pressing its hind end on the respective object, as if to sit on it. In this manner it marks stones, tree stumps, tree trunks and even bare ground on the regular pathways that traverse its territory. Other members of the Mustelidae mark their territory in a similar way. Red Deer have relatively large scent glands beneath the eyes, which, particularly during the rut, produce a greasy substance with a strong penetrating odour. The stag carefully marks the trees and shrubs in his territory by rubbing the gland against the branches. The scent glands of the Chamois are located on the back of the head at the base of the horns. During the rutting season they swell and produce a substance which the male rubs on shrubs and herbaceous mountain vegetation. The Domestic Dog has a characteristic method of marking. When let loose out of doors he does not leave out a single milestone, a single cornerstone. He sniffs every such spot, usually finding the scent marks of other dogs there, and then adds his own by urinating a few drops on the spot. He is very careful to use only a little urine so he has enough left for further spots. Such marked spots are visited by many dogs so that soon there is a veritable 'visitors' book'. When marking cornerstones each dog tries to leave his mark as high as possible above the marks of other dogs, to indicate his strength, greater territorial requirements and hence also a higher status. The Brown Bear uses a combination of visual and olfactory signs to mark his territory. At certain spots he strips the bark off the trees with his claws so that bared light wood is visible a long way away. Then he urinates on the ground and on his front paws, rolls in the urine, and rubs his hairy coat against the damaged tree, thus adding a scent mark to the visual sign.

In the case of acoustic and visual signs animals generally determine the duration of the signs themselves, but this they cannot do in the case of scent marks. Scent marks usually last a long time and thus serve as a protracted chemical protection of the territory. They also enable the territory's holder to find his way about the area more readily and quickly not only on his regular rounds but also in the case of sudden danger. Within the territory animals do not roam casually but use well-defined beaten paths called runways, runs, galleries or racks as the case may be. A close examination of these pathways in places where the ground is soft will reveal prints as well as droppings. The runs often intersect, divide and come together again, to form a whole network of pathways. In all types of habitat, whether fields, rocky mountain slopes, grasslands or swamps, these runs are conspicuous so that they cannot be overlooked. In aerial photographs of the African savannah the runways form a dense criss-cross pattern so that the whole landscape appears to be covered by a giant net. Even the runways of quite small animals may be extremely well beaten by treading.

Often the runs of two or more animals may follow the same path and overlap some distance. A Roe Deer's run may be joined by a Brown Hare's, a Partridge may use a Brown Hare's run as it scrambles through the thickets, and various voles and mice may use the same pathway. It is not uncommon for an animal run to join a man-made trail for some distance, most probably because the latter runs along the line connecting two important places on the animal's territory. And, of course, the converse has happened: many of our pathways, especially those in mountainous areas, were formed by the widening and adaptation of runs used for centuries by mountain animals travelling from one ridge to another. In North America the first highways and railway lines often followed the wide and well-beaten runs made by vast herds of American Bison as they travelled in search of food.

The runways of hoofed animals are most conspicuous at the edge of forests whose protective shelter they leave to graze in open grasslands. In general the most conspicuous paths are those made near a food supply. A run leading out of woodland into fields is wide and prominent at the start, then it gradually peters out, narrowing and dividing into a network of single branching pathways until it completely disappears somewhere far out in the open country. The animals follow the run to the food supply but then their paths diverge, each branching off by itself to find the choicest morsel. This dispersion of animals is easily seen after a snowfall (Fig. 1).

In open country, fields of fodder crops and woodland undergrowth you will find narrow paths made by mice and voles. These little runs, trodden or gnawed out by the small creatures, lead either from one burrow to another or else from a burrow to a food supply.

Fig. 1 — The runway of a Fallow Deer shows as a deep furrow in snow

The runs made by the Field Vole, hidden in the intricate labyrinth of plants at ground level, is usually concealed from view by the overlying vegetation and revealed only when the plants are parted. Voles remain active even in winter when the ground is covered by a deep layer of snow. The paths between food supplies and burrows are renewed, tunnelled out, and the Field Vole's normal life continues underneath the snow without any visible trace on the surface. The animal lines the walls of the corridors with grasses and herbaceous plants which it bites into small pieces and which probably serve as insulation against cold and damp. Then when spring comes and the snow melts a dense network of grassy tunnels is revealed.

Around ponds, streams and rivers on the Continent one will come across the runways of the Muskrat leading from the edge of the water to the shoreline vegetation where they gradually vanish from sight. It is along these runs that the Muskrat forages for food after emerging from its underground burrow. In a few places on the Continent the Beaver makes narrow canals from lakes to swamps below lake level down which it floats gnawed-off branches and saplings.

Dwelling Places

The central unit of every territory is the animal's permanent or temporary dwelling place, which serves as a hiding place or for rearing the young. The dwelling places most often encountered in the countryside are the nests of birds located in widely diverse places.

Ground-nesting birds include gamebirds, bustards, cranes, waders and many perching

11

birds. Gulls, ducks, geese and flamingos nest in muddy places in or at the edge of water. The simplest nests are those made by certain waders. These are unlined depressions made in sand or grass by the female who lays her eggs directly on the ground. Larks and gamebirds make sturdier structures, lining the hollow with dry plant material. The nests of buntings and pipits are cup-like structures made close to the ground; those of the Wood Warbler and the Wren, which are also close to the ground, are enclosed domed constructions with entrances at the side.

Nesting on the ground is accompanied by many dangers from predators, and that is why as species evolved many birds took to seeking more suitable places in trees and shrubs. The most primitive form of tree nest is a flimsy structure of dry sticks and twigs made by certain pigeons, such as the Wood Pigeon, Turtle Dove and Collared Dove. Such a nest does not provide much protection for the eggs and young nestlings and so the parent birds either set about making a hollow in the centre of the platform or else building up the edges of the nest. That is how nests of raptors, storks, cormorants and herons are constructed. Deepening of the nesting hollow led to the development of the deep cup-like nest of perching birds and rails.

Some birds make their nests in rock or tree cavities. Tits, the Nuthatch, Treecreeper, Jackdaw and the Hoopoe avail themselves of natural cavities. Others, like woodpeckers, are expert carpenters. They drill and chisel spacious cavities in the trunks of trees, providing themselves with an entrance hole just big enough for their bodies. A few birds lay their eggs in underground nests. The Sand Martin, Kingfisher and Bee-eater use their feet and beaks to excavate tunnels in vertical mud or sand banks and these terminate in a spherical nesting hollow.

Ground-nesting birds often conceal their nest in a clump of grass, under a bush or in a pile of stones. Buntings, pipits, larks, partridges, pheasants and the Stonechat and Whinchat are past masters in the art of concealment. Some waterbirds, for instance the Coot, Moorhen and many rails, conceal or mask their nests by covering them with a roof of broken plant stems. From this type of nest it is merely a step to the excellent camouflage of nests where the walls are woven in and around the plant stems of the surrounding vegetation so that they blend perfectly with and are an inseparable part of their environment. Examples are the spherical or domed structures with entrances at the side made by warblers, the Dipper and the Wren. The Magpie's nest is camouflaged and protected by a dome of thorny twigs in bushes and trees. The most protected nest is one that is fully enclosed, spherical, with an entrance at the side and further safeguarded by being located in the fork of a slender branch (Long-tailed Tit) or suspended from the very tip of a thin, arching branch (Penduline Tit).

The task of building the nest is shared either by both partners or the male's contribution is merely symbolic. In many instances the male simply stakes out the nesting territory, attracts a female to the spot — say with his voice and a partially built nest — and she then completes the structure. The material used by birds to build their nest is mostly pieces of plant material.

Large birds, such as raptors, storks and herons, use twigs and sticks to make the nest and they line the hollow with finer material such as dry grass, moss, animal hairs, feathers and rags. Doves and pigeons place dry, thin sticks and twigs haphazardly on top of each other in the fork of a branch without bothering to provide a lining of softer material. Crows and the Magpie build their nests with twigs of various thicknesses and line them with a layer of loam and then a soft inner layer of hairs and fine stalks. Small perching birds build nests of stalks, roots, leaves and bits of bark held together with moss and lichens and reinforced with spiders' webs and plant fibres. Feathers, fur and horse hair are used. The manner of building varies; the material may be woven, bound, tamped and often even mixed and cemented together with the bird's own saliva. Swifts catch feathers and bits of straw floating in the air, coat them with rapidly congealing saliva, and cement them together to form a simple, glued structure. The Swallow and the House Martin build nests of small bits of mud cemented with saliva and strengthened with plant stalks.

Large birds, such as raptors, crows, owls, gamebirds and ducks, have only a single brood; smaller birds, chiefly perching birds, such as sparrows and the Blackbird, have two and sometimes even several broods in one year and they build a new nest on each occasion. Storks, herons and raptors use the same nest again, sometimes for several years in succession.

As we have seen, bird nests vary widely in shape, size, material used and location. A closer look at the lives of birds, however, reveals that the location of the nest is governed by certain rules in each species. Each bird species selects a specific type of nesting territory in which it then builds its nest. The choice of nesting territory and the location and shape of the nest are so characteristic in the case of many species that an expert can tell at a glance what species of birds are nesting in a given area.

The structural design of the dwelling places of mammals is much simpler. This is due primarily to the different embryonal development in mammals and the way they care for their young. In some mammals the embryonal development or gestation period is so long that the young are born fully developed and require only the minimum of maternal care. The young of hares and all the hoofed animals are able to move about by themselves within a few hours after birth and do not need any sheltering nest. At birth they are usually placed on the bare ground in a spot sheltered from the wind or in a good plant cover, perhaps on a simple bed of grass.

Many mammals dig their dwelling places in the ground, using them as places of shelter, refuge, and for bearing and rearing the young. These burrows vary in depth and location according to the type of animal and its way of life. The Muskrat and Otter dig holes in the banks of rivers and other bodies of water with entrances under water. The Fox and Badger excavate holes usually in concealed places in woods. Small rodents inhabit fields, meadows and gardens as well as woods and their burrows are frequently encountered. The Mole lives permanently in an underground system of tunnels emerging only rarely. Members of the Mustelidae make their home in various niches in rocks, in hollow trees, human dwellings and sometimes in the abandoned nests of larger birds and squirrels. Only a few mammals, such as squirrels, dormice and the Harvest Mouse, make nests in bushes or trees.

All the mammals that dig burrows or make nests need to use them for rearing their young. These are born naked or only slightly hairy and are blind so that they need to be kept in a warm, sheltered place for a time, after which they leave the nest or burrow to fend for themselves. Large mammals, such as the Red Deer, Roe Deer, Wild Boar and Fox, bear young only once a year; smaller mammals, such as rodents, hares and the Rabbit, have several broods a year.

Mammal and Bird Tracks

A track, in the narrow sense of the term, is a single footprint made by an animal in soft ground. The shape of the footprint varies according to species and to the animal's mode of locomotion. The limbs of mammals are terminated either by paws or hoofs (cleaves); all birds walk on their toes. European land mammals with paws include insectivores (shrews and the Hedgehog and Mole), rodents (squirrels and mice), lagomorphs (hares and the Rabbit), and carnivores (dogs, cats and the Badger); those with horned hoofs include the perissodactyls or odd-toed ungulates (horses) and artiodactyls or even-toed ungulates (deer and the Mouflon, Chamois and Wild Boar).

Let us take a closer look at the anatomy of a mammal's foot. The toes are of different

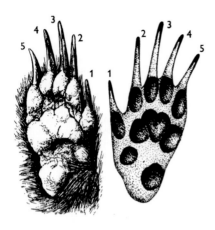

Fig. 2 — Right forefoot and fore track of the Badger. Designation of the toes: No. 1, thumb, inner toe; No. 2, second toe; No. 3, third, central toe; No. 4, fourth toe; No. 5, fifth, outer toe

length and are numbered from one to five (Fig. 2). To make this clearer we can compare them with the fingers of the human hand. No. 1 or inner toe is the shortest toe and is equivalent to the thumb on our hand; No. 5 or outer toe corresponds to our little finger. The longest toe is the central toe or toe No. 3, followed in order by Nos. 4 (our ring finger), 2 (our forefinger), 5 and 1. The position of the first toe is very important in reading tracks. When we come across a track with all five toes clearly imprinted (Hedgehog, Pine Marten) and with the print of the shortest digit on the left side (also usually lowest down) then the track must have been made by the right foot; conversely, the shortest digit of the left foot always appears on the right side of the print. However, if the ground is too hard, it sometimes happens that the print of the inner toe is very indistinct or may be absent altogether. The track then shows four toes of unequal length and the shortest toe will now be the outer toe.

When the first mammals evolved about 200 million years ago they walked on the whole sole of the foot and each of the four feet had five clawed toes. This primitive type of foot is found today in insectivores, some carnivores (bears and the Badger) and primates (monkeys, apes and Man). Mammals that walk on the whole sole of the foot are said to be plantigrade (Fig. 3a). In time, the plantigrade type of foot evolved into other types adapted for various methods of locomotion. The length of the limbs also changed. Plantigrade animals have relatively short limbs and therefore move at a relatively slow pace. Short legs do not allow for long strides or bounds and when the whole sole of a large foot touches the ground it acts like a brake in fast movement; undue energy is expended on friction between the foot and the ground. Changes in the shape of the limbs and feet began to appear in herbivorous animals that became dependent on swift or sustained running to escape from predators. The limbs lengthened and there was a corresponding reduction in foot size. This led to the evolution of digitigrade mammals (Fig. 3b), which walk on their toes with the heels not touching the ground, and finally unguligrade animals (Fig. 3c), which walk only on the tips of the toes — on the tips of horny hoofs. The full number of five toes also became an unnecessary brake to swift running and so some toes began to disappear. Some mammal groups developed a different number of toes on their hind limbs and forelimbs (dogs, cats, hares).

In specialized runners the first toe became reduced in size or it disappeared altogether so that the animals became four-toed; this was accompanied by an enlargement of those toes or parts of the toes on which the animal stepped most often. In swift and sustained running, however, even four toes were a hindrance and in time the second and fifth and even the

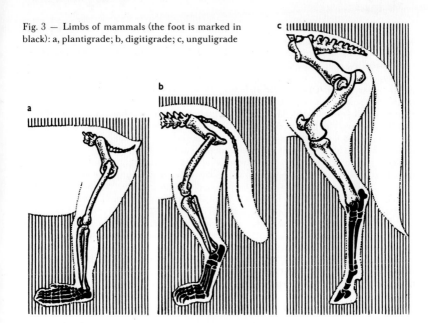

Fig. 3 — Limbs of mammals (the foot is marked in black): a, plantigrade; b, digitigrade; c, unguligrade

fourth toes disappeared and the weight of the body gradually shifted to the tips of the remaining toes. The artiodactyls (even-toed ungulates) walk only on the tips of their third and fourth toes. Dew claws, small horny projections above the hoof on the back of the leg, cover the atrophied remnants of the second and fifth digits. The most extreme development occurs in some perissodactyls (odd-toed ungulates). For example, in horses all the toes except the third (central) toe have disappeared and the animal walks on an enlarged terminal toe joint which is covered with a horny layer forming the characteristic hoof of these mammals.

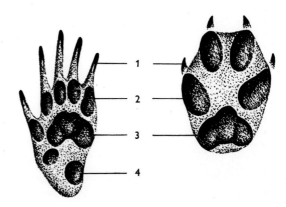

Fig. 4 — Footprints of mammals with paws: 1, claw marks; 2, toe pads; 3, hind pads; 4, wrist pads

When a footprint is made in wet sand you can see that it has various bumps and hollows which indicate how the foot is contoured. If you examine the foot of a dog or cat you will find pads on the underside covered with a thick but soft horny layer. They are elastic cushion-like parts reinforced with ligaments and serve to protect the foot from injury. Opening into these pads are glands whose secretion is transferred to the footprint when the animal walks, giving it a characteristic scent. The pads lack hair, and are clearly impressed in the track so that their size and arrangement serve as a means of identification (Fig. 4). In most mammals, however, the skin between the pads is covered with hair. In the Pine Marten and Red Squirrel the hair on the paws is so thick in winter that it completely covers the pads. Hares and the Rabbit lack pads; the soles of their feet are completely covered with a thick resilient cushion of short stiff hairs that prevent slipping.

Under the tip of each toe there is always a toe pad. Insectivores, bears and members of the Mustelidae have five such pads, like we do; other meat-eating mammals have only four. Rodents have five toe pads but only on the hind feet. Behind the toe pads there is another transverse row or group of pads fused in some mammals into a single, variously shaped pad called the hind or central pad. This is clearly visible in the tracks of cats, dogs and the Badger. The toes of the Badger and bears are positioned like our toes, that is they form a very shallow curve, and so the hind pad is similar — it is bean-shaped and positioned cross-wise behind the toes. The toes of dogs and cats are set clear of the hind pad in an arc on the periphery of the foot, because of their unequal length, and the hind pad is three-lobed. Plantigrade animals, such as the Pine Marten, Red Squirrel and Hedgehog, also have one or two proximal or wrist pads towards the back end of the foot.

Fig. 5 — Tracks of a Fallow Deer made in melting snow which froze; a fresh snow fall has transformed them into small craters that do not in the least resemble tracks made by an animal

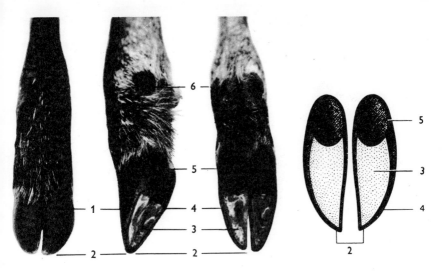

Fig. 6 — The toes (cleaves) of even-toed ungulates and cleave prints (right):
1, wall of toe; 2, tip of cleave; 3, sole of the foot; 4, ridge; 5, pad; 6, dew claws

This brief description of mammals' feet tells you what to notice when you find tracks. In the case of very small tracks it is particularly important to determine carefully the number of toe marks, the size and arrangement of the pads, and whether there are any claw marks. Thus, for example, claw marks are always present in a dog's track whereas in the track of a cat, which sometimes resembles that of a small species of dog in shape and size, they are absent. The reason for this is that the claws of cats are retractile and are usually retracted during walking so they do not scrape the ground and became blunted. It is also important to remember that the forefeet of most mammals (except rodents) make deeper, wider and sometimes also larger prints than the hind feet. Even when the animal is walking slowly the toes of the forefeet are more spread out (splayed) than those on the hind feet and this condition is more pronounced when running, when greater weight is brought to bear on the limbs. Another point to consider is the type or condition of the ground. On hard ground the track is always narrower, shallower and less clearly defined than in mud and melting snow. So tracks made by the same mammal can be surprisingly different in different ground conditions, which makes identification difficult (Fig. 5).

Identifying the tracks of hoofed animals is much easier, partly because there are relatively few European ungulates but also because all their limbs are terminated by a hoof that makes well-defined marks even in hard ground (Fig. 6).

The cloven hoof, or foot, is divided into two cleaves, or toes, which are essentially modified claws. Each is composed of two parts joined into a single whole enclosing the tip of the toe. The underside of the hoof is called the sole. On the sides is a curved covering of horn called the wall of the toe. The wall usually extends a short distance beyond the sole and forms a hard ridge at the bottom which impresses strongly in the track. The foot tapers into sharp points at the front but the back part is rounded and there is usually an elastic pad at this rounded end. In some cases the size and shape of these toe pads serve as a means of identification. If, for example, you are in doubt as to whether the footprint is that of

17

Fig. 7 — Cleaves and tracks of the Fallow Deer: forefoot and fore track (left); hind foot and hind track (right)

a female Red Deer or male Fallow Deer (the track of both may be the same length and width), then the size and shape of the pads will facilitate identification; the pads of the Fallow Deer are longer than those of the Red Deer.

The cleaves of even-toed ungulates are pressed tightly together when at rest. The inside edges are nearly straight whereas the outer edges curve outwards. The outside cleave is usually slightly larger than the other. The cleaves of the forefeet are always somewhat larger than those on the hind feet, even though one would expect the opposite in view of the size and length of the fore and hind limbs. Furthermore, the cleaves of the forefeet are usually slightly broader and more rounded at the tip. When an ungulate is in flight or moving on soft or loose ground, the cleaves splay out. Here again there are differences in the angle of spread between the front and back hoofs. The cleaves of the hind feet remain close together so that the hind track is almost parallel whereas the cleaves of the forefeet are splayed, even when walking, and the fore track resembles the letter V (Fig. 7).

On muddy ground a hoofed animal may slip forwards when stepping out, leaving a clear mark of the slip in the track (the cleaves are exaggerated in length) behind the heel. When lifting the feet the animal kicks up a bit of earth or snow with the tips of the cleaves and this is always seen at the front of the footprints. Both these signs help one determine the direction in which the animal was moving.

In most cases the dew claws are set so high up on the leg that they do not leave a mark in the track when the animal is walking, not even in soft ground, and often not even when the animal slips. It is only when the animal treads in thick snow or mud, or it crosses tilled fields with loose soil or comes up on to a sandy shore, that the hooves sink so deep that the dew

18

claws are impressed in the track (Fig. 8). This impression appears as two shallow depressions behind the cleaves. The dew claws may also show on hard ground when the animal is running or bounding; in this case the cleaves dig into the ground at more of a slant, are more wide apart and the dew claws touch the ground. Note that the dew claws of the Roe Deer and particularly the Wild Boar often leave a mark even when the animals are walking normally because they are set much lower on the limb than in other hoofed animals. The prints of the dew claws are larger and clearer in the fore track, partly because of the looser jointing of the front toes which causes the limb to sink deeper in the ground and partly because the dew claws on the fore legs are set slightly lower than those on the hind legs.

The shape and size of tracks by themselves are often insufficient for identification purposes. Many tracks are so similar that it is easy to be mistaken, particularly when the tracks are indistinct and distorted as, for instance, when the animal has walked in dry snow. It is therefore important to observe how the prints of the four feet are arranged in relation to each other so one can see the pattern of the tracks (trail) left by the moving animal. Mammals move in characteristic ways which are reflected in the arrangement of the tracks. The trail of a walking animal differs from that of a hopping or bounding animal. Often the trail is so typical and unequivocal that there is no need to examine the tracks in detail. A glance suffices to tell what animal made the trail and how it was moving. For example, the trail of the Red Squirrel is very uniform and unvarying.

The experienced tracker can tell from the tracks and their arrangement what the animal was doing even many hours previously. However, an exact reconstruction of what took place is possible only in winter when a large expanse of ground is covered by a deep layer of snow. All kinds of tracks and trails are left in such conditions. In other seasons tracking and reconstructing the animal's movements are not easy because the trail does not show up well and it is easy to lose it altogether. But in certain circumstances it is possible to track an animal when there is no snow on the ground, as every experienced hunter who has tracked a hoofed animal he has shot will tell you. If you do not have a hunting dog you can observe (crouched close to the ground if necessary) every little change in the places passed by the wounded animal. From the spot where it was hit you can follow the tracks of the fleeing animal, which are fresh and often deeply impressed, look for bits of hair, take note of broken twigs, broken-off branches or overturned stones, and look for signs of blood, which are often just a few drops on the ground or on the vegetation. Never hurry when tracking game. Haste can lead to loss of the trail or to the damaging or obliteration of the tracks. As a general rule you should always walk alongside the trail so as not to damage the tracks. If necessary you can then go back and start out over again if you should lose trace of the trail.

Essentially mammals have four gaits or types of locomotion: walking, trotting, galloping

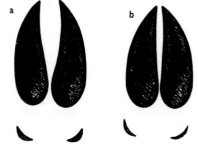

Fig. 8 — Print of the forefoot (a) and hind foot (b) of a hoofed animal showing the dew claws

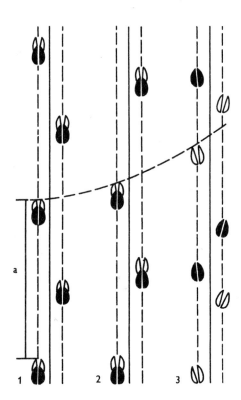

and bounding (Fig. 9). But not every mammal uses all these forms of movement; the Red Deer stag and dogs do, but hares and squirrels hop — they do not walk.

When walking mammals move their legs in a definite order. For example, the left hind foot of a Roe Deer moves first, followed by the left forefoot, then the right hind foot is moved, followed by the right forefoot and the whole sequence is repeated. The cleaves of the hind feet are placed more or less precisely in the tracks made by the forefeet. The hind track may be slightly in front of the fore track, it may be slightly behind the fore track or it may overstep or side step the fore track. If it coincides with the fore track so that the two overlap, they are said to be in perfect register. The trail of a walking mammal thus consists of two distinct parallel lines of tracks made at regular intervals by the right and left legs respectively. The distance between two successive tracks (the length of stride) and the distance between the left and right tracks (the width of stride or straddle) depend on the size of the animal and the type of locomotion.

Faster walking may change to trotting. This is a very economical form of movement that requires little physical effort and is widely used by mammals. Some can keep trotting for a long time without any visible signs of strain. In trotting the legs are lifted and set down in alternating diagonal pairs, always the forefoot and hind foot on opposite sides of the body (Fig. 10). The left forefoot leaves the ground together with the right hind foot, the right forefoot together with the left hind foot, and each pair touches the ground simultaneously. In trotting, unlike walking, the stride also becomes longer as the speed increases. However, the width of the stride (straddle) decreases, and in a very fast trot the tracks on the right and left sides lie almost in the same line. The hind feet may land on the track of the forefeet but usually they strike the ground in front of the forefeet, the distance increasing as the trotting gets faster.

Galloping is used less often than walking or trotting, mainly when danger threatens the animal or when it is attacking. The gallop is harder and faster than the trot. Whereas in walking the legs move in sequence one after the other on each side of the body and in trotting they are lifted in alternating diagonal pairs, in galloping first the two front and then the back legs leave the ground and for a while all four feet are airborne. The animal lands first on its back legs, one after the other, and then in turn on its front legs. The two tracks are not side by side but one is behind and slightly to the side of the other. The push-off is so strong in galloping that the hind feet always land in front of the tracks of the forefeet so the tracks are never in register. The strides are repeated regularly; the faster the gallop the greater the distance between the groups of four tracks.

Animals expend the greatest energy in leaping and bounding. The animal may leap from a resting position but usually leaping accompanies fast running or galloping, particularly when large obstacles have to be surmounted. In bounding the animal is airborne for a time, as in the gallop. After pushing off with its hind legs the animal flies forwards in a large arc to land on its forefeet which usually strike the ground one slightly behind the other. The animal then takes off again with its forelegs (the hind legs are still in the air) and the body again describes an arc, but this time a smaller one. The hind feet move in front of the forefeet, land in front and slightly to the side of the forefeet tracks and the whole sequence is repeated. In leaping and bounding the chief propulsive force comes from the back legs, the front legs being the ones on which the animal lands.

Mammals that have a long cylindrical body with flexible spine and short legs, such as martens, polecats, the Stoat and Weasel, can neither walk nor trot and their leaps and hops are different from those of other animals. They cannot move their hind feet far in front of the forefeet when bounding and so the hind feet land in or close to the tracks of the forefeet (Fig. 11). Their movement thus resembles the arched back movement of a caterpillar. The tracks of the forefeet are close beside or slightly diagonally one behind the other. This movement forms a pattern of tracks arranged close together in groups of two (when the

Fig. 10 — Group of running Fallow Deer

Fig. 11 — Trail of a bounding Stoat on snow-covered ice

hind track is over the fore track), three (when one hind track is impressed to the side), and naturally four (when the hind and fore tracks are impressed separately and do not overlap).

The feet of birds are far more uniform than those of mammals and they never have more than four toes (Fig. 12). Compared with mammals birds have lost their fifth toe if we use the same numbering. Birds' toes are not joined into a structure such as the paw or hoof. They are comparatively long and slender and are terminated by claws of various kinds, depending on the bird's way of life. The toes appear to grow from a single point; the first toe (thumb) usually points backwards and the remaining three toes, either close together or spread apart, point forwards. However, in some birds the first toe is absent (plovers, including the Lapwing); in others all four toes point forwards (swifts); owls, woodpeckers, cuckoos and the Osprey have two toes pointing forwards and two pointing backwards. The toes of birds have small horny cushions on the underside (analogous to the pads of mammals) and in some birds there is a more prominent pad at the point from which the toes radiate. Birds can be described as digitigrade, but keep in mind that the heel of a bird's foot ends relatively high up on the leg, that it never touches the ground in walking and that the tarsal (ankle) joint can be mistaken for the knee joint. In birds that live mostly on the ground or have lost the ability to fly, the foot has retained its characteristic shape.

Despite the great number of bird species we come across relatively few bird tracks, for most species move about in the air or in treetops and only rarely alight on the ground. The only birds that regularly leave tracks on the ground are those that seek their food there, for example gamebirds, waders, storks, herons, crows, ducks, geese and pigeons. The tracks of other species are encountered only occasionally. Some bird tracks are so typical that they can be identified quite easily (herons, storks, pheasants); others are more difficult, although it is usually possible to guess the group to which the bird belongs. Duck tracks, for example, can readily be identified by the webbing that joins the three front toes and shows clearly in the footprint. It is usually possible to distinguish between the tracks of diving and non-diving ducks and those of the Teal and the Mallard by their size, but it is far more difficult to distinguish between the similar tracks of the Mallard, Gadwall and Shoveler. Similar difficulties are encountered in identifying the tracks of perching birds. These birds have a prominent long hind toe but their tiny prints are very much alike.

On the ground birds move about in one of two ways: they either walk, in which case they leave alternate tracks of the left and right feet (crows, pigeons, waders, ducks, gamebirds), or they hop, in which case the tracks are always side by side in groups of two (some perching birds and woodpeckers). The greater the length of the stride or hop, the faster the movement. Faster movement may be compared to the trot or gallop of mammals, but the pattern of the tracks remains more or less the same.

Mammal and bird tracks can be looked for in a wide variety of places. The ground must be sufficiently soft to take an impression but remember that thin, runny mud causes distortion. You may even find tracks in a swamp where they appear as water-filled depressions in the plant cover. A good place to look for tracks is in fields and woods at the edge of drying puddles, on paths, and particularly at the edges of streams, rivers and lakes where in the sand or mud bordering the water will be not only the tracks of animals that live there but also those that go there to drink. Excellent in this respect are the flat muddy shores of dammed lakes that are exposed when the water level drops.

Snow, however, provides the best conditions for tracks. In a snow-covered landscape it is easy to follow a Brown Hare's trail for as much as several kilometres. Tracks are most clearly defined in snow that is neither too dry nor too wet and only several centimetres deep (Fig. 13). In light, dry, fluffy snow the tracks are indistinct, the thick layers of snow blur their edges and obscure their characteristic features. Furthermore, in deep snow, tracks look larger than they really are and like indistinct hollows. In such cases it may still be possible to identify the animal by studying the trail. Tracks are also well defined in old, settled snow after it has softened slightly or is covered by a thin layer of fresh snow, and in a light cover of snow on ice. In soft, melting snow a track is clear at first but after a while it becomes

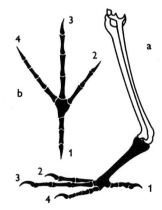

Fig. 12 — Left limb of a bird (a) with the foot marked in black. Designation of the toes on the foot and in the track (b): 1, hind toe; 2, inner toe; 3, middle toe; 4, outer toe

Fig. 13 — The tracks of the Red Squirrel are blurred in powder snow (left); in wet snow the claw and pad markings show clearly (right)

longer and wider making it seem as if it was made by a very large animal. In certain parts of continental Europe an ordinary dog track in melting snow can be mistaken for that of a Wolf, and the track of a Domestic Cat roaming in the woods may look like that of a Lynx. So when you try to identify uncommonly large tracks, take into account the habitat and consider if a Wolf track could appear in a low pine wood near human dwellings. This does not mean that you will never find tracks in places that are foreign to the animal's usual habitat; there have been cases of tracks of a Fox, Pine Marten and Badger even in large cities. As a matter of fact, many of the tracks shown in this book were photographed in an abandoned sand pit surrounded by houses.

Feeding Remains, Feeding Damage and Droppings

According to their diet animals are divided into three main groups: herbivores (plant eaters), carnivores (flesh eaters) and omnivores (animals that eat both plant and animal food). This division does not have exact limits. For example, deer are typical herbivores and yet they may also eat small animals in limited quantity; similarly the young of herbivorous birds eat insects fed to them. Conversely carnivorous animals may add variety to their diet by occasionally eating woodland berries and grass.

The amount of food consumed depends on the food's nutritional value. Meat is extremely nutritious and so predators do not need to eat very often. The amount of energy supplied by plant food is much smaller, sometimes almost negligible, and so herbivores must eat more often and in far greater quantities. A further important factor is the size of the animal. The smaller the animal the greater the relative body surface and the greater the amount of energy needed. Small animals thus need to eat relatively more food than large animals. Shrews die after several hours without food, whereas large carnivores and large raptors can go without food for several days without any deleterious effects.

Every animal is born with an instinctive knowledge of what to eat and how to go about gathering or capturing food, but as it grows older it adapts its behaviour as it becomes more experienced. The way an animal kills or the type of plant damage it does provides clues to the identity of the culprit, for these are usually characteristic for particular species. From the way in which a twig is bitten off one can tell if the damage was done by a rodent or a ruminant. Members of the Mustelidae attack prey larger than themselves and kill the victim by biting it in the back of the neck; the Wolf, which attacks in bands, sinks its teeth into the groin or belly region of the fleeing animal. The Peregrine bites off the flesh of its bird victim in small pieces and that is why the wings of its prey remain joined to the body skeleton and the long oar feathers remain on the tail even after the bones have been picked clean. The Goshawk and eagles first pluck their prey clean whereas owls do not; they try to swallow their prey whole along with the hair or feathers. Small perching birds crack hard seeds, nuts and snail shells on stones or stumps.

Mammals have four types of teeth, which differ in shape and function. The chisel-like incisors at the front of the jaw are used for biting food; the sharp-pointed canines are used for holding or killing prey; the premolars (front cheek teeth) are used for cutting up the food and together with the molars (back cheek teeth) for grinding food. The shape, number and arrangement of teeth correspond to the kind of food the mammal eats and are characteristic for each group of mammals as well as for individual species. The incisors of rodents and hares have loose roots, they grow continuously and the cutting edges are continually kept sharp for use as chisels in gnawing. Ungulates and rodents have ridged molars between which plant food is crushed and ground like between a pair of millstones. Omnivores and carnivores have molars with projections (cusps) on the chewing surfaces and much larger canines and incisors. Knowing how many teeth an animal has will help you to identify the species when you find a skull or when you examine feeding remains, such as owl pellets. The number of teeth is designated in the form of a fraction and always for only half of the upper and lower jaw. For example, the dental formula or the pattern of a cat's set of teeth is

$$\frac{3.1.3.1.}{3.1.2.1.},$$

which tells us that there are three incisors, one canine and one molar in both the upper and lower half of the jaw and three premolars in the upper but only two in the lower jaw. The number of teeth is the same for the other half of the jaws and so the entire set includes 30 teeth.

From the mouth food passes through the oesophagus to the stomach. Here again, the shape and size of the stomach depend on the species of mammal and nutritional value of the food. The stomach is shaped like a sac and in carnivores is relatively small. Herbivores have a much larger stomach in order to hold as much food as possible. Non-ruminant herbivores bite the food thoroughly into small pieces and grind it into a thick mush that is then chemically processed (digested) in the stomach and intestines. In ruminants (cattle, deer, sheep) the process is much more complex. The animals graze as if in a hurry and food

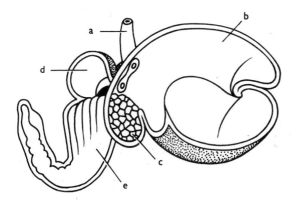

Fig. 14 — Section of the stomach of ruminants: a, oesophagus; b, rumen; c, reticulum; d, omasum, e, abomasum

25

is only coarsely ground by the molars. When swallowed, this coarse mixture passes to the stomach which consists of four parts: the rumen (or paunch), the reticulum, the omasum (or psalterium) and the abomasum (or reed), which corresponds to the stomach of other mammals (Fig. 14). The rumen serves as a large store house (a cow's rumen has a capacity of up to 200 litres). The food is churned and mixed there, then it passes from the rumen to the reticulum and is partially digested by the action of microorganisms and ferments. When the ruminant animal has grazed its fill it lies down to rest and about half an hour to one hour later begins to chew the cud or ruminate. The partially digested food is regurgitated from the rumen into the mouth, where it is completely masticated and then swallowed again, passing by the same route to the rumen and reticulum and from there to the omasum and abomasum. Ultimate digestion takes place in the abomasum and small intestine and undigested food remnants collect in the terminal section of the large intestine where excess water is absorbed and they are then passed out in the form of droppings through the anal opening.

The shape of the droppings is characteristic for each group of mammals (Fig. 15). The round droppings of hares, the Rabbit and many ungulates correspond to the form of the rectum — the terminal part of the large intestine. In the walls of the rectum there are hollows into which the faeces are pressed and moulded. In the case of Red Deer it is even possible to determine the animal's sex by the shape and size of the droppings. There may be seasonal changes in droppings. The droppings of herbivores are usually perfectly dehydrated; they are either round, sausage-shaped or bean-shaped and contain bits of plant remains. Carnivore droppings are longish, cylindrical, spindle-shaped and twisted like a rope; they are more mushy than herbivore droppings, contain remnants of bones, feathers and hair and generally have a pronounced odour.

Mammals differ in the way they deposit their droppings and are accordingly divided into two groups: those that place their droppings anywhere (hares, the Hedgehog) and those that place their droppings only in certain spots known as latrines (the Rabbit, carnivores).

Birds process food in a different way from mammals. Instead of teeth birds possess a bill or beak covered by a horny sheath. Birds cannot chew food like mammals do, and their bill serves only for collecting and capturing food and at most for tearing pieces that are too large. Bills are as varied as the food birds eat. Some bills serve as tweezers, awls, chisels or hatchets, others may be compared to nets, sieves, scoops, harpoons, nutcrackers or pincers.

In birds the function of teeth is taken over by the stomach. Food is passed from the beak via the throat to the gullet and thence to the stomach, which consists of an antechamber (or proventriculus) containing digestive glands and a gizzard (or ventriculus) with strong muscular walls. Some birds have a sac-like enlargement in the gullet called the crop where the

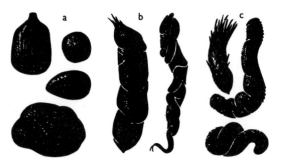

Fig. 15 — Animal droppings: a, droppings of plant-eating (herbivorous) mammals; b, droppings of meat-eating (carnivorous) mammals; c, droppings of seed-eating birds

food is retained and is sometimes also softened before it passes to the stomach. Gamebirds, pigeons, some perching birds, raptors and ducks have crops. In the proventriculus, the front part of the bird's stomach, the food is acted upon by digestive juices. Flesh, in particular, is almost completely digested here and only undigestible remnants such as bones, scales, feathers, hairs and claws, are regurgitated from time to time in the form of pellets. Best known are owl pellets because they are the ones most often encountered in the wild. After consuming their prey owls rest and digest the food in regular places where they also cough up the pellets and in time there may be quite a large pile beneath such a perch. Under trees where rooks roost the ground is literally covered with pellets, but those of many other birds are not regurgitated in any special place and so escape notice. Gull pellets are soon trampled to pieces in gull colonies, and those of shrikes, herons and the Kingfisher disappear from sight in the vegetation.

The gizzard of raptorial birds has thin walls and food is already well digested when it reaches this part of the stomach. In seed-eating birds, the gizzard has strong muscular walls which pulverize the hard, dry food by their powerful action. Furthermore, its inner walls are lined with a relatively thick, hard ceratoid (horn-like) layer that assists in grinding up the food. Finally many herbivorous birds swallow sand, grit or stones which enhance the grinding action of the muscular walls.

Undigested matter collects in the terminal section (cloaca) of the large intestine. The urinary tract also empties into the cloaca. Unlike mammals, birds do not have a bladder nor separate openings for the faeces and urine and this waste material is passed out of the cloaca mixed together. Bird urine is characteristically a thick, mushy, whitish fluid and the faeces top it like a white cap. Meat-eating birds (raptors, owls, herons and storks) produce thin, semi-liquid droppings; the droppings of seed-eaters, insectivores and omnivores are firmer and shaped like small cylinders or tear-drops. Piles of the droppings of seed-eating and insectivorous birds can be found at their roosting places; the white liquid droppings of raptors and herons are usually spattered round their resting and nesting places.

Recording Data on Bird Nests and Mammal Homes

If you keep your eyes open while you are in the countryside, you will certainly come across bird nests and mammal homes. They are well worth a close examination. Take along a large notebook and pencil to jot down any details of interest you might forget and a camera is also useful. What should you record and how?

Let's start first with bird nests. Besides a notebook and pencil you will need a wooden or metal folding rule, perhaps also callipers. When looking for and recording details of bird nests you must do so with the utmost care, for many birds are extremely upset when disturbed during the nesting period and may readily abandon the nest and the eggs it contains. So when you come across a nest with a bird sitting on it leave the spot as quickly and quietly as you can. You will have to abandon any thought of further, more detailed examination of the nest. If you then come across a nest containing eggs but without any sign of the female bird you can make the necessary measurements, but do so as quickly as possible. The female or both she and her mate will have left the spot for only a short while and may be back any moment. Your presence may cause them to abandon the clutch.

You will find bird nests in widely diverse places. For example, you may come across a Sand Martin colony in an old sand pit or steep river bank. First of all record the date and place of the find, then include a description of the spot in which the Sand Martin burrows are excavated and whether the entrances to the burrows face north, south, east or west. If you find the colony during the breeding period then this will have to be the full extent of the information you jot down in your notebook. Under no circumstances should you disturb

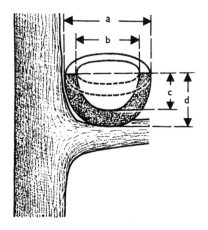

Fig. 16 — Measuring bird nests: a, outside diameter of the nest; b, inside diameter of the nest (the nesting hollow); c, inside height of the nest (depth of the nesting cavity); d, outside height of the nest; e, diameter of the entrance hole; f, distance between the entrance hole and the base of the nest

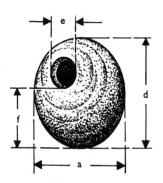

the birds. Further observations and measurements can be made after the young birds have fledged. It is best of all to wait until early autumn, then you will be able to measure the height of the entrance holes above the ground (this will also indicate how high up the burrows are generally excavated in the particular colony), the distance between two neighbouring entrance holes and last of all the dimensions of the burrows. Some are round, in which case record the diameter in centimetres; others are pip-shaped, in which case record the height and width of the burrow. If you are absolutely certain that all the birds have left the nesting colony then you can also measure the depth of the burrows with the aid of a long twig. Basic data on the burrows of the Kingfisher and Bee-eater can be obtained in the same way.

Most birds build their nests on the bare ground, in grass, in shrubs, or in trees. Here again, when you examine the spot, jot down in your notebook basic information about the character of the site, the height of the nest above the ground, how it is anchored (is it in the fork of a branch, close to the trunk of the tree or on a thick branch?) and about the material of which it is made. The figure shows how to determine the dimensions of a bird's nest (Fig. 16). The height is measured from the outside bottom to the upper edge of the nest, the depth is also measured from the bottom but on the inside to the upper edge of the nest. The difference between the height of the nest and the depth of the nesting hollow gives you an idea of how thick the base, or foundation of the nest is. Similarly, the difference between the outside and inside diameter of the nest will give you the thickness of the walls (you could also use callipers to determine this). In the case of dome-shaped nests, such as those built by warblers, the Long-tailed Tit, Wren, and Penduline Tit, you should also measure the diameter of the entrance hole (this is best done with callipers) and the distance between its lower edge and the bottom of the nest.

Birds of the same species build nests that are almost exactly alike in shape and size, with only negligible differences between the individual nests. This uniformity is an inborn trait. Nevertheless you may find the nest of, for example, a Blackbird that has an abnormally large inside diameter, probably because you measured it after the young birds had fledged. A newly made nest is always smaller inside and firmer. When the female incubates the eggs her weight causes the sides of the nest to spread and later the nest is further deformed by the nestlings, particularly if there are more of them. The Great Tit's nest is a neat, softly lined hollow, 7 to 8 cm deep and 3 to 4 cm wide, located in a cavity or nestbox. If you examine such a cavity after the young have fledged you will find no traces of the structure apart from the material of which it was made, for it will have been trampled flat by the nestlings. For this reason when you measure nests take into account the time of year when you do it.

Determining the size of cavities excavated by some birds in trees is very difficult. All you need do is to record the height of the entrance hole above the ground, the diameter of the entrance hole, and other basic information about the site — the type of tree in which the cavity was made and the direction in which the entrance hole is facing. In the case of the mud nests of swallows and the House Martin it is a good idea to measure the thickness of the walls with callipers.

Be extremely careful if you measure a nest which already contains eggs. The eggs of many small birds are very fragile and break even at the slightest impact. For that reason limit your observations and record only the number and coloration of the eggs.

Most mammal homes are located below ground, but some mammals build round nests above ground with a side entrance in vegetation, shrubs or trees. You can take the dimensions of such nests in the same way as you measure the dome-shaped nests of birds. The shape, arrangement and extent of underground burrows generally cannot be determined by the usual means of observation. All you can do is measure the entrances to the underground labyrinths, the same as you would for birds nesting in cavities. The entrances to the burrows of voles, mice and the Mole are usually round and not very big and so can be measured quite easily. Besides that measure the width and length of the runways treaded out by the rodents between the individual burrows and between the burrows and food supply. The entrances to the burrows of larger mammals, such as the Fox, Badger, Otter and Rabbit, may not be round, in which case you need to measure the height and width of the entrance hole.

Measuring the nests of birds or mammals built on the ground or within reach above the ground is easy. It is more difficult, and often dangerous, to examine nests built high up above the ground. Unless you are skilled at climbing or have a ladder, climbing irons or some other aid then it is better to abandon all thought of measuring such nests.

The nests of birds and some mammals can be systematically collected, but unless the collection is to be used for teaching purposes in, for example, a school or museum, there is little point in doing so. Apart from the fact that nests take up a lot of room they may also be the cause of much unpleasantness if the collection is kept at home. A bird's plumage harbours various parasites, some of which also attack humans (fleas, lice, mites). These parasites also live in the nest while the birds are developing and are present in increased numbers when the nestlings have fledged. For this reason the nest should be fumigated and left for 2 to 3 weeks in a box. For museum collections nests are usually taken together with a piece of the branch on which they are located for otherwise they lose their distinctive shape. However, cutting off a branch damages the tree to some extent and also deprives birds of a suitable foundation for building their nests in ensuing years. Such an act is therefore thoroughly undesirable from every viewpoint.

One other thing remains to be emphasized. Never, in any circumstances, collect eggs. This should be done only by experts and furthermore it is prohibited by law.

Plates

Symbols used:

  — print of the forefoot

  — print of the hind foot

Scent and Visual Marking of Territories Plate 1

Smell is without doubt the most highly developed of mammals' senses. It is so keen that it provides mammals with as much, perhaps even more, information than sight does in Man and birds. Communicating by means of scent marks thus plays an important role in the life of mammals, particularly in the marking out of territories.

Scent glands, which secrete the substance used for marking, occur in various places on the mammalian body. For example, Roe Deer (*Capreolus capreolus*) have scent glands in front of the eyes, at the base of the tail, on the outer side of the heel and between the cleaves on the hind limbs (2). In or at the edge of woodland all over Europe (including Britain, but not Ireland) you will find places up to 1 metre in diameter that look as if they have been scraped out with a rake. The vegetation has been removed and there are distinct furrows in the ground. These are the lying-up places of Roe Deer, scraped out regularly by the animals before lying down to rest and a characteristic sign that the territory is occupied.

Roe Deer have simple antlers (see Plate 108) that are shed and replaced by new ones every year. At the end of the year the old antlers break off from the frontal bone. The scar is soon covered by velvet — soft new skin with a dense network of veins that supply necessary nourishment to the growing antlers. These are fully grown after about 90 days and the deer removes the drying velvet by fraying (1) — rubbing the antlers on the trunks and branches of trees thereby stripping the bark (3, 4). At the same time the secretion produced by the frontal scent gland is deposited on the trees and the visual mark is combined with a scent mark.

The Red Deer (*Cervus elaphus*) has scent glands at the base of the tail, on the belly, on the outside of the heel and even in the velvet covering the antlers and in the skin round the antler stalks. When the male Red Deer (stag) rubs the velvet from his antlers, scent is deposited on the frayed branches. There is also a large scent gland beneath the eyes that is powered by strong muscles and can be flipped out to deposit scent on twigs.

Scent and Visual Marking of Territories Plate 2

On the Continent where it lives the Wild Boar (*Sus scrofa*) (1) likes damp places and above all enjoys wallowing. It regularly visits temporary or permanent puddles in wet ground where it wallows to its heart's content. On emerging from its bath, thickly coated with mud that sticks to its rough bristles, it rubs its back against the trunks of trees and against stones. The tree against which the Wild Boar rubs itself is readily identified even from a distance. The bark is partly scraped off and coated with dried mud. Bits of bark get caught between the bristles on the animal's back and if the tree is a conifer then resin clings there too. This, together with the mud, bristles and pieces of bark, forms a coat that is sometimes quite thick. When rubbing against trees the Wild Boar also deposits scent, thereby marking out its territory.

Red Deer (*Cervus elaphus*) also enjoy wallowing, particularly during the rut, and after rising up dripping water and plastered with mud they rub against trees, marking them with their scent. Even though wallowing and rubbing are mainly engaged in for purposes of personal hygiene (see Plate 23), they also serve for territorial marking. The rubbing places of the Red Deer are up to 2 metres high on trees (4), whereas those of the Wild Boar are about 1 metre high (2).

The stamping grounds of Red Deer stags often resemble wallowing places. They are shallow, sometimes wet depressions devoid of vegetation, which are scraped out by the stags with their hoofs or antlers. These stamping grounds are marked by the animal's pronounced odour in the rut and serve for territorial marking.

Scent perceived even by our imperfect sense of smell is produced by the glands of carnivores (bears, foxes, weasels, cats and their allies). These scent glands are usually located round the anal opening at the base of the tail and the secretion is deposited on the droppings as the animal defecates. The droppings themselves have a pronounced odour and this is further intensified by the secretion of the scent glands. That is why a carnivore such as a Fox (*Vulpes vulpes*) uses droppings (3) as effective territorial markings. They are also deposited in obvious, elevated places — on stones, stumps and piles of wood — so that the scent can be carried by the wind.

In Czechoslovakia the author came across the winter dwelling place of a Pine Marten (*Martes martes*) in a man-made nestbox for the Goldeneye (*Bucephala clangula*). The Pine Marten daily placed droppings on the nestbox's roof and by the end of the winter these formed a sizeable pile 20 cm wide and 10 cm high. The scent glands of the Western Polecat (*Mustela putorius*) are used not only for territorial marking but also for defense. When frightened or attacked the Polecat produces a secretion with a very pronounced and unpleasant odour that wards off the attack of even a much stronger enemy.

①

②

③

Acoustic Marking of Territories Plate 3

The Red Deer (*Cervus elaphus*) marks its territory with penetrating calls (1). This acoustic marking is, however, very limited in terms of time as it lasts only during the rutting season, from about the middle of September to the middle of October. At this time the stags roar and bellow, thereby denoting the boundaries of their territory and giving notice to other stags that trespassing is forbidden. The call varies in sound according to the age of the stag. An old stag's roar is like that of a lion and can be heard hundreds of metres away. The trumpeting call of a younger stag is a higher-pitched, moaning note. The efforts of juvenile stags usually end in a rattling bleat at the most, whereas a very old stag makes a hollow, rumbling cry.

Birds mark out their territories only with their voices. They do not use scent marks because their sense of smell is practically nonexistent. Territories are marked and defended chiefly during the breeding season. Each pair of birds stakes out a territory that is big enough for resting and building a nest and the provision of sufficient food for themselves as well as their offspring. The territory of a Robin (*Erithacus rubecula*) (2) includes open places, built-up areas as well as scrubland and woods. The male usually sings his song from an elevated spot so it will be heard as far as possible. The Stonechat (*Saxicola torquata*) (3), which makes its nest in grass on the ground, selects tall plants or shrubs for the purpose, and the River Warbler (*Locustella fluviatilis*) (4) (a very rare vagrant to Britain) a thick bed of reeds or nettles. Many warblers climb up reed stalks as they sing, larks and pipits do so in flight. The Roller (*Coracias garrulus*) (5), another rare visitor to Britain, perches on an elevated spot, its loud crow-like call sounding forth like a cry from a watch tower. It also accompanies the bird's acrobatic feats during the courtship flight.

①

②

③

④

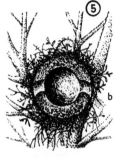

Nests in Trees, Shrubs and Grass Plate 4

Some mammals make nests in treetops, one example being the Red Squirrel (*Sciurus vulgaris*) (1). This rodent is found all over the Continent in woodland, large gardens and even in city parks. Sadly, in the British Isles, the range of the Red Squirrel has declined as the introduced Grey Squirrel (*S. carolinensis*) has spread. The Red Squirrel is now absent from most of England, but it still occurs in Wales, northern England, Scotland and Ireland. The behaviour of the two squirrels is broadly the same, but the Grey Squirrel tends to spend more time on the ground.

Squirrels make two types of nests called dreys — winter dreys in which they rear their offspring and summer dreys which serve as temporary resting places. The winter drey is a solid spherical structure measuring 30 to 40 cm across on the outside. It is made of strong twigs outside, thinner twigs inside and lined with soft dry grass, sometimes also some dry leaves and long, narrow strips of bark. There are one or two side entrances (5a, b — Red Squirrel). The whole structure is situated in the fork formed by a main branch with the trunk (3 — Red Squirrel), or on the terminal branches at the top of the tree. The walls of the drey are usually woven around the branches of the tree so that there is no danger of its being knocked down even by a strong wind. The Red Squirrel favours coniferous trees, while the Grey Squirrel typically inhabits deciduous woodland. Summer dreys are simple structures made of leafy twigs and located on side branches away from the main trunk. There are several such dreys within the territory and they are built mostly by the males. Besides dreys, squirrels also make use of natural tree cavities and even large man-made nestboxes for breeding.

The Harvest Mouse (*Micromys minutus*) (2), also builds a spherical nest. It is the smallest mouse in Europe, being only 5 to 7.5 cm long. It has a tail of equal length, which is used as a fifth limb in climbing among plant stems and thickets. It is not common anywhere in Europe and is rarely observed. It is absent altogether from Ireland and much of Scotland. The nest is made of grass leaves bitten lengthwise and woven around long grass, reeds or other herbaceous stems (4). It is barely 10 cm in diameter, and it is built up to 1 metre above the ground. Two types of elevated nests are made: one has a single side entrance and is used for breeding; the other usually has two entrances, one opposite the other, and is used as a resting place. In inclement weather, particularly in winter, the Harvest Mouse takes shelter in underground nests.

The Northern Water Vole (*Arvicola terrestris*) generally lives near fresh water and digs burrows in the banks of rivers, streams and ditches; these are used for shelter, breeding and storing food. It also builds spherical or ovoid nests of dry plant material in reed beds, bushes and in old bird's nests, always close to the ground or water (6). The species is found throughout Europe, except for Ireland and parts of France and Spain.

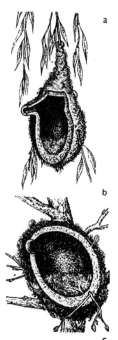

Although bird nests are temporary structures used to rear young for only a single season, sometimes just one brood, in many respects they are built with far greater care than those of mammals. Building a nest of a particular shape is an inherited trait so that a nest made by a pair of birds breeding for the first time will be almost as perfect as that of birds with years of experience. Each species has a characteristic type of nest. Some are simple and haphazard, others complex structures of excellent design, but saying that one is worse and the other better is a judgement made from our viewpoint and does not take into consideration the biological expediency of the respective type of nest.

Of European birds the most perfect nest is probably made by the Penduline Tit (*Remiz pendulinus*) (1), the term perfection in this case referring to the location of the nest which provides the nestlings with the maximum protection against enemies and bad weather. The task is begun by the male who starts by making a pear-shaped framework of grass stems at the tip of a drooping outer branch of usually the Goat Willow, Birch or Aspen. Then together with his mate he stuffs plant down, usually the downy seeds of Goat Willow, Aspen or a reed mace, into the framework to form a cottony cover. The finished nest, usually suspended above water, is bag-shaped, 12 to 18 cm long and 7 to 10 cm wide with a tunnel-like entrance in the top part of the structure. The walls are up to 2.5 cm thick, the bottom of the nest even thicker (5a). The nests of the Penduline Tit may be found in flood-plain districts with swampy landscape in central, eastern and southern Europe. The species is absent from the British Isles, Scandinavia and other parts of western Europe.

Just as perfect is the nest of the Long-tailed Tit (*Aegithalos caudatus*) (2), which inhabits thin mixed woods, parks and gardens and can be seen throughout Europe, including the British Isles. The structure, lodged firmly in the fork of a branch, is egg-shaped, 15 to 20 cm high and 10 cm wide, with a side entrance at the top. The thick walls of the nest are made of moss, lichen and spiders' webs. The outside is camouflaged with bits of bark and the inside is lined with masses of assorted small feathers, sometimes numbering as many as 2,000 (5b).

The Wren (*Troglodytes troglodytes*) (3), which is found throughout the British Isles in woods, parks and gardens with thick undergrowth, builds its nest in thick undergrowth near ground level, under the overhanging banks of streams, in piles of brushwood, and in fallen trees. It is made of grass, plant stalks, moss and small twigs. The side entrance is about midway between the top and bottom of the spherical structure, which measures up to 15 cm in diameter (5c).

A slightly smaller, dome-shaped nest is built by the greyish-green Willow Warbler (*Phylloscopus trochilus*) (4), a summer migrant to the British Isles. It is located in grass, heather, blueberry bushes or between the roots of shrubs and trees. It is hard to find because it is made of grass leaves, moss, velvet or lichen and viewed from above looks like a bunch of leaves. The entrance, located at the side, is very small but becomes enlarged through repeated use during the time the young are being fed by the parents (5d).

(5)

(4)

(5)

b c   d

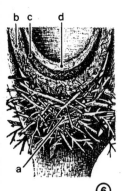

a

(6)

Nests in Trees, Shrubs and Grass Plate 6

The size of the nest and the material used in building depend on the size of the bird, its weight and strength. That is why big birds build large nests. Among the largest nest is that built by the White Stork (*Ciconia ciconia*). The White Stork usually occurs in country areas where there are ponds and marshes. The nest is built on rooftops, ruins, transmission towers as well as in trees (1). It is made of thick twigs and sticks reinforced with mud, turf, plant material and various bits and scraps and the hollow, which is flat and not very deep, is lined with fine plant material (for further details of the White Stork's nest see Plate 11).

Large nests are also built by raptors, for example by the Buzzard (*Buteo buteo*) (2). Its nest is usually built on a horizontal branch close to the trunk, from 10 to 20 metres up the tree and, like the White Stork's, is made of strong twigs at the bottom with sides woven of thinner twigs. The shallow depression is lined with leaves, moss and hair and the edge is covered with fresh twigs and leaves throughout the nesting period. Sometimes the same nest is used for several years in succession, in which case it is always repaired.

So well concealed is the nest of the Carrion Crow (*Corvus corone corone*) that it is hard to find amidst the branches of coniferous or deciduous trees and yet it is a solid, compact structure approximately 40 cm high and 60 cm wide. The Carrion Crow is extremely careful not to reveal its location — both during construction and when the young are in the nest. The nest is built either in the fork of a branch at the top of the tree at a height of 10 to 20 metres (4) or in the fork formed by a branch with the trunk (5). It is composed of four different layers (6): the base is made of dry twigs up to 2 cm thick (a), the sides are woven of thin flexible twigs (b) and these are topped by a 3- to 5-cm-thick layer of mud and turf (c). The hollow, about 10 cm deep, is lined with dry grass, hairs and inner bark (d). Nests of similar shape are also built by the Rook (*C. frugilegus*), but whereas crows always nest singly rooks live in colonies and their nests are placed close together in the rookeries.

The nests of doves and pigeons are flimsy structures made of much thinner twigs. The Wood Pigeon (*Columba palumbus*) (3) builds its nest in thick undergrowth or on the branches of trees, usually at a height of 5 to 20 metres. Selecting the flat fork of a branch it lays dry twigs several millimetres thick haphazardly on top of each other to form a low, unlined platform 7 to 14 cm high and 30 to 40 cm in diameter. As for the Turtle Dove (*Streptopelia turtur*) — a summer visitor to Britain — its nest is sometimes so flimsy that one can see the two white eggs through the gaps between the twigs.

①

②

③

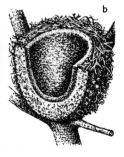

On the Continent, pleasant flutey whistling notes slightly reminiscent of yodeling reveal the presence of the Golden Oriole (*Oriolus oriolus*) (1). Its song is most likely to be heard in open broadleaved woods, parks and gardens in lowland districts. In Britain you might hear the Golden Oriole's song in south and southeastern England where the bird is an occasional summer visitor, if the climate permits. Although the nest is about 14 cm in diameter, it is hard to find among the leaves at a height of 10 to 20 metres. Unlike other birds the Golden Oriole does not build its nest on a branch but suspends it between the forks of a branch, weaving the upper edge of the hammock-shaped structure firmly round the boughs on either side (5a). It is made of grass stems lined with a cushion of feathers or hair.

The Chaffinch (*Fringilla coelebs*), one of Europe's commonest birds, always places the nest in the fork of a branch (2), though it may sometimes be built on a thick horizontal branch where it looks like some kind of tumour or stump. It escapes notice not only because of its small size — it is a neat, compact cup of moss, lichens and grass just 8 to 10 cm wide and 6 to 8 cm high — but mainly because the outside is superbly camouflaged with bits of Birch bark so that the whole looks like a worn part of the branch. The inside is lined with hairs, feathers and plant down.

The nests of the Blackbird (*Turdus merula*) and Song Thrush (*T. philomelos*) (3) are very similar in shape and size and occasionally also as regards their location. They are found in all sorts of woods as well as close to buildings and sometimes even directly on buildings. The outside diameter of both nests is 10 to 18 cm and the height between 7 and 10 cm. The nest is made of dry plant stems and grass and in the case of the Blackbird the nesting hollow, 4 to 6 cm deep, is lined with the same material. The Song Thrush, however, prepares the interior of its nest in a different way. It gathers mud, fine bits of plants and rotting wood, adding saliva to form a moist mixture which it then packs into the crevices on the inside, smoothing it until it forms a nearly hemispherical hollow, 6 to 8 cm deep, that soon dries and turns hard. It is provided with no further lining (5b).

Large reed beds in ponds, pools, lakes and estuaries are the favourite haunts of a large group of brown-coloured perching birds whose loud strident song can be heard from a distance. They are the swamp warblers, all of whom build nests that are very much alike. In continental Europe one of the commonest is the Great Reed Warbler (*Acrocephalus arundinaceus*) (4), which builds a fairly large nest (about 7 cm high and the same across) of reed leaves woven round several tall reeds growing side by side that serve as supporting 'pillars'. The inside is lined with fine plant fibres (5c). The Great Reed Warbler does not breed in Britain, but the related Reed Warbler (*A. scirpaceus*) is a summer visitor to England and its nest, a smaller one than the Great Reed Warbler's, can be found in reed beds.

44

Nests in Tree Cavities and Nestboxes Plate 8

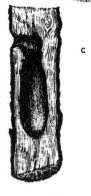

A relatively large group of birds abandoned nesting on tree branches in favour of cavities inside tree trunks. This improved shelter not only made the whole nest safer but also lessened the danger of possible harm to the clutch and nestlings. Birds nesting in hollows may be divided into two groups: passive inhabitants that occupy natural cavities and active builders that make their own cavities.

The first group includes certain species of owls. In Europe they are the Tawny Owl (*Strix aluco*) (1), Little Owl (*Athene noctua*), Tengmalm's Owl (*Aegolius funereus*), Pygmy Owl (*Glaucidium passerinum*) and sometimes also the Eagle Owl (*Bubo bubo*) (the last three species are not residents of the British Isles). Owls do not provide the nest with any special lining. The bottom of the cavity is always covered with rotting bits of wood and that suffices for the eggs as well as the nestlings. Owls also have no special requirements as to the size of the entrance hole; it may even be much bigger than their bodies. (For further details of owl's nests see Plate 11.)

Natural cavities are also occupied by certain small birds, chiefly tits. Their space requirements are very modest. A small crack in the bark of an oak through which the Great Tit (*Parus major*) barely manages to squeeze is enough and the cavity is occupied. Only an experienced eye can tell by the slightly frayed bark round the entrance hole that the cavity is inhabited (4). More active behaviour is exhibited by the Willow Tit (*P. montanus*). Although it also uses natural cavities, when it comes across a rotten tree stump it cannot resist its ingrained instinct and laboriously excavates a hole in it for its nest (3). Both these species of tit are found in the British Isles, but the Willow Tit has a more local distribution and it is absent in Ireland.

The nesting cavity of woodpeckers is readily recognized by the entrance hole which is almost a perfect circle and usually quite high up above the ground. The edge is furthermore perfectly smooth without any splinters. The Great Spotted Woodpecker (*Picoides major*) takes as much as 14 days to drill its hole (2) but in the end it has a spacious pear-shaped cavity inside the trunk with an entrance hole just big enough for it to slip through comfortably. A few chips always remain inside the cavity and these provide a soft layer for the eggs and nestlings. Gleaming white wood chips on the ground beneath the entrance hole indicate that the cavity has been drilled just recently. The Lesser Spotted Woodpecker (*P. minor*) chisels a nesting cavity 10 to 12 cm wide and 10 to 20 cm deep, with an entrance hole 4 cm in diameter (5a). The hole made by the Great Spotted Woodpecker is 12 to 15 cm wide and 23 to 30 cm deep with an entrance hole 5.5 cm in diameter (5b), and that drilled by the Green Woodpecker (*Picus viridis*) — the largest British woodpecker — is 15 to 20 cm wide and 25 to 50 cm deep with an entrance hole 6.5 cm across (5c). The largest cavities are those drilled by the largest European woodpecker, the Black Woodpecker (*Dryocopus martius*) — they are 15 to 20 cm wide and more than 60 cm deep with an entrance hole 9 to 10 cm in diameter (5d). The Black Woodpecker is not found in the British Isles.

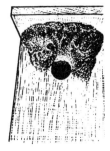

a

b

c

⑤

Woodpeckers nest only once a year, almost always drilling a new cavity for the purpose. Some birds also excavate cavities used for shelter after the nesting period. Sometimes they do not complete the task for one reason or another thereby providing numerous other cavity nesters with an excellent opportunity for taking up residence and rearing their young. Such abandoned cavities are frequently occupied by the Starling (*Sturnus vulgaris*) (1). It lines the cavity with various kinds of plant material, hairs or feathers and has two broods there in a year. Their place of abode is often revealed by the alarmed cries and nervous flight of the adult birds round the cavity and later also by the nestlings, which are also quite noisy. A cavity occupied by the Starling can also be identified by the liquid droppings on and beside the tree, squirted out by the nestlings through the entrance hole.

Another occupant of tree cavities is the Nuthatch (*Sitta europaea*) (3), a common bird of broadleaved and mixed woodlands as well as parks and gardens whose loud whistling sounds are often heard during the breeding period. The discovery of a cavity with an entrance hole that is too large awakens a compulsive urge to build. In its beak it brings mud mixed with saliva, sticks it to the edges of the entrance hole and packs it down firmly. It continues to narrow the opening until it is almost completely filled in, leaving only a hole big enough for it to slip through. When it has hardened the substance is extraordinarily firm and hard to break. The picture (4) shows such a hole walled in by the Nuthatch in a nestbox for the Goldeneye (*Bucephala clangula*). The entrance hole, which measures 11 cm in diameter, was narrowed by the Nuthatch to about 3 cm. The variously coloured spots in the 'masonry' indicate that the Nuthatch gathered its material in various places. Its urge to build did not cease even when the entrance hole was the required size. The bird continued plastering mud above the hole underneath the roof of the occupied nestbox (5a) and also on the inside walls (5b). Its behaviour is the same in the case of natural cavities. Sometimes the Nuthatch deposits unbelievable quantities of nesting material inside the cavity. In the case of the Goldeneye's nestbox the inside was filled with 12 litres of dry and rotten bits of wood, twigs and bark chips and the eggs lay on top of this 'mound'.

It has long been known and often proved in practice that many cavity-nesters also commonly occupy artificial cavities — man-made nestboxes. The commonest and most welcome occupants of such nestboxes are the tits, which destroy many plant pests and thus serve the purpose better than the often heedlessly used insecticides. A Great Tit (*Parus major*) (2) pair brings its nine nestlings approximately 0.75 kg of food during the 19-day nesting period, which represents about 7,500 caterpillars, butterflies, beetles and other insects. When the time of fledging draws near the parents bring food to the nest as often as 800 times a day. That is why it is worthwhile building a nestbox for tits. All that is necessary is to nail a few boards together, keeping in mind that the inside dimensions of the box should be 14 by 14 by 25 cm and the entrance hole 3 cm in diameter, and the box can be hung outdoors (5c); it is also possible to hollow out a log for the purpose (2).

a

b

c

⑤

Many birds have chosen to live in cliffside habitats and so it is quite natural that their nests are built on rock faces. Some avail themselves of suitable cracks and cavities, others select inaccessible ledges. This habitat is also the nesting site of a small group of birds of the swallow family. The Swallow (*Hirundo rustica*) and House Martin (*Delichon urbica*), however, have become permanent companions of Man. Their nests are built on buildings, which serve as a substitute for steep rock faces. Both species are migratory and both make nests of mud.

On its arrival from wintering in Africa, the Swallow sets about building its nest. Both partners visit drying puddles or other wet places where they gather bits of mud in their beaks. This they mix with saliva, which increases its adhesive properties, and paste little balls of the sticky mass in rows one above the other like bricks. To strengthen the structure they put various plant stems between the balls and these often hang from the nest like long whiskers. Only rarely is the Swallow's nest stuck on the outside wall of a house. As a rule it is located inside — in a barn, granary, corridor or even a room. The Swallow often builds its nest on a foundation such as a water pipe, electric wire (1) or jutting beam (2). The finished nest is a cup-shaped structure (actually a half-cup or quarter sphere), open at the top (5a). It is approximately 10 cm high and measures 8 to 14 cm in diameter. The walls are 1 to 2 cm thick so that the actual nesting hollow, richly lined with feathers, hairs and fine grass, measures 7 to 10 cm in diameter. The Swallow has two, and sometimes three, broods a year. When the young first leave the nest they return to it for the night for a few days more.

The nest of the House Martin is built in the same way as the Swallow's and yet the two are readily identified. For one thing the House Martin builds its nest on the outside, rather than on the inside walls of houses, usually under eaves so that it is well protected from above (4), and secondly it generally nests in colonies (3). The principal identifying feature, however, is the shape of the nest. The House Martin's nest is a hemispherical structure stuck to a vertical wall with a small entrance hole at the top (5b). It is about the same size as the Swallow's and the entrance hole is approximately 4 cm in diameter.

The Red-rumped Swallow (*H. daurica*) builds its nest on ceilings and on the underside of roofs and rock ledges. The nest is shaped like a half retort with a tube for entrance at the side instead of a simple hole (5c). This bird nests in parts of the Mediterranean region and is only a very rare visitor to Britain.

①

②

③

④

Nests on Cliffs and Buildings Plate 11

The White Stork (*Ciconia ciconia*) has been a favourite of Man since time immemorial and is thus not at all shy. On the contrary it is attracted to human habitations because they provide it with a suitable foundation for its nest. It has a preference for rooftops and chimneys and that is also where the nest is usually located (1), for there is not always a suitable tree on hand with branches strong enough to support the weight of such a large and heavy structure. Building the nest is no easy task for the White Stork. Many twigs fall to the ground or are knocked off by the wind before the foundation is finished and that is why the nest is often used for several years and defended so vigorously against other interested parties. When the White Stork returns to its nest from its winter quarters in Africa duels fought over nests are quite a common occurrence.

Repeated use of the same nest in no way lessens the bird's building instinct. Every year the nest is repaired and added to by the White Stork on its return and the inside lined anew with fresh grass, turf and rags. After several years the White Stork's nest is a gigantic structure (2). A newly built nest is roughly 30 cm high and approximately 80 cm in diameter. The oldest known nest in Germany used by storks for some 400 years is more than 2.5 metres high and 2.25 metres in diameter and its weight is estimated at 1 tonne.

The Eagle Owl (*Bubo bubo*), the largest and strongest European owl, has no such problems with building a nest. It inhabits spreading woodlands with rocky locations, nesting on cliff ledges or in caves. It does not build a nest in the true meaning of the term, for it lays its eggs on bare ground covered only with a thin layer of pine needles, scraps and feathers (3). The shallow nesting hollow is about 30 cm across at first, but when the young hatch no trace of its original shape remains for it is trampled by the nestlings and filled with food remains (4).

Cliffs are also favourite nesting sites of raptors — vultures, eagles and falcons. The nests are located in inaccessible places, under rock overhangs (5a) and on rock towers (5b). They are only sparsely lined and edged on the outside with plant material.

Many birds nest in so-called partial cavities — cavities in cliffs or houses that are open in front. A hole in the wall of a house due to a missing brick is often used for the purpose by the Spotted Flycatcher (*Muscicapa striata*) (5c), a regular summer visitor to Britain. It builds its nest about 15 cm wide of rootlets, grass and moss.

52

90–150 cm

50–250 cm

① ② ③ ④

Many mammals and birds do not construct any abode for shelter at all, not even for breeding and rearing the young. They use only some sheltered spot and at most merely fix it up a bit.

One such animal is the Brown Hare (*Lepus europaeus*) (1), a common inhabitant of both lowland and upland areas. A twilight (crepuscular) or nocturnal mammal, it spends the day resting (lying up) under cover. Only during the mating period does one see groups of hares running about in the fields in daytime. A Brown Hare that makes its home in the woods has no difficulty finding a suitable cover — under a small tree, amidst tall grass, dense thickets or between the roots at the base of a large tree, where it is excellently camouflaged by its brownish-rusty colouring which blends perfectly with the surroundings. The Brown Hare also seeks shelter in the open countryside. In summer it lies up in fields among forage, cereal or root crops. However, when the fields are devoid of vegetation in autumn they no longer provide suitable places of concealment and the Brown Hare then lies up in clumps of old grass (6) or in a ploughed furrow. Often, however, it prepares a lying-up place for itself by scraping out a shallow depression (about 12 cm deep) with its forefeet (2). In winter it often lets itself be covered by a snowdrift. The picture (3) shows a winter lying-up place from which a hare was started up. It bounded off in the direction of the bottom right corner of the photograph, then turned and headed in the direction shown by the fresh footprints.

The Wild Boar (*Sus scrofa*) is a roaming animal that travels considerable distances by night, sometimes even several tens of kilometres. For that reason it does not have any permanent dwelling places. Occasionally, however, it makes a roomy lying-up place in dry grass (4) where it rests during the day. A similar lying-up place is regularly prepared by the female (sow) just before dropping the young.

Foothills and mountain districts with moors and heaths are inhabited by the Black Grouse (*Lyrurus tetrix*), which forages for food both on the ground and in trees but at dusk always flies up into the treetops to roost. In winter in severe frosts the Black Grouse hurtles from the treetops into the snow, digging itself in and closing the hole behind it to pass the night in a warmer shelter (5).

⑥

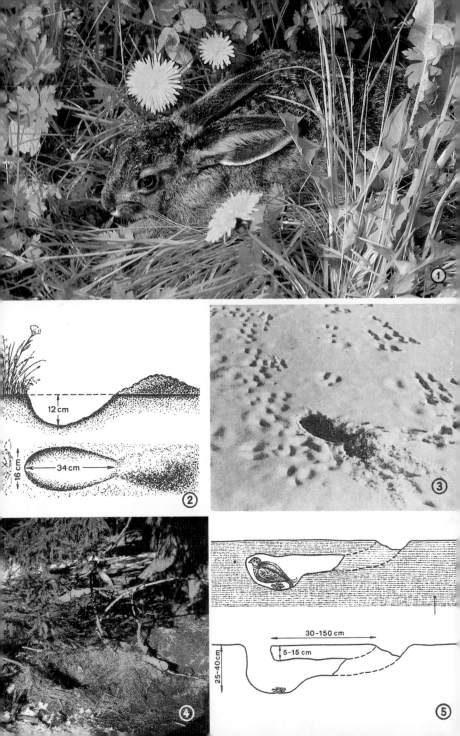

①

② 12 cm
16 cm 34 cm

③

④

⑤ 30-150 cm
5-15 cm
25-40 cm

Birds that nest on the ground never build such complex woven structures as do those that dwell in treetops. Instead they make use of suitable depressions in the ground, making a simple nesting hollow by circling with the body or scraping out the earth with their feet.

One such is the nest of the Little Ringed Plover (*Charadrius dubius*) — a simple scrape in sand (4) or gravel. The clutch always consists of four eggs coloured like pebbles, which makes them practically invisible among the surrounding pebbles.

Typical ground-nesters are the gamebirds, which forage for food on the ground (some also on shrubs and trees) and are mostly plant eaters or omnivores. A common inhabitant of mixed and coniferous forests in lowland districts is the Pheasant (*Phasianus colchicus*), a very adaptable bird which has become increasingly common during the past decades even in unforested districts in fields, meadows and shrubby hillsides. The hen (1) scrapes a simple hollow in the ground (about 5 cm deep and 20 cm wide) which she lines with a few grass stems. The nest is concealed in a clump of grass, in a standing forage crop, under a shrub or under a woodland tree, usually at the edge of a clearing. The clutch consists of 10—20 olive-green eggs (2).

A similar but better-built nest is made by the Partridge (*Perdix perdix*) in fields and meadows, hedgerows, on slopes and by waysides. The nesting hollow is deeper than that made by the Pheasant and is lined with a thicker layer of grass or leaves. It is 7 to 10 cm deep and about 15 cm in diameter. The clutch usually consists of 15 olive-green or brownish eggs which are incubated for 24 days. Within 24 hours of hatching the nestlings are dry and able to leave the nest to forage for food with the parents, leaving behind only empty egg shells. These serve to indicate whether the nestlings hatched successfully or whether the eggs were destroyed by an enemy. While still inside the egg the chick grows a so-called egg tooth on the tip of the upper beak with which it pecks at the shell when the time comes. While doing so it turns round its longitudinal axis and the space at the rounded end of the egg becomes increasingly bigger (5). Finally the pressure from within causes the pecked portion of the shell to break away allowing the nestling to emerge. The movements of the chicks cause the two parts of the shells to slip inside each other and that is an unfailing sign that the eggs were not destroyed (3).

Dwelling Places above Water and in Shoreline Vegetation

Plate 14

Many mammals and birds make their homes on or beside water. One such inhabitant of streams, rivers, ponds and lakes is the Muskrat (*Ondatra zibethicus*). This is a North American species that has become established in Europe through escapes from fur farms. At one time it occurred in Britain, but it has been successfully eradicated. This large rodent builds two types of dwelling places: burrows dug out in river banks (see Plate 20), and mounds or fortresses resembling huge ant-hills, constructed of aquatic vegetation among reeds at the edges of ponds and other calm bodies of water. Because it is an expert diver the Muskrat collects building material for its mound mostly under water. With its sharp teeth it bites the stems and roots of aquatic plants into pieces about 20 cm long and lays them in a single place. The structure rises from the bottom above the surface and when completed protrudes up to a metre above the water and measures about the same across. The whole structure may measure as much as 170 cm from top to bottom (1). Inside this wet pile of rotting material the Muskrat digs out the nesting burrow. The entrance is below the water with a corridor leading upwards to a spacious dwelling or nesting chamber above the water surface. This is lined with a dry cushion of fine plant fibres. The Muskrat's mound usually has two entrances and adjoining the nesting chamber is a small chamber for storing food supplies (2). Only rarely does the Muskrat build an open uncon-cealed nest in a clump of reeds just above the water (3).

The Great Crested Grebe (*Podiceps cristatus*), a common bird of lakes and large ponds, builds its nest in a similar manner. It, too, is an excellent diver, for its diet consists of various aquatic animals, and it collects the material for its nest underwater. When doing so it dives to the very bottom where it gathers rotting aquatic vegetation with its awl-like beak. This it brings to the surface and attaches to reeds, shrubs growing in the water or other aquatic plants. The finished wet structure, with a foundation sometimes as much as 80 cm below the surface, is shaped like a flat, truncated cone (5). The part above the water, with a nesting hollow about 15 cm wide and 5 cm deep, looks like a large pie and measures approximately 60 cm in diameter (4). Occasionally the Great Crested Grebe builds a nest in shallow water and then the foundation rests directly on the bottom of the pond or on the roots of aquatic plants. If it is not firmly attached to the plants, such a nest sometimes tears loose from its moorings and floats freely on the water. The eggs are white at first but then gradually acquire a brownish hue from the damp and rotting vegetation.

⑤

a

b

c

Dwelling Places above Water
and in Shoreline Vegetation

Plate 15

The wealth and diversity of animal and plant food is the main reason why so many birds have opted for the waterside habitats of ponds, lakes and rivers. They include the large group of waterfowl — swans, geese and ducks — that regularly nest in these places.

The Mute Swan (*Cygnus olor*) (1), which has been rapidly increasing in number during the past years (it is not hunted by Man and has few natural enemies), builds a huge nest in beds of reeds and rushes or on small islets. It is a haphazard pile of dry reeds in the middle of which the female makes a nesting hollow with her body that measures 40 to 60 cm across and is about 10 cm deep. The nest's foundation may be as much as 2 metres in diameter and it may rise as much as 1 metre above the water. The large, green-tinted white eggs are laid on a layer of fine material to which a little white down from the swan's breast is gradually added later, during incubation. The clutch consists of five to nine eggs.

On the Continent, you may find the nest of the Greylag Goose (*Anser anser*) on the remains of a Muskrat mound, otherwise it will be on a bed of cast-up reeds or on small islets. In Britain the Greylag Goose is normally only a winter visitor, but pairs do breed in parts of Scotland. Their nest is made of the same material as the Mute Swan's nest but is smaller — barely 1 metre in diameter and approximately 40 cm high. In the top of the flat conical structure is a shallow nesting hollow lined moderately with greyish-white down in which the female lays three to ten eggs. They are coloured dingy white or yellowish and all together may weigh as much as 1.5 kg. If the goose is suddenly alarmed she sprays the nest and the eggs with her liquid, foul-smelling droppings as she takes off; this perhaps protects the eggs from possible destruction (2). The cygnets (5a) and goslings (5b) remain in the nest only a short while, after which they roam the neighbourhood in the company of their parents. Their toes are connected by a web so that they are also able to swim by themselves. The down feathers of cygnets are whitish grey, the down of goslings dingy yellow.

The Coot (*Fulica atra*) is one of the commonest of waterbirds. Its nest may be found on practically every lowland pond with a bit of plant cover. It is located among reeds or in a clump of sedges (3) and is constructed of dry reedmace, sedge and reed stems. As a rule it is anchored to broken plant stems and is sometimes covered by a thin roof of reeds. The nest, which rises 20 to 40 cm above the water, measures approximately 40 to 50 cm in diameter, and is sparsely lined. Six to nine pinkish, black-speckled eggs (4) are laid. The newly hatched nestlings are covered with black down and the toes, like those of the adult birds, have a leathery fringe (5c).

①
②
③
④

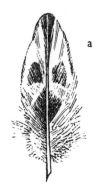

Dwelling Places above Water
and in Shoreline Vegetation

Plate 16

One of the largest groups of birds that make their home on lakes, ponds, rivers and swampy ground are the ducks. In Europe there are a great many species, which are very plentiful and may often be encountered even on rivers and bodies of water in cities. Introduced species can often be seen in wildfowl reserves. Ducks, which are omnivores, are divided into two groups according to the manner in which they obtain their food: non-diving ducks and diving ducks. Non-diving or dabbling ducks generally obtain their food on the surface, submerging only on occasion, whereas diving ducks forage for food on the bottom and dive regularly.

Ducks build their nests in shoreline vegetation (sedge, grass and herbaceous plants), on islets and some even in trees or tree cavities, often far from water. Commonest of the dabbling ducks is the Mallard (*Anas platyrhynchos*) (1), which inhabits even very small bodies of water. The nest is a very simple affair. In a suitable spot among vegetation, selected with the aid of the drake, the duck makes a rather deep hollow by circling with her body and fills it with plant material from around the hollow, pushing it in over the edge. The picture shows a duck's nest at the edge of muddy islet (4, left) and the nest of a Black-headed Gull (*Larus ridibundus*) (4, right), which is not at all unusual as ducks often nest in gull colonies (see Plate 18 for more detail about the Black-headed Gull's nest). The eggs of all ducks are relatively large and coloured greenish, yellowish or whitish. During incubation the duck covers them with a layer of down which she plucks from her breast. The colour of the down and coloration of the breast and belly contour feathers covering the down, which may also be found in the nest, serve as a means of identifying the species of duck.

The down in a Mallard's nest is greyish white and the belly feathers intermingled with the down not only have a narrow dark tip but also a pair of dark spots in the middle and a single spot at the base of the feather (5a). The down in the nest of the Gadwall (*Anas strepera*) is dark grey, making the ring of feathers round the edge seem almost black; the belly feathers have a wide triangular spot at the tip (5b). The Teal (*A. crecca*) fills its nest with dark down; the belly feathers have two dark stripes along the quill (5c). The Shoveler (*A. clypeata*) (3) has greyish-brown down feathers and dark belly feathers edged with white (5d). A duck that is found or captured can be identified by the colouring of the wing patch. The Mallard's is violet-blue edged with white at the front and back (2a), the Gadwall's (2b) is all white, the Teal's is green and black edged with yellow at the front (2c) and the Shoveler (2d) has a green wing patch edged with white at the front.

⑤

62

① ② ③ ④

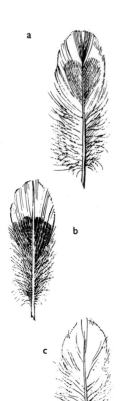

a

b

c

d

⑤

Dwelling Places above Water and in Shoreline Vegetation

Plate 17

Unlike dabbling ducks which often nest even far from water, for example in meadows, fields and even the edges of woods, diving ducks build their nests on islets, floating marshy vegetation and waterside vegetation. Only on the rare occasion do they nest farther from water. Diving ducks often build their nests in the midst of a gull colony, perhaps because the hundreds of gulls' eyes are more likely to perceive imminent danger and also because they warn of approaching danger with loud cries.

When ducks leave the nest they cover the eggs with down feathers. In addition to this they camouflage the whole nest by bending the surrounding vegetation to form a protective cover. The nest of the Pochard (*Aythya ferina*) (2) is relatively large and massive and is later edged with a thick layer of down (3). This is blackish at first, later brownish grey. The belly feathers are light-coloured with an imperceptible dark spot (5a). The whole nest is 29 to 49 cm wide, the nesting hollow between 13 and 24 cm in diameter and 5 to 15 cm deep. The Ferruginous Duck (*A. nyroca*) builds a nest 20 to 35 cm wide and 7 to 12 cm deep with a nesting hollow 14 to 18 cm in diameter. The down is similar to that of the Pochard, the belly feathers are darker but conspicuously light-coloured in the upper third (5b). The Ferruginous Duck does not breed in Britain but it occasionally visits southern England in winter.

The nest of the Tufted Duck (*A. fuligula*) (1) is similar to the Pochard's but somewhat smaller. The outside diameter is 23 to 35 cm, the nesting hollow is 14 to 18 cm across and 5 to 8 cm deep. It is edged by a thick layer of down coloured dark brownish-black; the belly feathers are whitish without any markings (5c). The Red-crested Pochard (*Netta rufina*) builds a large nest edged with a large quantity of down. The outside diameter is 34 to 45 cm, the nesting hollow 9 to 19 cm across and 5 to 13 cm deep. The down is light buff and grey dotted with whitish and brownish belly feathers which are also scattered round the nest (5d). Like the Ferruginous Duck, the Red-crested Pochard is likely to be encountered in Britain only in wildfowl reserves.

The wing patches of diving ducks are not so brightly coloured and have no conspicuous demarcation; they look like a long, light-coloured band, which often extends from the body to the tip of the wing. The Pochard (4a) is greyish white on the back and its large chestnut-coloured head is striking even in flight; there is only an inconspicuous light-coloured band at the hind edge of the wing. The Ferruginous Duck is smaller than the Pochard and coloured dark brownish-red throughout, with a white band extending roughly to the bend of the wing (4b). The plumage of the Tufted Duck is a stark contrast of black and white (4c); the head is crowned with a tuft of feathers and the black wing is marked with a conspicuous white stripe. The Red-crested Pochard has a broad white band running the length of the whole wing (4d).

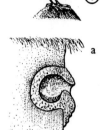

Dwelling Places above Water and in Shoreline Vegetation

Plate 18

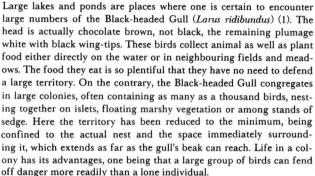

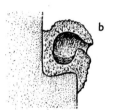
a

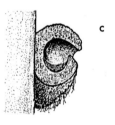
b

c

d

Large lakes and ponds are places where one is certain to encounter large numbers of the Black-headed Gull (*Larus ridibundus*) (1). The head is actually chocolate brown, not black, the remaining plumage white with black wing-tips. These birds collect animal as well as plant food either directly on the water or in neighbouring fields and meadows. The food they eat is so plentiful that they have no need to defend a large territory. On the contrary, the Black-headed Gull congregates in large colonies, often containing as many as a thousand birds, nesting together on islets, floating marshy vegetation or among stands of sedge. Here the territory has been reduced to the minimum, being confined to the actual nest and the space immediately surrounding it, which extends as far as the gull's beak can reach. Life in a colony has its advantages, one being that a large group of birds can fend off danger more readily than a lone individual.

The Black-headed Gull's nest is a relatively simple structure. It consists of a larger or smaller pile of dry aquatic plants placed on top of one another lined with fine dry grass, sedge or reed leaves (2). It is approximately 30 cm wide, the nesting hollow is some 15 cm across and only several centimetres deep.

The abundance of food provided by lakes and ponds attracts a great many species of birds in large numbers and these, in turn, attract the notice of their enemies — raptors or birds of prey. Many raptors visit lakes and ponds to hunt but some also nest there. The Marsh Harrier (*Circus aeruginosus*), a slender, relatively long-legged, brown and grey raptor, is a regular inhabitant of reed beds on the Continent; in Britain it is resident only in eastern England south of the Wash. Its nest is concealed in the impenetrable tangle of reeds and usually rests on bent reeds just above the water. It consists solely of the dry stems of aquatic plants and measures approximately 80 cm across. The shallow nesting hollow is visible only at the beginning of the nesting period, later it is trampled flat by the young nestlings (3). Although it was once quite widespread in Britain, the Marsh Harrier now breeds regularly only in a few parts of southeastern England and so it is unlikely that you will encounter its nest.

In streams in mountains and foothills the Dipper (*Cinclus cinclus*) (4) makes its home. About the size of the Blackbird, it is coloured brown all over except for the white patch on the breast. Its nest, made of aquatic plants, moss and grass, is a large, thick-walled spherical structure with an entrance at the side (5). It is concealed close to the water in a hole in the stream bank (6a), under trailing tree roots (6d), often even under a waterfall or on the jutting ledge of a footbridge or in the wall of a canal (6b, c). It is approximately 20 cm in diameter and the entrance hole always slants downwards towards the water.

①

②

③

⑤

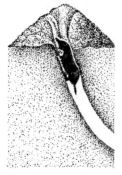

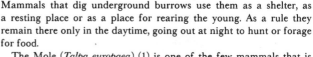

Dwelling Places below Ground

Plate 19

Mammals that dig underground burrows use them as a shelter, as a resting place or as a place for rearing the young. As a rule they remain there only in the daytime, going out at night to hunt or forage for food.

The Mole (*Talpa europaea*) (1) is one of the few mammals that is adapted to a permanent underground existence. It is widespread throughout Europe in meadows, fields, gardens, open woodlands, lowland as well as mountain districts and also in quite wet places. The only place it is not found is where the ground is too stony.

Molehills — mounds of earth thrust up on the surface by these animals — are known to everyone but far less familiar is the extensive and elaborate system of underground tunnels (4 to 5 cm in diameter). The Mole is an insectivore measuring 13 to 16 cm in length and covered with a thick coat of fine black hairs. Because these do not grow at an angle but straight up the Mole is able to move with equal ease both forwards and backwards in the tunnels, which it often does. It can crawl backwards just as fast as it runs forwards.

The Mole has very short legs. The hind feet are small and the forefeet are modified into very efficient excavators (4). The front limbs point forwards and outwards and the foot is broad and shovel-like with five long, strong claws (6a); the front limb is furthermore turned so that the animal tends to walk on the side of the forefeet with the underside facing backwards (6b). The Mole pushes the earth to the surface with its head (5) where it is thrust up into molehills. Small heaps 10 to 20 cm in diameter are thrust up from hunting tunnels (3a) which the Mole checks on and repairs several times a day and where it collects the animals that have fallen inside. The nest, lined with dry grass, moss and leaves (3b), is located beneath a larger heap which may be between 40 and 60 cm in diameter. The largest molehills (fortresses) are usually thrust up in the autumn. They are up to 1 metre wide and 50 cm high (2) and located beneath, at a depth of 30 to 60 cm, are the Mole's winter quarters surrounded by concentric tunnels and connected with the whole underground system. Here it waits out the winter. When it captures a large number of earthworms it paralyses them by biting them in a nerve centre and carries them to its food store beneath the main fortress (3c). The Mole also tunnels for worms and other prey close to the surface. In this case it does not make molehills but continually thrusts the earth up with its feet and head leaving an erratic trail behind in the form of a long ridge about 4 to 5 cm high.

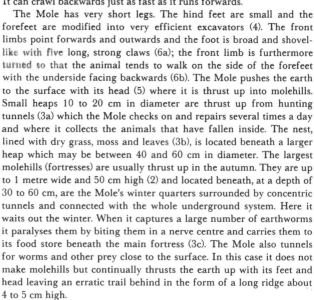

a

b

(6)

Dwelling Places below Ground   Plate 20

The Muskrat (*Ondatra zibethicus*) (1) builds its large fortresses (see Plate 14) only in calm bodies of water where there is no danger of sudden torrents of water. If it does make its home by a river or stream it digs a burrow in the bank. The entrance to the burrow is always underwater, roughly at a depth of less than 1 metre, so that the burrow and its inhabitants are protected from enemies. Runways several centimetres deep are tunnelled in the ground at the bottom, all radiating from the burrow. These are clearly visible, for example, when water is drained from a pond where there is a Muskrat burrow (2), although even when it is filled it is possible in clear water to see cloudy bands which are infallible signs of the Muskrat's underwater runs. From the entrance the burrow extends upwards at a slight angle for as much as several metres, terminating in a large chamber or den, lined with dry plant material. Besides the den there are also several smaller chambers for storing food (3). The burrows and dens are located about 50 cm below the ground; sometimes the burrow is so close to the surface that the roof caves in after a rainfall.

Another aquatic animal, the Otter (*Lutra lutra*), builds its dwelling place in a similar way. Whereas Muskrat burrows are 10 to 15 cm wide, the Otter's measure about 25 cm across. The burrow extends from the entrance, which is underwater, upwards at a slant into the bank and several metres from the entrance widens into a large den lined with fine, dry plant material. Besides the main entrance there are one or two more exits at ground level that also serve as a means of ventilation (4).

The Fox (*Vulpes vulpes*) is a common predator but few people are aware of its presence because of its wariness and concealed way of life. It lives in lowland to high mountain districts in woods, on rocky slopes overgrown with thickets and often even in open country, in fields. In such places it digs out earth for its den which has many tunnels underground and several entrance holes (5b). Sometimes it takes cover in an abandoned Badger's den. Besides breeding dens the Fox also digs simple seasonal dens (5a) used as an occasional shelter for the adults and the older cubs. The entrance hole to a newly dug den measures 20 to 25 cm in diameter; dens used for several years in succession are bigger and the entrance hole is about 50 cm across. The excavated earth is piled up into a large mound in front of the den and an occupied den is readily recognized by the feeding remains outside the entrance as well as by the strong smell produced by the Fox's scent glands.

The Orkney or Common Vole (*Microtus arvalis*) digs an elaborate system of underground tunnels, removing the earth with its hind feet (6a). Besides these passageways it also excavates chambers for breeding and sleeping as well as chambers for storing food (6b). This vole is ubiquitous on the Continent, where it can be quite a pest (see Plates 33 and 85), but in the British Isles it occurs only in the Orkneys (hence its alternative name) and Guernsey. It is also absent from Scandinavia.

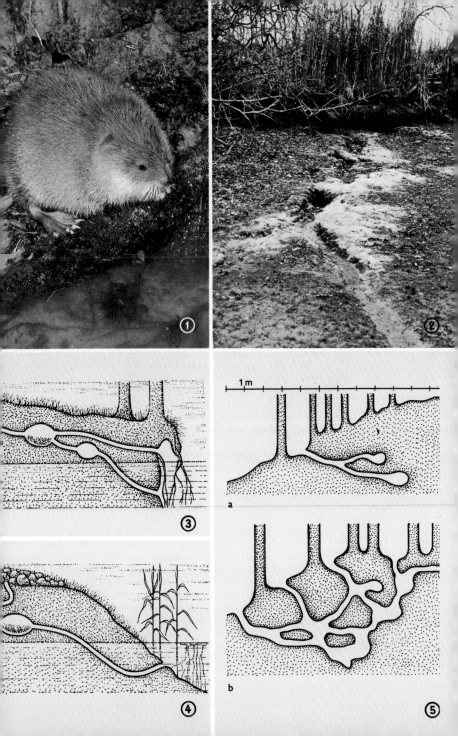

1

2

a

1 m

3

4

b

5

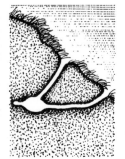

a

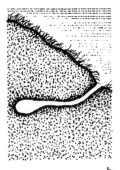

b

c

Dwelling Places below Ground Plate 21

The Rabbit (*Oryctolagus cuniculus*) (1) is closely related to the Brown or Common Hare (*Lepus europaeus*). Originally an inhabitant of grasslands and open woodland, the Rabbit is also found in dry sandy places in lowland districts; it is rarely encountered at heights above 700 metres. Despite the close ties between the two species the Rabbit differs from the Brown Hare in its way of life. The Brown Hare is generally solitary, whereas the Rabbit is definitely a social animal, always living together with several other individuals and sometimes forming large colonies numbering several tens of individuals. The Rabbit usually chooses dry, sandy shores and banks and slopes with a light cover of trees and shrubs for its burrows, which it digs out with its front feet. At the end of the burrow is a spherical chamber which the Rabbit uses for shelter in bad weather and when danger threatens. These burrows are often elaborate affairs with sometimes several passages leading from the den (6a) and forming an extensive intertwined system. The entrance hole is 10 to 15 cm wide with often a small mound of trampled earth outside (3). Such a burrow is dug by the Rabbit from the outside, but some burrows are dug out from the inside so that there is no earth outside the entrance hole (2). On the ground between the separate burrows there are conspicuous runs treaded by the rabbits (2), which with years of use may become deep grooves. Runways and entrance holes are regularly marked with small, round droppings (4).

In addition to the elaborate burrow system which is the Rabbit's home or dwelling place, the Rabbit also digs simple nesting burrows — small dead-end tunnels about a metre long called stops — where the young are nursed until they are weaned (6b). Stops made by younger females (does) of lower rank are located on the outskirts of the colony whereas those of older, higher-ranking does are placed in the middle of the colony. The nesting burrow is likewise terminated by a spherical chamber lined with dry grass, moss and leaves, which may also be mixed with wool plucked by the doe from her body to increase the insulating properties of the layer. Unlike the Brown Hare, the young of the Rabbit are born blind and almost naked (the Brown Hare young have a full coat of hair and can see at birth) and must be kept in a warm wrapping; another reason for this is that the doe does not keep the young warm with her body but visits them only to nurse. When she leaves the nesting burrow the doe seals the entrance with a relatively thick 'plug' of earth and grass (6c). A circle of freshly scraped earth is an indication that the burrow still contains very young rabbits (5). Besides this the doe usually marks the sealed burrow with several droppings of urine and this territorial marking is respected by the other members of the colony. When the young are near weaning the doe no longer seals the entrance and the young go outside for brief periods.

a

b

(5)

Southern and southeastern Europe is the home of the Bee-eater (*Merops apiaster*) (1), a gregarious bird that breeds colonially and is one of several that nest underground. It is generally found in open country with plenty of earth and sand banks in which it digs a burrow ending in a nesting chamber. As a rule the Bee-eater seeks out old brickworks, sand quarries and vertical river banks as nesting places.

The burrow is excavated by both partners, which fly at the wall striking it with their beaks until they have made a small hole. When it is big enough for them to perch on the edge they peck at the earth with their beaks and scrape it out with their feet. The finished burrow is 5 to 6 cm wide and often up to 2 metres long, and the task is completed in 10 to 12 days, though it may take as long as three weeks if the earth is hard. The amount of material excavated is between 10 and 15 kg. At the end of the burrow the Bee-eater excavates a nesting chamber 10 to 12 cm high and approximately 30 cm wide. The eggs are laid directly on bare earth. Later, however, they rest on a bed of undigested food pellets regurgitated by the adult birds. When danger threatens the young nestlings can eject a foul-smelling liquid from the anal opening.

The Kingfisher (*Alcedo atthis*), a bird of streams, rivers and lakes but found there in ever fewer numbers, nests in much the same manner as the Bee-eater but singly, not colonially. The burrow, often more than 1 metre long and ending in an egg-shaped nesting chamber (2), is dug out in a vertical bank by both birds with their beaks and feet. The entrance hole is about 5 cm across and is located at least 60 to 80 cm above the water. The young regurgitate undigested food remains (fish bones) in the nest and also defecate there. The liquid droppings, smelling of ammonia, run out of the burrow and down the wall and are thus an infallible sign that the burrow is occupied. The Kingfisher reveals its presence by its shrill whistling cry and the liquid white droppings it leaves in the places where it waits for prey.

The Sand Martin (*Riparia riparia*) (5a) is a gregarious bird that nests in colonies often numbering several hundred pairs. It differs from the related Swallow and House Martin chiefly by its manner of nesting. It is found only in places with vertical banks, usually round the lower reaches of rivers, in old sand quarries and in old clay pits, in which it excavates its burrows (3). This it does with its beak and feet in much the same manner as do the Bee-eater and Kingfisher. The tunnel, 0.5 to 1.5 metres long and about 5 cm wide, terminates in a spherical nesting chamber (4) which is approximately 10 cm in diameter and lined with feathers and plant material (5b). The task of excavating the burrow takes from three to five days. The individual burrows are often so close to each other that the birds break through into the adjacent nesting chamber during the process.

74

Health and Hygiene Facilities

Plate 23

The territories of many birds and mammals include places where they tend to their personal hygiene — where they groom themselves in one way or another. Ducks use the whole expanse of the pond for this purpose and take a bath several times a day, cleaning and trimming their feathers with their beaks and oiling them with the secretion from the preen gland at the base of the tail. Small perching birds bathe in puddles, pools and shallows, gamebirds clean their feathers in a dust or sand bath. The Jay (*Garrulus glandarius*) flies to anthills where it captures large ants, squeezes the formic acid from their bodies with its beak and spreads it on its feathers. The reason for this behaviour is not precisely known but undoubtedly it has to do with and is an important part of the bird's personal hygiene because it spreads the formic acid primarily on those places that usually harbour the greatest number of parasites.

All mammals like a good rub and every now and then rub their bodies against some hard object for quite some time. In this way they get rid of various parasites, rub itching spots and also rub off old hair. Red Deer (*Cervus elaphus*) (1) have their favourite trees located near their regular pathways which they visit occasionally to rub themselves on all sides. These trees also serve for territorial markings (see Plate 2). After lengthy use such trees are almost entirely stripped of their bark up to a height of 2 metres and often dry up completely. It is interesting to note that in a spruce wood Red Deer always select the occasional pine tree for this purpose, perhaps because the rough pine bark serves as a better rasp for the removal of dead hairs than the spruce bark. Closer examination of such a tree will always reveal hairs adhering to the trunk (5).

Mention has already been made of the wallowing places of Red Deer (Plate 2). These are various muddy expanses in the woods in which the stag always rolls about and then rises plastered with mud (2). It rubs this coat of mud off on the bark of surrounding trees, at the same time ridding itself of old dead hairs and flaking skin. After such a mud bath the animal's hair is extraordinarily clean and shining. The wallowing places of Wild Boar (*Sus scrofa*) are similar (3) (see also Plate 2) and can be identified by the tracks left by the animals as well as droppings and sometimes also by the smell. The Wild Boar has a pronounced odour like that of domestic pigs and the wallowing place or rubbing trees (4) in its vicinity are marked with this smell for a brief period. The Wild Boar can rub the bark off down to the bare wood.

①

②

③

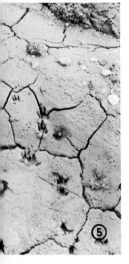

Tracks of Mammals with Paws Plate 24

The Hedgehog (*Erinaceus europaeus*) (1) is found in gardens, parks, scrub, thin deciduous as well as mixed woods, also at the edge of coniferous woods and often even in open fields. In the daytime it rests in thickets, a pile of stones or in a nest of leaves. During its nocturnal rambles it gathers insects and often hunts small vertebrates as well.

Hedgehog tracks can be found in such places as muddy woodland and field paths, the edges of drying puddles, muddy shores and wet vegetable beds. The best time to look for tracks is after a rainfall; they never occur in snow because the Hedgehog hibernates for about five months in winter.

The forefoot (2a) and hind foot (2b) have five relatively long toes with strong claws. The pads are large and the pad markings are clearly visible in a strongly impressed print. The Hedgehog is a plantigrade animal and walks on the whole sole of the foot, though often the thumb mark is very faint. In a strongly impressed track it is evident that the toes of the hind foot are narrower and closer together, whereas the toes of the forefoot are stronger and more widespread. The Hedgehog is one of the few exceptions in which the hind foot is larger than the forefoot.

The track of the forefoot (3) is approximately 2.5 cm long (the length is always measured without the claws) and 2.5 to 3 cm wide, measured from toe to toe at the widest spread. The hind track is somewhat narrower, approximately 2 cm wide, but on the other hand it is longer than the fore track — up to 3 cm on average (3b). Remember that the measurements of all tracks are average figures and that the size of the tracks made by a given species is determined by the animal's age, its condition and development, and even its sex.

The Hedgehog moves only by walking, or at most by fast walking which may be reminiscent of a slow trotting gait. The trail is a wavy double line with the prints of the forefeet turned inwards and the prints of the hind feet turned outwards (6). When walking the hind foot is placed partially over the fore track so that the claws of the hind toes are impressed in line with the toe pads of the fore track. This results in a double track (4), which in harder ground may show only four toe marks (5). In fast walking the hind foot moves farther forwards and is placed in the same position as the forefoot or else slightly oversteps the forefoot. The stride is 10 to 15 cm long and 3 to 6 cm wide.

78

The Brown or Common Hare (*Lepus europaeus*) (1) is one of the most widespread mammals. It is found in all types of landscapes from lowland to wooded high mountain districts. Its coloration corresponds to that of its environment. As a rule it is coloured rusty brown, but in areas with rich black earth its brown coat has a black tinge and in areas with red soil a reddish tinge. The Brown Hare is a very active animal and may travel long distances (up to several kilometres) in a single night. Brown Hare tracks are found less frequently in the period from spring to autumn and then usually only in soft, bare places, but immediately after the first snowfall the whole countryside is covered with tracks and that is the best time to track the Brown Hare.

The Brown Hare is a typical runner that moves only by bounding — by short or long leaps (Plate 26) — and it does not walk or trot. Compared with the Rabbit (see Plate 28) it has much stronger and longer hind limbs and these provide the chief propulsive force in locomotion (2c). There are five toes on the forefeet but the thumb is usually atrophied, so that it does not show in the track (2a, left). The outer, or fifth toe thus appears in the track as the shortest toe. The hind foot has only four toes and is longer as well as slightly wider than the forefoot (2a, right). The fore tracks are approximately 5 cm long and 3 cm wide; the hind tracks are much longer, 6 to 12 cm in length, and average 3.5 cm in width. In soft ground the tracks may be much longer and wider. The sharp claws are impressed strongly in all the tracks and on harder ground are the only prints that show. At a normal gait all four feet make pointed impressions. The sole of the Brown Hare's foot is without pads. Instead it is completely covered with thick stiff hairs (4), which are most prominent on the underside of the toes. That is why in soft ground these impress as four hollows resembling the prints made by toe pads (2a; 3). This thick hairy cover serves an important purpose — it prevents slipping. If we were to examine the hare's foot through a magnifying glass we would discover that the hairs are of several different kinds. Those on the upper side of the foot are smooth (5a, d) whereas those on the underside of the foot are rough at the tip (5b). The hairs on the underside of the hind feet are the longest and are fringed at the tip (5c). They are nearly square (5e) and the fringe is so thick that it prevents slipping when the animal is running.

In all types of locomotion the Brown Hare moves the hind legs ahead of the front legs (2c) and therefore the larger hind tracks are always placed in front of the fore tracks (2b). Only when it stops and postures is the fore track in front of the hind track.

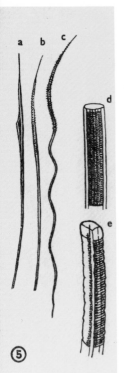

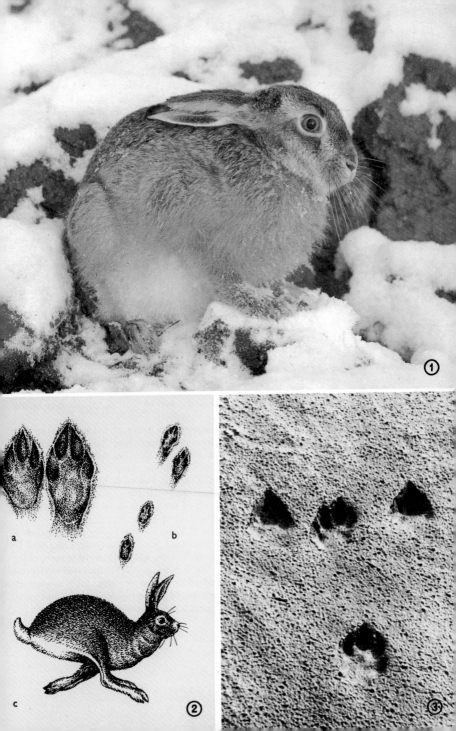

a b c

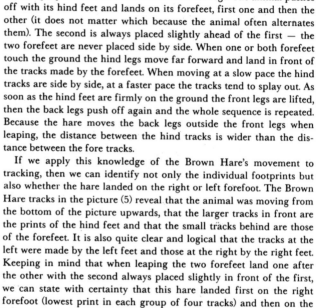

Tracks of Mammals with Paws

Plate 26

The Brown Hare (*Lepus europaeus*) (1), as we have seen (Plate 25), travels by leaps of varying length. This movement has various phases (2). The propulsive force comes from the back legs. The animal pushes off with its hind feet and lands on its forefeet, first one and then the other (it does not matter which because the animal often alternates them). The second is always placed slightly ahead of the first — the two forefeet are never placed side by side. When one or both forefeet touch the ground the hind legs move far forward and land in front of the tracks made by the forefeet. When moving at a slow pace the hind tracks are side by side, at a faster pace the tracks tend to splay out. As soon as the hind feet are firmly on the ground the front legs are lifted, then the back legs push off again and the whole sequence is repeated. Because the hare moves the back legs outside the front legs when leaping, the distance between the hind tracks is wider than the distance between the fore tracks.

If we apply this knowledge of the Brown Hare's movement to tracking, then we can identify not only the individual footprints but also whether the hare landed on the right or left forefoot. The Brown Hare tracks in the picture (5) reveal that the animal was moving from the bottom of the picture upwards, that the larger tracks in front are the prints of the hind feet and that the small tracks behind are those of the forefeet. It is also quite clear and logical that the tracks at the left were made by the left feet and those at the right by the right feet. Keeping in mind that when leaping the two forefeet land one after the other with the second always placed slightly in front of the first, we can state with certainty that this hare landed first on the right forefoot (lowest print in each group of four tracks) and then on the left.

When hopping the groups of four tracks are so close together that there is no appreciable distance between them (3a). The tracks of the hind feet are side by side, almost parallel, and the tracks of the forefeet are in the same line one behind the other. If at this slow gait the Brown Hare travels across a layer of fine mud, the tracks it makes are perfect and undistorted and the underside of the individual toes as well as the hairs on the sole of the foot show (4). When hopping the space between the hind tracks is 7 to 10 cm.

When bounding, which in terms of speed may be compared to trotting, the distance between each group of four tracks lengthens (it is approximately 50 cm long), but the width of the stride remains the same. The pattern of the tracks remains roughly the same or else one of the hind tracks is placed a little farther forwards (3b). When bounding at speed the distance between each stride lengthens as the speed increases and may be between 1 and 3.5 metres (3c).

①

②

a

b

c

③

Tracks of Mammals with Paws Plate 27

Like all mammals the Brown Hare (*Lepus europaeus*) has regular pathways in its territory along which it travels when it leaves its shelter in search of food. The pathways in such a territory are not the property of a single animal but are used by many. In summer they are easily overlooked because they are concealed by the tall vegetation. Nevertheless they are there and are continually kept in good condition by the Brown Hare. Do take the trouble to try and find such a summer run in a meadow, forage or cereal crop. It winds like a deep tunnel and if you bend down to take a closer look you will see how the plants that were in the way have been carefully bitten off and removed.

In winter, if the ground is covered with snow, the Brown Hare's run is visible for a long distance. It zig-zags through the snow like a deep furrow, which may sometimes be as much as 30 to 40 cm wide — often for hundreds of metres (4). Diverging from the run to all sides are individual tracks that generally lead to supplies of food covered by snow, which the animals dig out with their front feet. Sometimes the runs divide into several pathways and frequently they are also used by other mammals. Even when there is no snow on the ground in winter, the Brown Hare's runs appear in the form of muddy, treaded pathways and where an individual has turned off on to drying mud there may be a well-defined group of tracks (6).

In fresh snow, which has not yet been trampled by lots of various feet, a Brown Hare's trail can be followed for a long time. It will show when the animal hopped (1), when it sat on its haunches (thereby also marking the spot with scent from the gland at the base of the tail), when it dug food from the snow and when it was forced to move at a fast pace (5). When the snow stops falling shortly before daybreak a Brown Hare can be tracked all the way to its nest, for that is the time when it retires to rest after foraging for food during the night. Before it lies down in the excavated depression (there are several such lying-up places throughout its territory — see Plate 12), it behaves in an interesting manner, employing tactics aimed at deceiving a possible pursuer following the scent of its tracks. The Brown Hare does not run directly to the nest but in an irregular circle around it, retracing its steps for a few metres every now and then and then leaping off to the side (2). The leap may be as much as 2 metres long. The animal repeats this manoeuvre several times, almost always leaping in the direction away from the nest. In this manner the Brown Hare slowly approaches the nest, entering it with a long leap the last time it retraces its steps (3).

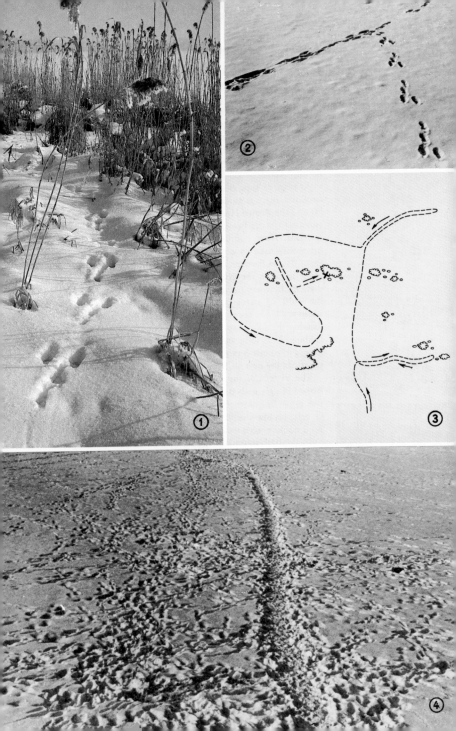

The Rabbit (*Oryctolagus cuniculus*) (1) resembles the Brown Hare (*Lepus europaeus*) but differs in the size of the back and front legs. The hind legs of the Brown Hare are much longer and stronger than the forelegs, whereas in the Rabbit the disparity between the two is far less pronounced. The Rabbit's larger front legs may be attributed to the fact that it is a burrowing animal and a proficient excavator (see Plate 21). Nevertheless, here, too, the main propulsive force comes from the back legs; the rabbit pushes off with the hind feet and lands on the forefeet — the latter are not used to push off.

As regards type of locomotion, size of the tracks, stride and trail, here, too, there is evidence of the close relationship between the Rabbit and the Brown Hare (see Plate 26). However, because the Rabbit is smaller than the Brown Hare, all these features are likewise on a smaller scale. When running, or rather bounding (the rabbit moves in no other way than by a series of leaps), the hind feet regularly move in front of the forefeet (3). When hopping there is no appreciable distance between the groups of tracks (3a). At a slightly faster pace the distance between the groups of four tracks lengthens to about 30 cm; the width of stride is approximately 7 cm (3b). When bounding at speed the leaps are shorter than those of the Brown Hare (the stride is usually no more than 1 metre) and far more frequent. The fore track is about 3 cm long and about 2.5 cm wide, the hind track about 4 cm long and about 3 cm wide. As with the Brown Hare, in distinct impressions the hair on the underside of the toes will show.

The pattern of the tracks may be of two kinds. It may be like the Brown Hare's with the tracks of the forefeet one behind the other in the same line and the tracks of the hind feet placed side by side (2, left) or like the Red Squirrel's (Plate 29) with both the fore and hind tracks placed side by side in pairs (2, right; 5).

In the first, hare-like trail (2, left) we can see a change in the order in which the forefeet landed on the ground. In the first group of tracks at the bottom the Rabbit landed on the right forefoot but in the next group of four tracks it landed first on the left and then on the right forefoot. In the third leap the order was again reversed and remained the same in the next three leaps, and the last time there was once again a change in the order.

The runs of the Rabbit (4) are like those of the Brown Hare (Plate 27) and serve the same purpose, but they are much shorter. The Rabbit is basically a timid animal and never strays far from its colony.

①

②

③

Tracks of Mammals with Paws

Plate 29

The Red Squirrel (*Sciurus vulgaris*) (1) inhabits coniferous, mixed and deciduous woods from lowland to high mountain districts, but as we have seen (Plate 4) its distribution in Britain has become restricted. It spends most of its time in trees, descending to the ground only occasionally. Its limbs are well adapted for climbing on tree trunks and branches. The long slender toes on all four feet are furnished with equally long, narrow, needle-sharp claws curving downwards like sickles. These enable the squirrel to keep a firm grip not only on rough but also on smooth bark because they readily penetrate even the smallest fissure. Also important in climbing are the pads on the feet whose rough surface prevents slipping. In winter the hair between the toes is longer and this, too, serves to prevent slipping by providing greater adhesion.

The forefoot has four toes; the thumb is so greatly reduced that it is only a negligible remnant (4a, left). On the palm there are three distinct pads at the junction with the toes (the two middle toes — the third and fourth — are set on the central pad) and two distinct wrist pads at the opposite, back end of the palm. All five pads show clearly in tracks made in soft ground (4b, left). On the hind foot (4a, right) there are five toes and four pads at the junction with the toes so that the third toe issues from the point between the two middle pads (4b, right). There are no pads at the heel of the hind foot, which is smooth and usually impresses whole — from front to hind end.

The fore track is about 4 cm long and about 2 cm wide, the hind track is about 1 cm longer and from 2.5 to 3.5 cm wide. In general the width of the track always depends on the type of ground, which affects the degree to which the toes spread. The long claws always show distinctly in both the fore and hind tracks.

The Red Squirrel's trail is so characteristic and typical that it cannot be mistaken for that of any other mammal. The Red Squirrel always moves in the same manner as the Brown Hare and Rabbit — by hopping, the hind feet landing in front of the tracks made by the forefeet. The fore tracks and hind tracks are always placed side by side — the space between the hind tracks measures 5 to 10 cm, whereas that between the fore tracks is only 2 to 3 cm (4c; 3).

The tracks and trails of the Red Squirrel are seen only in snow and muddy forest rides. The trail is never very long, only several tens of metres, and as a rule always begins and ends at the bottom of a tree. In both the group of four tracks (4c) and the trail (2) we can see that the tracks made by the hind feet are turned slightly outwards. The distance between the sets of four tracks depends on the speed of locomotion. At a leisurely pace the hops may be from 30 to 50 cm in length, at a faster pace they may be up to 1 metre long (2).

c

④

Tracks of Mammals with Paws Plate 30

The Common Hamster (*Cricetus cricetus*) (1) is a typical grassland rodent found in eastern and central Europe, but it is rare in western Europe and is not found at all in the British Isles. It is a solitary animal that lives in fields, on treeless slopes and at the edges of woods beside spreading stands of grain in lowland and hilly districts. It digs underground burrows which have a relatively big pile of earth in front of the entrance. These burrows often form an extensive system; some may be inclined, others run straight downwards to food supply chambers where the animal stores 10 to 15 kg of food. The Common Hamster's diet consists mainly of plant food but it also feeds on insects and small vertebrates. Before the onset of winter it excavates a hole as much as 2 metres deep ending in a large sleeping chamber, which it lines with dry grass and where it hibernates, waking from time to time from its winter sleep to feed from its underground stores.

Because it hibernates, the Common Hamster is encountered only in summer, in fields, and after a rainfall. The toes are long and have relatively strong claws. There are five toes on each foot but the thumb on the forefoot is so greatly reduced (2a) that it rarely shows in the track or does not show at all (2d). The toes on the hind feet (2b) impress very strongly (2c) and the prints of the pads beneath the toes and at the heel are also very distinct. The fore track is about 1.5 cm long and about 1 cm wide, the hind track is 2 to 3.5 cm long and 1 cm wide. The trail is distinctive in that the tracks of the hind feet are outside and slightly behind the fore tracks (5). The length of the stride is 7 to 10 cm and the width of the stride — straddle — is about 3 cm between the fore tracks and 5 to 6 cm between the hind tracks.

The European Beaver (*Castor fiber*) is nowadays found only in nature preserves in Germany, France, Poland, Scandinavia, Russia and Mongolia. This robust rodent with broad flat tail is adapted to life in water. In the banks of streams it digs long burrows furnished with ventilation holes and underwater entrances or else it builds large lodges of twigs, reeds and mud in shallow water like those of the Muskrat (see Plate 75).

Beaver tracks are found only in the vicinity of a Beaver colony, in other words in muddy river banks. The forefoot has five relatively short toes with relatively long, pointed claws (3a), used to dig the burrows. All five toes of the forefoot may show in the track (3c), but on harder ground sometimes only four are seen. The toes are not webbed. The hind foot, which is much longer, is also five-toed, the claws are shorter and more blunt and all five toes are joined at the tips by a rigid web (3b). In soft ground the webbing is impressed in the track (3d), on harder ground it does not show. The forefoot is approximately 5 cm long and 4 cm wide, the hind foot is up to 11 to 15 cm long and about 10 cm wide. In the trail (4) the hind track is usually inside and partially covers the fore track (there is thus a lateral register of the tracks). The stride is quite short — the distance between each group of tracks is 15 to 50 cm. In mud and snow the Beaver's broad tail may leave a drag mark down the centre of the trail.

90

1

2

3

a

b

c

d

a

b

c

d

Tracks of Mammals with Paws Plate 31

Beside streams and millraces, on muddy pond and river banks and especially on the muddy bottoms of drained ponds in continental Europe one will find trails of closely set tracks made by the Muskrat (*Ondatra zibethicus*) (1). It is an aquatic animal whose way of life depends on the presence of water and so its tracks are not encountered elsewhere. It is chiefly found in lowland and hilly country, occurring less often at heights up to 1,000 metres above sea-level.

The front toes are slender and long in proportion to the length of the forefoot and end in long, narrow claws (2a). The underside of the foot is bare and hairless with prominent palm pads beneath the toes as well as on the heel that are clearly defined in the track (2c). The fore track, which is characterized by the four widely spread toes, may not show the whole foot and so appears very short because the heel is not impressed. The hind foot is larger — as is generally the case in rodents — and has five toes (2b). The palm pads show in a track made in thick mud (2d) and sometimes so do the short stiff hairs that form a thick fringe round all the toes. Though one would expect an aquatic mammal to have webbed feet, the Muskrat does not; the function of a web or lobes is taken over by the thick fringe of hairs on the toes.

The fore track is about 3.5 cm long and about 3 cm wide. The hind track is 6 to 7 cm long and 3 to 4 cm wide. Because the Muskrat generally moves about in muddy terrain all the tracks seem wider and often also longer than they really are. In shape the tracks of the Muskrat slightly resemble those of the Red Squirrel (Plate 29), but there is a marked difference in the pattern of the tracks in the trail. The Muskrat moves either by walking or trotting. When walking the stride is relatively short; at a slow pace it measures only 5 to 6 cm, at a faster pace it is 10 to 13 cm long. The width of the stride is less than 5 cm. The trail consists of a series of regularly repeated paired prints in which the hind track covers the heel of the fore track (3) to a lesser or greater extent and often completely overlaps it. (The three diagonal trails in the picture are the tracks of a beetle: on either side are the prints of the feet, the groove in the centre was made by the insect's body.) The Muskrat is active even during winter and so its track may also be found on snow or snow-covered ice (4). In deep mud the trail shows a deep groove in the centre made by the drag of the tail (2e).

The Muskrat's habitat is also populated by the Brown Rat (*Rattus norvegicus*) and Northern Water Vole (*Arvicola terrestris*) and their tracks will be found there too. These are readily distinguished from the Muskrat's because the hind track of the Brown Rat is 3 to 4.5 cm long and that of the Water Vole only 2 to 2.5 long. You will, of course, only find this combination of tracks on the Continent because the Muskrat does not occur in the British Isles (see Plate 14).

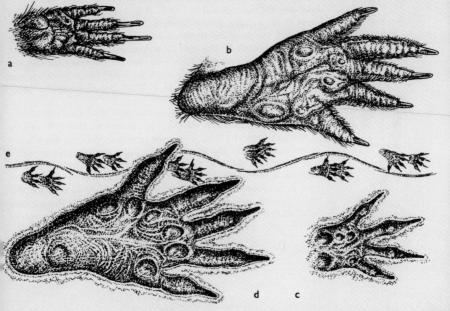

Found throughout practically all of Europe are two very similar rodents — the Yellow-necked Mouse (*Apodemus flavicollis*) (1) and the Wood Mouse or Long-tailed Field Mouse (*A. sylvaticus*). The Wood Mouse inhabits deciduous and coniferous woods but is also often found in shrubberies, hedgerows, large gardens and shoreline vegetation by ponds and rivers, which are the typical habitats of the Yellow-necked Mouse. The Yellow-necked Mouse is, however, less frequent than the Wood Mouse in open woodland and is only patchily distributed in England and Wales. In winter both species frequent buildings and often end up in mouse traps. They differ from the grey-coloured House Mouse (*Mus musculus*) in having brownish-rufous hair on the back, large black eyes and large ears. Distinguishing between the two themselves is, however, a different matter. The Yellow-necked Mouse has a distinct line of demarcation between the brownish-rufous hair of the back and the white hair on the belly and a brownish-rufous spot on the throat. The hair on the Wood Mouse's back has a slightly greyer tint and the transition between this and the dingy-white hair of the belly is not clearly defined; the spot on the throat is small and yellowish and may be absent altogether. The Yellow-necked Mouse is 9 to 12 cm long, the Wood Mouse 9 to 10.5 long. The tails of both species are the same length as the body.

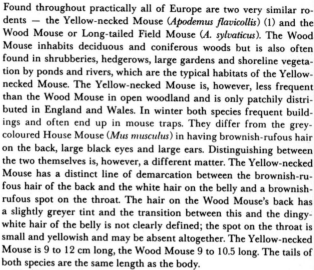

The Wood Mouse has five toes on both the forefeet and hind feet but the thumb on the forefoot (2a) is placed high up, is greatly reduced and does not show in the track (2b); the fore track is therefore always four-toed. The fore track is about 1 cm long and because the toes splay widely when the animal puts its weight on the foot it also measures the same in width. The hind foot is five-toed and is almost three times as long as the forefoot. The thumb and outer toe are shortened, the three middle toes are very long with tips practically in the same line (3a). All five toes show clearly in the track, which is 2.3 to 2.7 cm long and roughly 1 cm wide (3b). The hind foot has six pads but these show in the track only when the Wood Mouse travels across fine, soft mud because otherwise it is not heavy enough to leave clearly defined prints.

Field mice are fast and excellent jumpers. The hind feet always land in front of the tracks made by the forefeet (6). Down the middle of the trail there is a shallow narrow groove — the drag mark made by the long tail (5). The drag mark may also show as arcs on either side of the trail made by the tail as it switches from side to side. In deep snow the prints of the forefeet and hind feet merge to form a single long print (7). When moving at a leisurely pace (4) the distance between each group of tracks is about 6 cm and in flight it may be as much as 50 to 60 cm. The size of the tracks may be compared with the snow-covered tracks of a Brown Hare (see Plate 27).

① ② ③ ④ ⑤

b

b

The Orkney or Common Vole (*Microtus arvalis*) (1) lives in fields, meadows and hillsides as well as in thin groves, woodland margins, parks and gardens throughout Europe (but not Britain except for the Orkneys and Guernsey). Because of its extraordinary fertility (the female has several broods of 4 to 12 young each year), it reaches plague numbers from time to time on the Continent and the whole country-side is then inundated with voles, which can cause great damage to field crops (see Plate 85). The rate of reproduction is furthermore increased by the extraordinarily rapid rate of sexual maturation — females are capable of being fertilized at about the age of one month, when they themselves are still being nursed by the mother.

The forefeet have five toes (2a) but only four toe prints show in the track (2c) because the thumb is rudimentary and set close to the tarsal (ankle) joint. The third and fourth toes are usually the longest; the second and fifth toes are only slightly shorter and thus do not lie in the same line as the other two toes. In the track the two outer toes point far outwards; sometimes they are almost in a straight horizontal line. The hind foot (2b) is much longer and has five toes, with thumb and outer toe set farther back. The three central toes (the second, third and fourth) are approximately the same length and in the track (2d) lie in practically the same line. When the weight is brought to bear on the foot the two outer toes point far outwards, often far more than shown in the figure (2d).

The fore track is about 1 cm long (if the print is clearly defined); the hind track is almost twice as long and measures 1.5 to 1.8 cm. The Common Vole moves by long or short jumps with the hind feet landing in the fore track or close beside it. The trail then appears as a series of double tracks in the form of deep or shallow depressions (5). The trail of the Common Vole is never as long as that of the Yellow-necked Mouse (Plate 32) and generally leads from one tunnel entrance to another or from the furrow to a food supply. In dry, deep snow the drag mark made by the short tail also shows as a narrow interrupted groove between the left and right tracks (4).

The Common Vole is active throughout the year. During the growth period 3- to 5-cm-wide runs appear in the ground vegetation. Similar runs, or tunnels, are dug out by the animals beneath the snow cover in winter. The walls of these tunnels are lined with gnawed grass which leave a pattern of deep grassy furrows in the ground when the snow melts (3).

The tracks of the small insect-eating shrews are very similar to those made by the Common Vole. However, they are half as large and a clearly defined print always shows five toes in both the hind and fore tracks (2e).

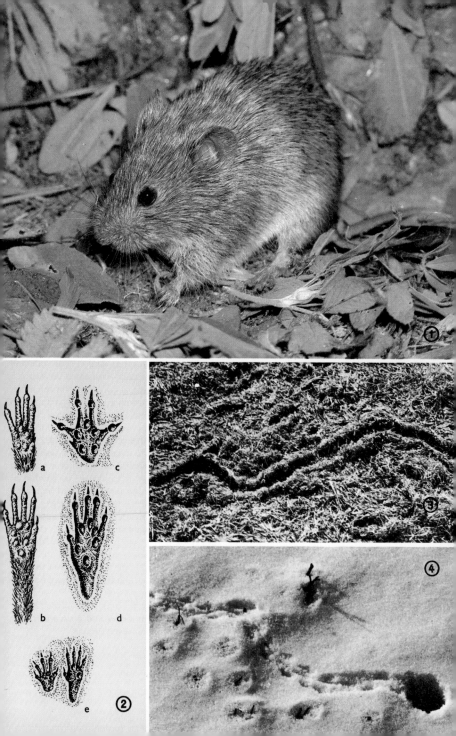

Tracks of Mammals with Paws

Plate 34

Three members of the cat family are found in Europe. The first and most common is the Domestic Cat (*Felis catus*); the second, the Wild Cat (*F. silvestris silvestris*), is a rare breed which only occurs in parts of central, eastern and southern Europe and Scotland; and the third, the Lynx (*Lynx lynx*), (Plate 35) is encountered only occasionally. The common house cat is descended from the African Cat *Felis silvestris libyca* which was domesticated by the ancient Egyptians and is interfertile with the Wild Cat. Over the ages breeding and selection have produced many different breeds of cats differing in size, shape and colour. The shape of the feet and their prints, however, have not changed much.

The Domestic Cat (1) has five toes on the front foot and four on the hind foot, but the thumb on the forefoot is set so high up (4a) that it leaves no print (5b). The sharp, hooked claws on all the toes are carried in a retracted position in sheaths so that they show in the track only very occasionally, for instance when the cat is leaping upon prey. The prominent toe pads are shaped like small grapes and are arranged in a regular arc on the slightly oval foot. In the track they are impressed close together (5b; 6). The pad beneath the toes is distinctly three-lobed and its hind edge has three regular curves that in a clear print are almost always in line (5a). The hind foot (4b) has four toes arranged in the same way as the front toes and only slightly smaller.

The track of the Domestic Cat is almost as long as it is wide and appears circular. The fore track of a medium-sized cat is between 2.5 cm and 3.5 cm long and about 3 cm wide. A cat's footprint resembles that of a small dog but its toe prints are rounder and no claws show.

When stalking the Domestic Cat both creeps, in which case the feet are placed very close together, heel to toe (6), and walks, in which case the hind feet are placed on the toe prints of the forefeet (2a). When walking the tracks may occur in various combinations, as double tracks and even as single tracks depending on whether something attracted the cat's attention and caused it to change its rhythm of movement (7). When trotting (2b) the hind feet are placed in exactly the same position as the forefeet so that the two tracks register — the trail appears as a single line. Sometimes a five-toed print appears in the trotting trail, but this is a normal double track in which the hind foot side-stepped the fore track by one toe print. When walking the length of the stride is about 30 cm, when trotting between 35 and 50 cm and when jumping (2c), in which case the hind feet land in front of the fore tracks and form an irregular quadrangle, it may be from 1 to 2 metres.

The feet of the Wild Cat (3a, b) are larger than those of the Domestic Cat and the track (5a) is about 1 cm longer and 1 cm wider. The gait, pattern of the tracks and trail are, however, similar.

Tracks of Mammals with Paws

Plate 35

The European Lynx (*Lynx lynx*) (1) is found in eastern Europe, Spain, Scandinavia and sporadically also in other European countries where it has been reintroduced. It is absent from the British Isles. It is the rarest of the European cats and to come across its tracks is most unusual. It inhabits large continuous woods with thick shrub layer and avoids open spaces. It is particularly fond of rocky country which is best suited to its manner of pursuit and attack.

The tracks of the Lynx resemble those of the Domestic Cat but are two to three times the size. The toe pads are bare, hairless and regularly oval in shape. The pad beneath the toes is shaped like a rounded triangle with the apex pointing towards the four toe pads set in an arc above it. The hind edge of the pad consists of three slightly projecting lobes. The forefoot is wider and sometimes also shorter than the hind foot. The track made by the forefoot (2a) is 5 to 7 cm long and 5.5 to 7.5 cm wide; that of the hind foot is 4.5 to 6 cm long and about 5 cm wide (2b).

a

The trail of a walking Lynx consists of a double line of left and right double tracks because the hind feet are placed in the track of the front feet, they therefore register (4a). When the speed of walking increases, however, the hind foot oversteps the forefoot, the pad of the hind foot is placed roughly in the same line as the front toes and the back end of the fore track is exposed (2c). When trotting at a leisurely pace — the Lynx's normal gait — the trail is similar. When the animal runs (4b) the hind feet are placed in front of the forefeet and the feet do not register — all four are impressed separately so that there are no double tracks. In normal walking the length of the stride is 30 to 80 cm; it increases to about 130 cm when the Lynx is trotting and may be as much as 150 cm or more when the animal is running. A solitary predator, the Lynx does not stalk its prey but usually lies in wait for it on a high rock or in a tree and pounces on it with a powerful leap that may span a distance of 5 to 7 metres.

All members of the cat family are digitigrade — they walk only on the tips of the toes with the rest of the foot not touching the ground. When they sit the tracks are different (3). The dark prints in front of the figure were made by a Lynx's forefeet, behind these are the prints of the toes and the whole of the hind feet all the way to the heel. In the corner at the extreme left are the Lynx's droppings.

b

①

②

③

The Fox, or Red Fox, (*Vulpes vulpes*) (1) is the most widespread wild species of the dog family. It lives mainly in woodland, but can be found in open country; it may even pass through towns and cities where it escapes notice because it is a wary and shy animal. It occurs throughout Europe, except for Iceland, and is common over most of the British Isles.

The front foot (2a) has five toes but the thumb is placed so high that it leaves no mark in the track. The only visible part of the thumb is the claw which protrudes slightly from the hairy coat. The hind foot (2b), or rather the front part of the hind foot for the whole foot is much longer, is furnished with four toes. The forefoot is usually slightly larger, longer and wider than the hind foot.

The track has a very regular, ellipsoidal shape with clearly defined claw marks (2c). The two middle toes are impressed close together and lie in the same line. Impressed just as symmetrically are the outer toes placed farther back and the triangular hind pad is also regular in shape (2a). This nearly perfect bilateral symmetry makes it difficult to distinguish between the tracks made by the right and left feet. The forefoot track (3) is about 5 cm long and 3 to 4 cm wide, the hind track is almost the same length but appears more slender. The pads of the two central toes are set far forwards and their hind edge is almost in the same line with the front edge of the two outer toe pads (compare the Domestic Dog track in Plate 39). Because the hind pad is set far back there is a relatively large space between the toe pads and the hind pad. Both these characteristics are typical of the tracks of wild species of dogs and are also an important means of identification. Perfect prints may be found in hardening mud and in wet snow in winter. But winter tracks are sometimes blurred because the pads become covered by thick, long hair that grows between the toes. In winter, therefore, it is possible to mistake the track of a Fox for that of a Brown Hare (Plate 25) because the two are approximately the same size. But that happens only in the case of a single track, because both the stride and trail of the two mammals are very different.

The Fox has a variety of gaits (see Plate 37) — walking (4), trotting, running, bounding and creeping. When creeping the feet are placed only a few centimetres apart and the trail appears as two lines. In deep snow a broad, shallow drag mark is made by the body as the animal creeps.

Tracks of Mammals with Paws Plate 37

Members of the dog family — and cats too — often move in a manner called lining (2a), which is so named because the feet are placed close together and the tracks form a single line. The right hind foot is placed in the track made by the right forefoot and the left hind foot in the track made by the left forefoot. The tracks are regularly spaced and create the impression of single footprints, although they are double tracks which are in perfect register, that is they completely overlap. One exception is the Domestic Dog (*Canis familiaris*); its tracks are not precisely in one line but are placed slightly to either side of the median line with a space in between (Plate 39).

In deep snow the tracks made by the Fox (*Vulpes vulpes*) (1) look like round pockets and the trail may superficially resemble that of a Roe Deer (Plate 51). On closer inspection, however, a deer track can be identified by the prints of the hoofs and dew claws. The length of the Fox's stride is variable and may be anywhere between 20 and 40 cm, but it averages 30 cm.

When members of the dog family trot (2b) the tracks occur in pairs with one track placed slightly ahead of the other. The paired tracks are of several kinds: the two prints placed side by side may be those of the two hind feet, the two forefeet, or the fore- and hind foot on the same side of the body. The last example, where the paired track consists of prints of the forefoot and hind foot, is very common in the Domestic Dog (3). This track shows the difference in size of the hind and fore tracks (the hind track is in front and is smaller). It may seem unusual for the fore and hind tracks, both right or both left, to be placed beside each other. But look at a trotting dog and you will see how often the hind quarters are carried slightly to one side of the fore quarters and the hind feet are always placed alternately beside the forefeet.

When running slowly the Fox makes short bounds and the hind feet land close in front of the tracks made by the forefeet (2c) to form a group of four tracks. Sometimes the four tracks are arranged in a straight line placed diagonally across the median line. This form of movement is called crossing (2c; 4). In fast running, which consists of regularly repeated bounds, the tracks of the Fox are arranged in a rhomboid pattern (2d).

a

b

c

d

Tracks of Mammals with Paws   Plate 38

The Wolf (*Canis lupus*) (1) is the largest European representative of the dog family. It occurs on the Continent, mainly in the Soviet Union and other eastern European countries but isolated populations are found in Spain and Italy. It may lead a solitary life but usually it lives in family groups or packs. It hunts for its food, chiefly herbivores, and can travel more than a 100 km in a single night when stalking prey.

The forefeet have five toes but because the thumb is placed high up only four leave marks in the track. The feet have large oval toe pads and strong claws (2). The hind feet have only four toes and are similar to the forefeet in shape, but are slightly shorter and narrower.

The track is very regular, as is usually the case in members of the dog family, and the toes and pads clearly show in the prints. The prints of the third and fourth toes are at the forward end of the ovate track and are placed close together with tips (and hence also the claw marks) turned inwards (3a). The outer (second and fourth) toes are set farther back, towards the middle of the track so that the track has a slender, elongate shape. Furthermore, the front edge of the outer toe prints is roughly in the same line as the hind edge of the two central toe prints. The pad beneath the toes is typically three-lobed and set far back so that there is a relatively large space between the toes and the pad, as in the track of a Fox. There is no difference in the shape of the hind foot track and forefoot track and sometimes not even in their size (3b). The fore tracks are 8 to 11 cm long and 6.5 to 10 cm wide, the hind tracks about 8 cm long and 6 to 7 cm wide. In those parts of Europe where the Wolf occurs, the track may easily be mistaken for that of a large Domestic Dog, but its distinguishing feature is its slender outline and conical tip.

Although the Wolf may occasionally walk, its commonest gait is a sustained trot; running is usually used in pursuit of prey, which is downed by a giant leap. The trail is the same as that of other members of the dog family. Lining is the commonest pattern made by the Wolf, both when walking and trotting, with the hind and fore tracks in a single line and the hind foot placed in the track made by the forefoot (5a). When walking the length of stride is about 40 cm, when trotting it is between 60 and 100 cm. When running (4; 5b) the Wolf leaves a trail consisting of groups of four tracks in which the first two prints — made by the hind feet — are placed one slightly ahead of the other; the two behind — made by the forefeet — are likewise placed one slightly ahead of the other but in reverse order.

Although opinions differ the most likely place to seek the origins of the Domestic Dog (*Canis familiaris*) is among the animal's closest relatives, the Wolf (*C. lupus*) and the Jackal (*C. aureus*). The young of these predatory animals were tamed by prehistoric man, probably in many parts of the world at the same time, the animals gradually became domesticated and cross-bred to produce after thousands of years the many breeds we know today. Some dogs are so small that they almost fit into a coat pocket; others, like the mastiff, St. Bernard and Newfoundland dogs, weigh about 80 kg. No matter how different the various breeds are in size and coloration (1), their feet and tracks are the same shape.

The front foot has five toes but the thumb does not show in the track because it is rudimentary and placed high up. The hind foot is four-toed. The forefoot track (3, right) is usually longer and wider than the hind foot track (3, left). The claw marks are clearly defined in each. The length of the tracks ranges from 2.5 cm to 10-13 cm.

On the Continent the tracks of the Domestic Dog can be confused with those of the Fox and Wolf. The Fox track is not likely to be mistaken for a Wolf track (Plate 38) because the two differ markedly in size. However, distinguishing between the track of a Domestic Dog and that of a Fox or Wolf of the same size is a different matter. For accurate identification it is necessary to find a perfect print, in mud or damp snow, with clearly defined pad and claw marks. In Britain there is, of course, a likelihood of confusion only between Fox and Domestic Dog tracks.

In the Domestic Dog (2a) the underside of the toes is impressed close to the hind pad. The track is almost completely filled with the pad marks and there is no space between the toes and the hind pad. The two central toes spread outwards and when the line joining their base is extended to either side it always intersects the prints made by the outer toes. In the Fox track (2b) the two central toes are set far forwards, their hind edge is almost in the same line with the front edge of the two outer toe prints, and there is a relatively large space in the middle of the track between the toes and the pad. The Wolf's track resembles that of the Fox in shape; the two central toes point inwards, the two outer toes are pressed to the inside of the foot and there is an elongated space between the toe prints and hind pad (2c).

In lining the tracks of the Fox and Wolf are arranged in almost a perfectly straight line (4b); in the lining of a Domestic Dog there is a space between the tracks (4a).

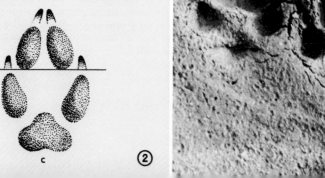

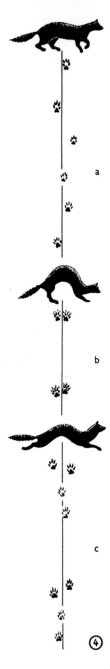

The Mustelidae have the greatest number of species of any mammalian group in Europe. They include the Pine Marten (*Martes martes*) (1) and the closely related European, or Beech Marten (*M. foina*), both of which have a wide distribution on the Continent, but the Beech Marten is absent from the British Isles and Scandinavia and the Pine Marten is found only in remote parts of Britain and Ireland. The Pine Marten is found in forests with tall trees and without a thick shrub layer. During the day it conceals itself in tree holes and old birds' and squirrels' nests. The Beech Marten was originally an inhabitant of rocky country and remains so to this day, although it now also frequents buildings, which provide it with the safe shelter it needs. Despite their great similarity the two martens exhibit differences in their feet and hence also in their tracks.

The foot of the Pine Marten is quite similar to that of the Brown Hare. The forefoot is five-toed but neither the toe pads nor the hind pad are visible. Relatively long, thick hair fills the spaces between the toes and completely covers the pads. The hair is thicker in winter than in summer. The Pine Marten hunts prey in tree tops and the hairs on the feet prevent slipping on branches that are wet or covered with hoar frost. In a well-defined print all five claw marks show, often also the pad markings, but the track as a whole is blurred because of the hairy covering. The hind foot also has five toes and equally thick hair. The fore track (2, right) is the larger of the two being 4 to 4.5 cm long and 2.5 to 3.5 cm wide; the hind track (2, left) is 3 to 3.5 cm long and about 3 cm wide.

The underside of the Beech Marten's feet is partly covered with hair but the pads show. All four feet are five-toed and all five toes and the claws show in the track. A well-defined print of the forefoot (3) will show not only the five toe prints and three-sectioned pad beneath the toes but also one or two pads at the heel, which are absent on the hind foot. The tracks of the Beech Marten are about the same size as those of the Pine Marten.

The Pine Marten's tracks and trails may be found in and around woods, those of the Beech Marten near villages and in parks and gardens. The trail of the Pine Marten often ends at the bottom of a tree where the animal leaped up on to the trunk in pursuit of squirrels.

Martens rarely walk (4a), usually only when worming their way through difficult places and when stalking prey. In open areas the normal gait is the characteristic caterpillar-like 'gallop' with arched back (4b), the tracks being in groups of two. When moving at high speed (4c) the hind feet land in front of the tracks made by the forefeet making hare-like tracks.

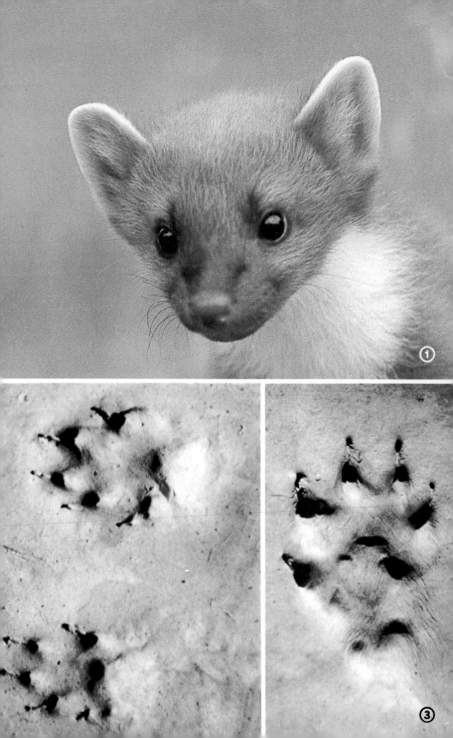

Tracks of Mammals with Paws

Plate 41

The Western Polecat (*Mustela putorius*) (1) is more common on the Continent than the two species of martens. In Britain it is found in Wales and neighbouring parts of England, but elsewhere in Europe it has a widespread distribution, except for Ireland, Iceland and northern Scandinavia. It is found in fields, copses, scrub and on rocky slopes. Small rodents are an important part of its diet and so it is often found also in buildings where mice, voles and rats are plentiful. Its tracks may therefore be found in farmyards and gardens. It will also hunt frogs, stalking them beside ponds, rivers and streams and leaving its prints in the mud at the edge.

The forefoot (2a) and hind foot (2b) both have five toes with prominent claws. They are only lightly covered with hair so that the toe pads, the large, irregular hind pad and the pads at the heel usually show clearly. In a well-defined print made by the whole foot in soft ground all the pads are impressed very strongly (3a, b); in a less distinct print only the front part of the foot is impressed and some tracks show only four toes (4).

The tracks of the Polecat resemble those of martens (Plate 40) not only in shape but also in the pattern made by the moving animal; however, they are smaller. The fore track (3a) is 2 to 3.5 cm long and 2 to 2.5 cm wide, depending on the condition of the ground. In mud (4) the tracks are always much wider because the toes sink into the ground and spread wide. The hind track is about the same size as the fore track, but if the whole underside of the foot is impressed (3b) then it may be 4 to 4.5 cm long.

The trail may be of several kinds with the typical pattern of the weasel family. The commonest gait is the arched-back gallop in which the hind feet are placed in the same position as the forefeet and the tracks are in groups of two, either close beside each other or with one double track slightly ahead of the other. The stride depends on the speed and may be between 40 and 60 cm long. When the Polecat enters the muddy bottom of a drained pond in quest of frogs or fish the prints are deep and indistinct (6), but precise identification is still possible.

When galloping the back is arched and the animal's movements slightly resemble those of the Brown Hare (Plates 25 and 26). When bounding at speed the body begins to stretch out more, the hind feet land in front of the tracks made by the forefeet (5), and the four tracks are arranged in various patterns, which may be rectangular, irregular, rhomboid, or reminiscent of the Brown Hare's. The usual pattern is rectangular (5, bottom). The Polecat's trail often ends at a Rabbit's burrow, sewage canal or crack in a wall.

2

a   b

3

a   b

4

The Stoat (*Mustela erminea*), one of the smallest members of the Mustelidae, is relatively common and widely distributed in lowland and upland areas throughout Europe, including the British Isles. It may be encountered in fields, at the edges of woods, round heaps of stones, on overgrown banks and in hedgerows — wherever voles and mice are to be found. In summer the Stoat is coloured cinnamon brown on the back and white on the underside; in winter its fur becomes entirely white (1) except for the black tip of the tail. The male is always conspicuously larger than the female and this is reflected in the size of the feet and footprints.

The front foot (2a) has five toes with prominent toe pads and hind pad composed of three tight bumps. The third and fourth toe are approximately the same length, the second and fifth toes are at the front and in the same line. The thumb pad is in line with the hind pad. This arrangement of the pads is seen in a clearly defined print (3a). The hind foot is longer (2b) and the print (3b) more slender.

The forefoot track is usually about 2 cm long, about 1.5 cm wide and is oval in outline. The hind track is about 3.5 cm long, 1.3 cm wide and because the toes are pressed close together it is more pointed. The Stoat's track resembles that of the Western Polecat (*M. putorius*) (Plate 41) but is much smaller and hence more like the prints made by the Weasel (*M. nivalis*) (Plate 43).

The Stoat moves in the manner characteristic of the weasel family — by short or long bounds (5a) with the hind feet placed in the same position as the forefeet and the tracks in groups of two either close beside each other or one double track slightly ahead of the other. The stride width is very small and the space between the tracks is only 4 to 5 cm. At a slow pace the strides are 20 to 40 cm long, at a more rapid pace they are up to 70 cm long. When bounding at speed the hind feet are placed in front of the forefeet and the resulting tracks may be arranged in a triangular, quadrangular (5b) or rhomboid pattern or they may resemble the Brown Hare's (4), with all four prints practically the same size.

The Stoat moves in a zig-zag line and the length of stride continually changes. The trail frequently ends at the bottom of an old hollow tree. Although it mainly hunts prey on or under the ground, the Stoat is also able to climb trees, where it not only seeks prey, for example birds in their nests, but also stores supplies of food (captured mice and voles) in cavities.

① ② ③ ④

a

a

Tracks of Mammals with Paws Plate 43

The commonest and smallest European member of the Mustelidae is the Weasel (*Mustela nivalis*). It is found throughout Europe except for Iceland and Ireland. Like the Stoat (*M. erminea*) the male is larger than the female. The Weasel can easily be mistaken for the Stoat for the female Stoat is about the same size as the male Weasel and in summer both have the same coloration. If you come across one of these animals and are uncertain of whether it is a Stoat or a Weasel you can distinguish them by the colour of the tip of the tail. The Weasel's is cinnamon brown the whole year (1) whereas the tip of the Stoat's tail is black both in summer and winter. The tracks of the Weasel can be found in fields, hedgerows, on slopes, round heaps of stones and by haystacks. It avoids damp places.

The Weasel's feet and also the prints resemble those of the Stoat. Both the forefoot (3a) and hind foot (3b) have five toes with prominent toe pads and sharp claws and an irregular or three-lobed pad beneath the toes. The fore track (3c), when clearly defined, is practically no different from the hind track (3d) in size and shape, though the hind print is slightly more slender and a bit more pointed. The fore and hind tracks are about 1.5 cm long and 0.7 cm to 1 cm wide.

The tracks of both martens (Plate 40), the Western Polecat (Plate 41), Stoat (Plate 42) and Weasel are strikingly similar in shape. There are slight differences between them but these do not usually suffice for precise identification. It is thus important to know the size of the tracks of each animal. This at least serves as a rough guide. The track of the Pine Marten (*Martes martes*) and Beech Marten (*M. foina*) is between 4 and 4.5 cm long, the Polecat's is 2.5 to 3.5 cm, the Stoat's only 2 to 2.5 cm and the Weasel's 1.5 to 2 cm long, depending on the condition of the ground.

The pattern of the Weasel's tracks is similar to that made by the Stoat, but the prints are smaller (4). The commonest gait is bounding with the tracks arranged in groups of two (2a). The distance between the groups of tracks varies depending on the speed of movement. The stride is 15 to 50 cm long and less than 4 to 5 cm wide. When bounding at speed the stride is longer, the hind feet are placed in front of the tracks made by the forefeet and the trail may consist of groups of three or four tracks or even patterns resembling those of a small Brown Hare (2b).

It is rarely possible to follow a Weasel's trail for a long distance. Usually it extends only a few metres in the snow and then ends at a mouse's nest, in a heap of stones or in old grass; it is often marked with drops of blood from captured voles.

④

①

②

③

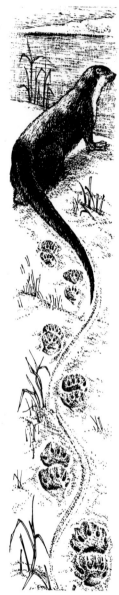

Tracks of Mammals with Paws

Plate 44

The Otter (*Lutra lutra*) was once widespread throughout Europe (except Iceland) but is now much less common and is absent or rare in many lowland areas. Its spindle-shaped body with short legs and long 'lizard-like' tail indicate that it is excellently adapted for moving about in water. The toes of all four feet are webbed and used as paddles; the tail serves as a powerful rudder. The Otter feeds chiefly on fish which it is able to catch even in clouded water thanks to the long tactile hairs round its nose.

The front foot has five toes joined by hairless webbing and terminated by long but not very strong claws. The large pad beneath the toes is composed of four cushions bunched together and is irregular in shape (2a). The hind foot is similar but longer (2b) with a more prominent heel pad.

The track made by the front foot (3a) is nearly circular, 5 to 6.5 cm long and roughly the same in width. The webbing shows only in a well-defined print; this applies to the hind foot as well. The thumb sometimes does not show in harder ground. The hind track is longer than the fore track (3b) and measures between 6 and 9 cm in length; when the whole foot is clearly impressed it may measure as much as 12 cm from toe to heel. The width of the hind track may be as much as 6 cm.

The Otter's tracks can be found on the muddy shores of lakes and rivers and on snow-covered ice, sometimes quite far from water for the Otter is a great wanderer. It has a wide variety of gaits. It walks at a slow pace only rarely, for example when stalking prey on land, in which case the hind foot is placed close in front of the track made by the forefoot (4a) or the fore- and hind feet nearly register (5). The normal gait is the typical arched-back gallop of the weasel family with the tracks in groups of two — the hind tracks completely overlapping the fore tracks (4b).

The pattern of tracks is extremely variable and sometimes the Otter seems to have alternated various gaits without any apparent reason, perhaps purely out of mere playfulness. In deep snow one can find a trail consisting of regular double bounds followed suddenly by a creeping trail with a groove made by the body drag and then by groups of four tracks with hind tracks impressed in front of the fore tracks. On snow-covered or muddy banks the Otter will even make slides — long troughs 40 to 50 cm wide down which the animal slides into the water.

When running at a fast pace the feet are placed in an unusual manner. The forefeet are placed at a diagonal, one farther forwards than the other, and the hind feet are placed alongside, also with one farther forwards than the other. All four prints thus appear close together in a short straight line at a diagonal to the median line of the trail. In the group of four tracks (4c) the right fore track is in front, behind it the right hind track, then the left fore track and left hind track.

118

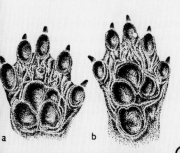

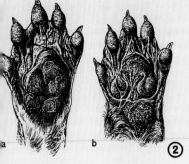

a

b

a

b

a

b

c

①

②

③

④

The Badger (*Meles meles*) (1) is found throughout Europe (except northern Scandinavia and Iceland) though nowhere in great numbers. Woodland is the preferred habitat, but open ground must also be accessible. Its home or 'set' consists of an extensive system of subterranean tunnels dug out in sloping ground in a concealed spot.

The Badger walks on the whole underside of the foot and is thus a plantigrade animal. The front foot has five strong toes with prominent toe pads and long, strong claws. The strong front feet are chiefly used to excavate its burrows and dig out prey, such as rodents and insects. The underside of the foot is hairless. There is a large kidney-shaped pad beneath the toes and another pad visible at the heel. The claws of the hind foot, which is also five-toed, are much shorter and there is a large pad beneath the toes and another at the heel.

In soft ground all five toes of the forefoot show in the track but in harder ground the thumb print is usually faint. The claws are impressed either in their entirety (2a) or only their tips show far in front of the toes (4, right). The fore track, if the whole of the foot is impressed, is about 7 cm long, but if only the front part shows the track is about 5 cm long and 4 to 6 cm wide. The hind track (2b) is 8 to 10 cm long if the whole foot shows (from the tips of the claws to the heel) but as a rule only the toes and hind pad are impressed and such a track measures about 6 cm. The claw marks in the hind track are shorter than those in the fore track. The width of the hind track is 4 to 5 cm. A Badger's tracks resemble those of a small bear, and the two could be confused in those parts of Europe where the Brown Bear (*Ursus arctos*) and Badger occur together.

Because of its thick-set build the Badger generally moves at a slow, leisurely gait, with the hind feet behind the fore tracks (4), partially covering the fore tracks — the claw marks of the hind track are roughly in a line with the hind pad of the fore track (5) — or completely overlapping the fore tracks. When trotting (3a) the kidney-shaped pad of the hind feet is roughly in line with the front toe prints, the hind tracks appearing farther in front of the fore tracks the faster the pace. When walking the stride is from 25 to 50 cm long; when trotting, used by the Badger when travelling greater distances, it may be as much as 70 to 80 cm. In fast running the hind feet are placed in front of the tracks made by the forefeet, all prints are distinctly separate (3b) and are arranged in a rhomboid pattern. A typical characteristic of the Badger's trail is that the toes of all feet point inwards.

⑤

①

②
a
b

③
a
b

④

Tracks of Mammals with Hoofs Plate 46

The structure of hoofs — cleaves — is more or less uniform but still there are slight differences that make it possible to identify the various species of even-toed ungulates.

The Wild Boar (*Sus scrofa*) (1), a robust animal with thick-set body and relatively short legs, is found in wooded regions in most of Europe, except the British Isles, Iceland and Scandinavia. The males are always larger and heavier than the females. The limbs of the Wild Boar are distinctive in that the dew claws are set very low on the back and to the side of the limb and are relatively large. Unlike the tracks of other even-toed ungulates it is the dew claws, which in soft ground are impressed even when walking slowly, that serve to identify Wild Boar tracks (2). Because they are set low to the side they appear in the track outside and to the back of the cleave prints, thus giving the whole track a rhomboid shape. In young animals the dew claws sometimes do not show or are not to the outside of the cleave prints (3).

The size of the tracks depends on the sex and age of the animal. The track of an adult male Wild Boar is 5 to 8 cm long and 4 to 6 cm wide. That of a younger animal is 3 to 4.5 cm long and 2.5 to 4 cm wide. It is impossible to determine the animal's sex by the shape of the track. In young individuals the cleaves are pointed, in older specimens they are definitely rounded at the front.

The Wild Boar moves by walking, trotting, galloping and bounding. When walking the length of the stride is 20 to 30 cm in young individuals and 30 to 40 cm in adult males. The width of stride in old males is 10 to 20 cm, in young animals 5 to 10 cm and in females 10 to 15 cm. At a slow pace, when walking or trotting, the feet register, overlapping partially to form double tracks, with the hind track over the fore track and the front end of the fore track exposed (4a). When galloping or bounding the feet are impressed separately and the tracks are in groups of four. The hind feet are placed in front and slightly outside the forefeet with one hind foot slightly farther forwards than the other. The tracks made by the forefeet are set farther back and in a straight line — one behind the other on the median line of the trail (4b).

The movement of a herd of Wild Boar in deep snow is distinctive. The animal at the head of the herd ploughs through the snow drifts making a deep groove with its chest and belly and the others follow after him.

The Red Deer (*Cervus elaphus*) (1) was originally an inhabitant of grasslands but was forced to move to large forests as Man's agricultural activities intensified. Nowadays it is found in woods, and on open moorland and mountains. It has a scattered distribution throughout most of Europe except Iceland and Scandinavia. In the British Isles indigenous wild herds occur in Scotland, the Lake District, Somerset, Devon and parts of Ireland. Red Deer are distinguished by marked sexual dimorphism (differences between the sexes). The male, or stag, has huge antlers and weighs from 120 to 250 kg; the female, or hind, does not have antlers and is about two-thirds the weight. The differences in size and weight are also reflected in the size and shape of the tracks (Plate 48).

The cleaves (or two main toes) of Red Deer are well developed (3) and set above them at the back are the dew claws. The cleaves on the forefeet are slightly larger, longer and wider (3, right) than those on the hind feet (3, left). As a rule the two cleaves that make up the set on one foot are not the same size. The outer toe is always slightly longer than the inner toe and its outside wall is more convex. At the back end on the underside of each toe is a large pad called the heel. It is shaped like an egg cut lengthwise and is about a third of the length of the toe. The front end of the toe is covered by a hard horny layer and is slightly hollowed on the underside. The dew claws of the forefeet are set slightly closer to the heels than those on the hind feet.

When walking or trotting (4), particularly on hard ground, both toes, or at least the front part of the toes, show clearly in the track. The dew claws do not touch the ground and so do not show in the track (2). The marked difference in the size of the fore track and hind track behind it can be seen in the double track. When walking in deep snow or mud or when running the hoofs sink deeper into the ground, the whole track is much deeper, more strongly impressed, and the oval prints of the dew claws show. In soft ground the toes tend to splay, with the tips far apart, and the print resembles the letter 'V'.

The fore and hind tracks of Red Deer can be distinguished not only by their size but also by the position of the cleaves. In the hind track, which is usually smaller, the cleave prints extend in the same direction and their inner edges are parallel. The fore track is generally longer, more rounded and broader, the cleaves are joined more loosely than in the hind feet and because more of the animal's weight is brought to bear on the fore- than on the hind limbs the cleaves splay out, the spread increasing in proportion to the speed of movement. The difference in the spread of the cleaves is evident even in slow walking.

④

The size of tracks of the Red Deer (*Cervus elaphus*) (1) naturally corresponds to the size and age of the animal. In addition it is also possible to tell by their shape whether the tracks were made by a stag or a hind. The print of a stag is more oval than a hind's; the outer walls of the toes extend from the heels in almost a straight line at first, converging to form a blunt, rounded tip at the very front (4a). The hind's track is not only narrower and shorter than the stag's but is ovate in outline, with the outer walls of the toes converging roughly from the heel to a sharper point in front (4b).

The track of an old stag, seven years old or older, is 7.5 to 9 cm long and 6 to 7 cm wide. That of a three-year-old to six-year-old, in other words a middle-aged stag, is 6.5 to 7 cm long and 5 to 6 cm wide. Young stags up to three years of age make the smallest tracks ranging from 4 to 5.5 cm long and from 3.5 to 5 cm wide. The tracks of a hind are usually 6 to 6.5 cm long and 4.5 to 5.5 cm wide.

The width of stride in old stags is 15 to 20 cm, that of middle-aged stags about 15 cm and that of young stags from 5 to 10 cm. In hinds the width of stride is 10 to 15 cm. The length of stride in old stags is from 60 to 70 cm, in middle-aged stags 50 to 60 cm, in young stags 35 to 45 cm and in hinds 50 to 60 cm.

When walking the whole cleaves are impressed with tips pointing outwards (5a). The older the stag the greater the angle of spread and thereby also the broader the stride. The hind feet are placed roughly in the tracks made by the front cleaves thus giving rise to various double tracks (Plate 49). When galloping the hind feet are placed in front of the prints made by the front cleaves and the tracks show in groups of four with each set of two at a diagonal — one fore track ahead of the other and one hind track ahead of the other (5b). When leaping the hind feet are placed far in front of the fore track and side by side, whereas the front prints are placed one ahead of the other (5c).

The Red Deer track sometimes resembles that of the Wild Boar (*Sus scrofa*) in size and shape but can be distinguished from the latter by the prints of the dew claws. In the Red Deer these are set high up (2a) and do not show in hard ground (3a), whereas in the Wild Boar (see Plate 46) the dew claws are large and set low down (2b) and are impressed outside the cleave prints (3b). Should the dew claws of the Red Deer show they are not impressed outside the width of the track.

① ② ③ ④

The trails of all Europe's even-toed ungulates are very similar. The gaits used by ungulates are walking, trotting and galloping. Leaping is used only in extreme cases — when danger threatens or when it is necessary to clear an obstacle.

The walking trail of Red Deer (*Cervus elaphus*) (1) consists of double tracks which show many variations in the position of the front and hind feet. Hunters and gamekeepers can distinguish these variations, but we need to know only a few of them.

In essence a Red Deer makes two types of double tracks: registered and non-registered tracks. You will recall that a register is where two tracks — the hind and the fore — overlap to greater or lesser degree; non-registered tracks are double tracks in which the hind and fore tracks are placed side by side but do not touch.

A track where the hind foot is placed in front of the forefoot (2a) is called a non-registered overstepped track. If the hind foot covers the fore track then it is an over-register — the hind track may cover only the tip of the front track (2b) or the whole track so that only the back end of the fore track is exposed and the heels' prints are close together forming a set of four (2c). When the hind foot is placed beside the fore track it is a non-registered sidestepped track — the hind track may be side by side in line with the front track (2d) or it may be to the side and back of the front track (2f). In the latter instance it may happen that instead of being impressed separately to the side of the front track the hind track partly covers the fore track and this is then a partial register (2e; 4). Another example of partial register is where the tip of the hind foot is set on the back end of the fore track (2g). When the tip of the hind foot is close behind the back end (heel) of the fore track it is a non-registered retarded track (2h). In the picture (3) the tracks on the left are the partial register of a Red Deer hind; those on the right, placed one behind the other, are an example of a non-registered sidestepped track made by a Roe Deer (*Capreolus capreolus*).

Some may think that such a detailed analysis of the tracks of the Red Deer is unnecessary or merely an end in itself. However, the experienced tracker and gamekeeper know that an over-register of the type shown here (2b) is a track made by a young animal or by a weak stag or hind, and the older the animal the more often its tracks are a partial register (2g) or a non-registered retarded track (2h), that a partial register (2e) is typical of old stags and gestating hinds, whereas middle-aged stags make tracks of the over-register type (2c) or else a perfect register where the hind feet are placed in almost exactly the same position as the fore track. The gamekeeper can identify his charges according to their double tracks as precisely as if the animals were there before him.

Whatever the type of double track, the tracks of the Red Deer stag are distinctive by being larger, with greater length and width of stride and greater angle of spread (5a) than the hind's. The hind's tracks are nearly parallel with the median line of the trail (5b).

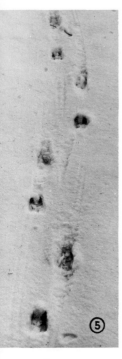

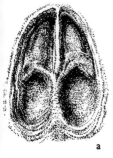

Tracks of Mammals with Hoofs Plate 50

In the geological epoch known as the Pleistocene, between about two million and 10,000 years ago, the Fallow Deer (*Dama dama*) (1) occurred in central Europe as a native animal. Then it disappeared, but from the end of the Middle Ages onwards it was reintroduced by Man to parks all over Europe, including Britain and Ireland. These Fallow Deer were from the northeastern parts of the Mediterranean region and adapted well to their new homes. Originally they were kept for their tender meat but nowadays Fallow Deer are popular with tourists and hunters as trophy game because of the buck's handsome antlers which are flattened at the extremities and form decoratively notched blades.

The Fallow Deer is smaller than the Red Deer (*Cervus elaphus*). In summer its coat is coloured cinnamon brown spotted white on the back and side (the spots are arranged in bands). In winter it is replaced by longer, thicker, greyish-brown hair in which the spots show up faintly or are almost absent altogether .

The cleaves of Fallow Deer are broadly similar in shape to those of the Red Deer but are smaller, longer and sharply pointed at the tip. The cleaves of the forefeet (2a) are larger, broader and more oval than the cleaves of the hind feet (2b). The pads are large and well developed and are almost half the length of the cleaves. It is the size of the heel that makes it possible to distinguish between the track of a young Red Deer stag or hind and that of a male Fallow Deer or buck when they are of similar size, but only if the track is well defined. In Red Deer the heel is roughly a third of the length of the cleave (3a) whereas in Fallow Deer the heel takes up the whole back half of the cleave (3b). The outer cleaves are slightly longer than the inner cleaves.

The outline of the fore cleave prints (6a) is ovate, that of the hind cleave prints is smaller and pear-shaped (6b). The track of strong bucks is about 7.5 cm long and 4.5 cm wide, that of royal bucks, that is old individuals with magnificent antlers, is up to 8 cm long and 5 cm wide. When walking the stride is 45 to 50 cm long and the space between the tracks (the width of stride) measures 10 to 15 cm, though sometimes it may be as much as 20 cm.

The track of an old and strong female Fallow Deer (doe) is up to 5.5 cm long and 3.5 cm wide, though the average is about 5 cm in length and 3 cm wide. The stride is 35 to 40 cm long and about 10 cm wide. The tracks of young fawns are about 4.5 cm long and 2.5 cm wide.

When walking or trotting at a leisurely pace (the commonest gaits), Fallow Deer place the hind cleaves in or almost in the same position as the fore cleaves giving rise to double tracks of various types as in Red Deer (4) (see also Plate 49). When walking in deep snow (5) or mud the cleaves splay out and their tips make long furrows in the snow as they are thrust forward. The dew claws are impressed only when the Fallow Deer walks in deep snow or mud or makes lengthy leaps.

⑤

a

b

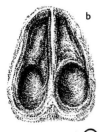

⑥

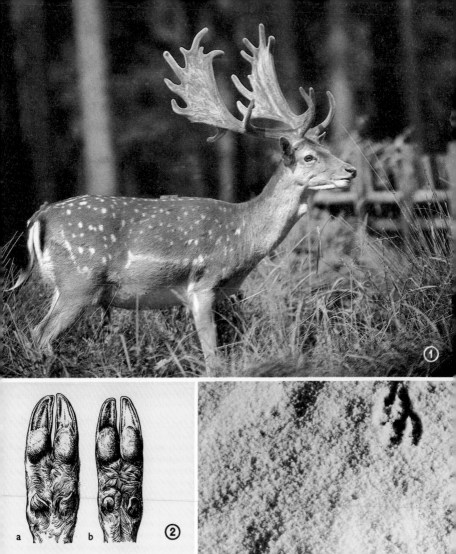

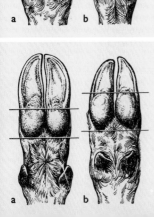

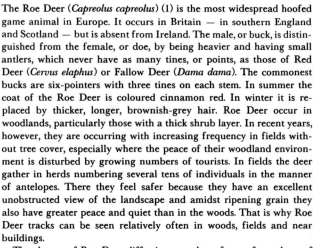

Tracks of Mammals with Hoofs Plate 51

The Roe Deer (*Capreolus capreolus*) (1) is the most widespread hoofed game animal in Europe. It occurs in Britain — in southern England and Scotland — but is absent from Ireland. The male, or buck, is distinguished from the female, or doe, by being heavier and having small antlers, which never have as many tines, or points, as those of Red Deer (*Cervus elaphus*) or Fallow Deer (*Dama dama*). The commonest bucks are six-pointers with three tines on each stem. In summer the coat of the Roe Deer is coloured cinnamon red. In winter it is replaced by thicker, longer, brownish-grey hair. Roe Deer occur in woodlands, particularly those with a thick shrub layer. In recent years, however, they are occurring with increasing frequency in fields without tree cover, especially where the peace of their woodland environment is disturbed by growing numbers of tourists. In fields the deer gather in herds numbering several tens of individuals in the manner of antelopes. There they feel safer because they have an excellent unobstructed view of the landscape and amidst ripening grain they also have greater peace and quiet than in the woods. That is why Roe Deer tracks can be seen relatively often in woods, fields and near buildings.

The cleaves of Roe Deer differ in a number of ways from those of Red Deer and Fallow Deer. First, they are much smaller and more slender and the heels are more elongate — about one-third the length of the toe (2), with a long tongue extending to the hollow horny front part of the foot. The dew claws of the fore limbs are set relatively low (4, left) and their covering is turned 180° against that of the cleaves; those on the hind limbs (4, right) are set higher up and their covering is turned slightly to the side.

It is usually impossible to tell from the size of the tracks whether the animal was a buck or doe, but tracks about 5 cm long are probably those of a buck. The track made by the forefoot is slender and oval, 3.5 to 4.5 cm long and approximately 3 cm wide, the cleave prints are elongate and slightly open at the front (2a). The hind track is only slightly smaller but the tips of the cleaves are closer together (2b).

The normal gait is a leisurely pace at which the length of stride is between 30 and 70 cm, the width of stride between 8 and 15 cm, and the tracks point outwards from the median line of the trail (5) (see also Plate 52). The buck usually has a greater width of stride than the doe, but the space between the tracks decreases when walking at a faster pace and so it is very difficult to tell if the tracks are those of a buck or a doe. At a leisurely gait on soft ground the hoofs sink in so deep that the dew claws also show (3) (see also Plate 53).

⑤

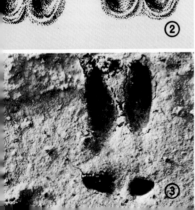

When Roe Deer (*Capreolus capreolus*) (1) go out to graze in the evening they not only go to the same place but also at the same hour. They
are creatures of such regular habit that often a gamekeeper can say
with certainty: 'A six-pointer about six years old will emerge from the
woods in the upper right-hand corner of the clearing about 50 metres
from the big spruce between 7.15 and 7.25 p.m.' Such regular habits
are also welcomed by the tracker. When he observes a Roe Deer from
a raised platform or well-concealed hide on the ground he can estimate its age and subsequently determine the size of the animal's
tracks. If the animal comes out of the wood into a field or if the
countryside is covered with snow then it is possible to observe not
only the individual tracks but also the pattern of the tracks and the
trail.

When walking slowly in snow that is not very deep the fore and
hind tracks of the Roe Deer impress together and at the back of these
are depressions made by the dew claws (3); when walking is very slow
and loitering the feet are barely lifted off the ground and the tips of
the cleaves make two parallel grooves in the snow. Because the gait is
slow and the ground relatively hard the two cleaves (the two halves of
the hoof) do not splay out but remain close together and almost
parallel.

On soft wet ground the double tracks are much clearer. The cleaves
of the front foot, particularly their tips, dig fairly deep into the
ground and spread out so wide that the gap between them may be as
much as 1.5 cm (2). The hind foot is placed on the back end of this
fore track in various ways and the print made by the hind foot is
distinctive in that the cleaves do not splay out but are almost parallel.
The whole hind track is nearly three-quarters of the width of the fore
track.

When trotting the hind foot is placed in the same position as the
fore track (4a) or slightly ahead of it thus making various kinds of
over-registers, and non-registered overstepped tracks. At this gait
(trotting) the length of stride naturally increases and may be as much
as 100 to 130 cm, while the stride width is somewhat narrower. If a Roe
Deer is started up suddenly it flees by galloping with long bounds.
The hind feet move outside and far ahead of the forefeet and land on
the ground one slightly ahead of the other in front of the fore tracks
(4b). When galloping the feet land on the ground with great force, the
cleaves splay out wide (the gap between the tips is 3 to 4 cm) and
because the feet land at a sharp angle the dew claws may show even
in hard ground. Roe Deer are excellent jumpers; when galloping their
leaps may be up to 6 metres long and they can jump over an obstacle
more than 1.5 metres high.

As we have seen the tracks of a Wild Boar (*Sus scrofa*) always show the dew claws which are impressed so far to either side that the track is rhomboid in outline (see Plate 46). The dew claws of other even-toed ungulates show only at a faster gait and on soft ground and are impressed in the same line as the cleaves so that the track is rectangular or square in outline. Despite this it may sometimes happen that the track of a Roe Deer (*Capreolus capreolus*) has the characteristics of a young Wild Boar's track. The picture (3) shows the prints made by two does running side by side over an icy expanse covered lightly with snow. At this fast pace with long bounds the cleaves were impressed in practically the same line with no appreciable width of stride and because each foot slipped a little as it landed the cleaves as well as the dew claws splayed out widely on all the limbs. Several tens of metres farther on the tracks of the two does appear separately, the pace has slackened and the prints show the distinctive features of the Roe Deer track. That is why you should follow a trail for as long as possible, study the individual prints and not allow yourself to draw hasty conclusions.

A characteristic feature of Roe Deer tracks is the strongly impressed ridging. On both the fore (4a) and hind (4b) limbs the hard horny layer covering the toes has a sharp raised edge on the perimeter. On very hard ground often only the tips of the toes are impressed — the heels do not show; all that shows clearly are the pointed arcs made by the edges of the cleaves. Clearly evident in such prints is the difference in the size and length of the two cleaves that make up the hoof; the outer cleaves are slightly longer and more curved than the inner cleaves.

Like other mammals the Roe Deer also treads out many regular runways on its home range leading to resting and feeding places. These runways can be found even in summer, particularly when they extend from the edge of a wood into a field, but they are most distinct in winter (1). In snow the animals tread out wide and deep lanes in which there are hundreds of tracks of various sizes. Roe Deer runs, which usually lead to feeding stations, are often used by other hoofed animals as well, but because it is difficult to identify the individual tracks in the trampled snow the best clue to determining what animals passed there are droppings.

In deep snow the tracks of Roe Deer walking at a normal gait are deep hollows in which the cleave prints often show poorly (2). When the foot is put down the cleaves scrape over the snow before they sink into it and then when the foot is lifted a small mound of snow is piled up at the front of the track. The trail in the photograph was made by a doe moving from the bottom in the upward direction.

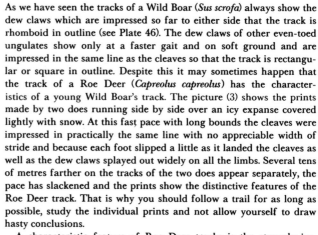

④

①

②

③

Tracks of Mammals with Hoofs Plate 54

The Mouflon (*Ovis musimon*) (1) is the only living wild sheep in Europe. Unlike the males of the Red Deer, Fallow Deer and Roe Deer, which cast their antlers every year, the Mouflon's curved horns remain attached throughout the animal's life and increase a bit in length every year (see Plate 109). The females have no horns, or only small nobs. The Mouflon is slightly larger than the Roe Deer — males (rams) weigh up to 50 kg, females (ewes) weigh 10 to 20 per cent less. It is native to southern Europe where it is found in the mountainous regions of Corsica and Sardinia. From there the Mouflon has been introduced to game preserves in western and central Europe. The animal has since spread and become established in deciduous and mixed woods. It prefers warmer regions with rocky slopes. It is absent from the British Isles.

The limbs of the Mouflon are adapted to moving about in rocky terrain. The legs are relatively short and strong — a must for running and leaping in such territory. The forefeet have prominent heels that are almost half the length of the cleaves. The cleaves are broad and close together at the heel, slender and elongate in the front part with pointed tips and sharp edges on the periphery. The tips of the cleaves are spread wide (2). The cleaves on the hind feet (4) are similar in shape but the heels are usually not as prominent.

The cleave prints are oval or ovate in outline; the fore prints (3a) are not much different from the hind prints (3b). In a well-defined fore track one can see the heavily impressed heels and more widely spread cleave tips. The splay of the cleaves is typical of the Mouflon track and shows in the trail of slow-moving animals even on hard ground. There is usually a prominent ridge in evidence on the edge of the track and the outer tips of the fore and hind cleaves point inward.

The track of the ram is 5.5 to 6 cm long and about 4.5 cm wide; that of the ewe is smaller and more slender, 4.5 to 5.5 cm long and 3.2 to 3.7 cm wide; the ram's stride is 40 to 60 cm long and between 10 and 15 cm wide; the ewe's stride is 35 to 40 cm long and about 10 cm wide. However, it is impossible to tell with certainty whether the tracks belong to a male or female.

At a walking gait the hind feet are placed in the same position as the fore tracks and the tracks point markedly outwards from the median line of the trail (5a). When running the Mouflon makes long leaps, moving the hind limbs in front of the fore limbs (5b); the dew claws show only in very soft ground.

138

① ② ③ ④

a

b

The Chamois (*Rupicapra rupicapra*) (1) is native to the high mountain regions of Europe above the tree line. It is not found in the British Isles. In summer its coat is coloured light brown or rusty red with a prominent dark band on the back; the hair is about 3 cm long. In winter the hair is three times as long, much thicker and coloured dark grey to nearly black. Both males and females have short, smooth, rounded horns, the shape and size of which indicate the age and sex of an animal (see Plate 109).

The skeleton of the Chamois is superbly adapted to climbing on steep mountain slopes, mountain ledges and screes. Movement in this difficult terrain is aided by the muscular legs terminated by hard, upright hoofs. The ridging is elastic and extends slightly beyond the sole of the foot to form a sharp edge that enables the animal to retain a foothold even on a minute rock ledge. That is why Chamoix are able to run with unbelievable sure-footedness on steep slopes and nearly smooth surfaces. Their physical attributes are supplemented by the ability to judge distances precisely. Chamoix can jump from one boulder to another over a gap of up to 7 metres and leaping downwards several metres is likewise no problem.

The cleaves of Chamoix are elongate, the same width throughout, and blunt at the front. The shape of the cleave tips is affected by the wear and tear of moving about in rocky terrain and of digging for food in snow. There is always a prominent gap between the cleaves, the heels are not pronounced and there is a tuft of hair between the heels. The dew claws are set relatively high up and are often hidden amidst the thick hair.

The cleave prints, particularly those of the front toes (2), are a longish wedge shape with a relatively wide gap the entire length that shows even at a slow walking gait. The prints of the hind cleaves (2b) are similar in shape but slightly more oval. Because the middle part of the foot is the one most subject to wear the parts that are most heavily impressed are the heels, the tips and the edges of the cleaves (3). The length of the track is between 5 and 6 cm, the width between 3 and 3.5 cm. The width of stride is relatively large and may be anywhere between 10 and 18 cm. When walking at a leisurely pace the stride is 30 to 50 cm long and the dew claws do not show (4a). The trail consists of double tracks either in normal register (one almost completely covering the other) or lateral register (one covering the other from the side). When running and jumping (4b) the hind feet are placed in front of the tracks made by the forefeet. As the foot lands the cleaves splay widely (3) and the foot bends so sharply that the dew claws are impressed as well. Because they are set so high up on the legs the prints made by the dew claws may be as much as 10 cm behind the heels.

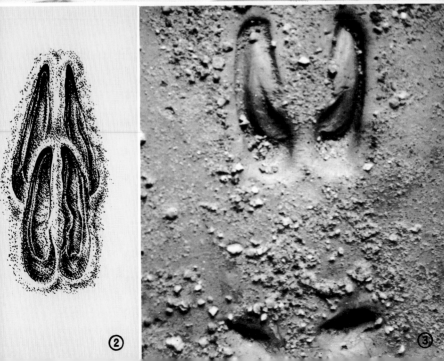

Plate 56

Tracks of Mammals with Hoofs

Size of tracks of domestic and wild ungulates (1)

	Animal	Sex	Length of track (cm)	Width of track (cm)	Width of stride (cm)	Length of stride when walking (cm)
a	European Elk or Moose (*Alces alces*)	♂	13-16 (20)	11-13	20-25	120
		♀	10-14	9-11	20-25	90-120
b	Domestic Cow (*Bos taurus*)	♂	10-12	9-10	20-40	~100
		♀				
c	Domestic Horse (*Equus caballus*)	♂	~10	8-9	10-15	~100
		♀				
d	Red Deer (*Cervus elaphus*)	♂	4-9	3.5-7	5-20	35-70
		♀	6-6.5	4.5-5.5	10-15	50-60
e	Alpine Ibex (*Capra ibex*)	♂	7-10	~6	~20	30-60
		♀				
f	Wild Boar (*Sus scrofa*)	♂	3-8	2.5-6	5-20	20-40
		♀	3-6.5	2.5-5	10-15	20-40
g	Domestic Sheep (*Ovis aries*)	♂	5-6	4-5	15-20	23-35
		♀				
h	Chamois (*Rupicapra rupicapra*)	♂	5-6	3-3.5	10-18	30-50
		♀				
i	Fallow Deer (*Dama dama*)	♂	7-8	4-5	10-20	45-50
		♀	5-5.5	3-3.5	10	35-40
j	Mouflon (*Ovis musimon*)	♂	5.5-6	4.5	10-15	40-60
		♀	4.5-5.5	3.2-3.7	10	35-40
k	Wild Goat (*Capra aegagrus*)	♂	5-6	~4.5	~15	30-60
		♀				
l	Domestic Goat (*Capra hircus*)	♂	4.5-6	3	15	25-35
		♀	4.5-5	3	15	25-35
m	Roe Deer (*Capreolus capreolus*)	♂	3.5-5	~3	8-15	30-70
		♀	3-4.5		8-15	30-70

Trail of the Wild Goat (2)

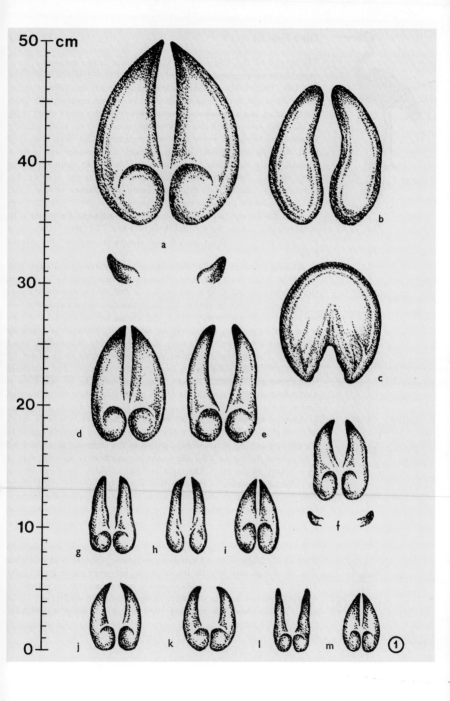

Bird Tracks

Plate 57

The tracks of the Common or Grey Heron (*Ardea cinerea*) (1) are found only on the muddy or sandy shores of rivers, ponds and lakes. The Grey Heron is particularly attracted by the autumn fishing-out of ponds when the bottoms of the drained ponds are covered with shallow pools of water containing small white fish, the bird's chief food. At this time one may encounter great numbers of these birds walking slowly over the mud, every now and then extending their S-shaped neck towards the ground and practically always coming up with a small fish in their long beak. Although fish are the mainstay of the Grey Heron's diet (this bird mainly takes fish that are dead or diseased, rarely healthy fish) the Grey Heron also catches various other small animals in the vicinity of the ponds. It is then that the Grey Heron's tracks can sometimes be found in adjacent fields, usually, however, only where the ground is slightly wet. The Grey Heron is the commonest of European herons and occurs throughout the British Isles.

Walking in deep mud is never easy because the feet always sink deeply into the mud. The feet of herons are thus adapted to provide the greatest spread so that the weight of the bird is distributed over a large area. The Grey Heron has three toes facing forwards and one backwards. The toes are so long and are so widely spread that the track of a single foot may cover an expanse of 150 cm² and may be 15 to 17 cm long. The middle toe is about 9 cm long, the hind toe 6 to 7 cm long. The middle and outer toes are connected at the base by a short web which also shows clearly in the track (2). The relatively long claws also impress strongly. The print made by the hind toe is not in line with the middle toe but is altogether closer to the median line of the trail. This helps one to identify the left and right footprints. If the hind toe shows to the left of the middle toe then it is the track of the right foot (2) and vice versa. Beside the Grey Heron's tracks in the picture are the much smaller prints of the common Black-headed Gull (*Larus ridibundus*). All the tracks are marked by 'ageing', that is by cracking of the mud. The right and left tracks of the Grey Heron can also be identified by the direction in which they are turned. When walking the stride is short, only 20 to 40 cm long, and the toes are turned towards the median line of the trail (5). If the middle toe points leftwards towards the median line then it is the track of the right foot and vice versa.

Similar tracks, but approximately 3 to 6 cm shorter, are made in mud by the Night Heron (*Nycticorax nycticorax*) (3), which also catches fish. In the picture (4), the tracks at the top were made by a Night Heron as it landed, then walked slowly forwards, stopped, shifted its weight from one foot to the other several times and walked off to the side. This bird breeds in southern Europe and is a rare passage visitor to the British Isles.

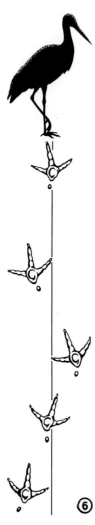

Bird Tracks

Plate 58

The White Stork (*Ciconia ciconia*) (1) makes tracks that are similar in shape and about the same size as those of the Grey Heron (*Ardea cinerea*). However, they are not found as often beside ponds because the White Stork's diet is slightly different from that of the Grey Heron. Walking slowly on the edges of ponds, in wet places in fields and in meadows, the White Stork catches various small vertebrates (frogs, lizards, snakes, rodents, insectivores and young birds) and insects with its long beak. Its tracks are therefore found more frequently in fields and meadows.

A clearly defined track (3) shows the prints of four toes; the three front toes are arranged in the shape of a widespread letter V and the relatively short hind toe shows as a short oval depression about 1 cm behind the pad at the base of the toes. In a perfect track the short blunt claws on the front toes also show as does the pad, which impresses in the shape of a round depression. Generally, however, the White Stork's track is not distinct, the toes show without the claws and there is only a faint indication of the foot pad. All the toes are relatively strong and those facing forwards are connected at the base by a short stiff web.

The whole track is approximately 15 cm long and up to 13 cm wide. The middle toe is 8 cm long, the outer toe about 6 cm and the hind toe 2 to 2.5 cm long. The toes are 10 to 13 mm thick at the base. The length of stride shows marked variation and may be anywhere between 10 and 40 cm. If the print of the hind toe points leftwards away from the imaginary prolonged axis of the middle toe then it is the track of the right foot and vice versa. The prints of the middle toes are turned slightly inwards towards the median line of the trail; the right foot is turned to the left, the left foot to the right (6).

Also found in fields and meadows in some parts of Europe (but not the British Isles) are the slightly smaller tracks of the Great Bustard (*Otis tarda*) (2), the largest European bird. There are marked differences between the sexes, the male being much larger than the female, and this is reflected in the size of the tracks. The track of the Great Bustard is distinctive in that the toes are much shorter than the White Stork's, though they may be up to 2 cm thick at the base. The whole track is 7 to 10 cm long and almost the same in width, the lesser dimensions being those of the female, the larger ones those of the male, or cock. The middle toe is 5 to 7 cm long, the outer toe (which is longer than the inner toe) is 4 to 5.5 cm long. The hind toe is absent (5). When walking the stride varies in length from 10 to 30 cm and the middle toes are turned slightly inwards towards the median line of the trail (4). When running the stride reaches up to 1 metre in length.

①

②

③

④

⑤

To find the tracks of the Mute Swan (*Cygnus olor*) (1) one need not go very far. These swans usually inhabit lakes and ponds (see Plate 15) where they build their large nests in beds of reeds and their tracks can be found in the mud and alluvial deposits on the shore. Their tracks may even be found in cities with a river or body of water within their confines.

In recent years the Mute Swan has rapidly increased in numbers all over Europe and it is becoming quite a common bird. It has practically no natural enemies, its handsome plumage and regal bearing are admired by Man, who provides the bird with protection, and because it raises four to seven young every year the increase in its population is not at all surprising. Swans quickly perceived and took advantage of Man's friendship. In winter they regularly visit densely populated cities where large numbers of birds crowd the shores of lakes and rivers waiting patiently for a titbit to be thrown to them by passers-by. Man's feeding of the birds may also play a role in increasing their numbers for it lowers the losses that commonly occur in winter because of lack of food. At this time the Mute Swan is also completely devoid of its shyness and takes food directly from the hand.

In winter, after a fresh snowfall, tracks of the Mute Swan appear like large triangles on snow-covered ice (2) , shores and embankments. Because of their size it is impossible to mistake Mute Swan tracks for those of any other waterfowl. Four toes show in the track which is 17 to 20 cm long. The middle and outer toes are about 16 cm long, the hind toe is quite short — 2 to 2.5 cm long. The three forward-facing toes are connected by a web up to the short claws, the hind toe is free. The two toes on either side of the middle toe curve slightly inwards towards the middle toe and impress heavily in the track. Because of the Mute Swan's great weight the webbing also impresses clearly, making a prominent groove in the snow at the front along the line joining the tips of the toes and forming triangular cushions in the middle of the track between the toes. When walking at a very slow pace the feet are lifted only slightly and then the claw on the middle toe makes a narrow groove in the snow (3). Like other waterfowl the Mute Swan turns the toes inwards towards the median line of the trail when walking (4) thus making it easy to identify the left and right tracks. If the hind and middle toes are turned leftwards then it is the track of the right foot and vice versa.

① ② ③

Bird Tracks

Plate 60

The Greylag Goose (*Anser anser*) (1), like the Mute Swan (*Cygnus olor*), inhabits larger bodies of water, building its nest (see Plate 15) in lakes, large ponds, oxbow lakes and marshes with old reed beds where it will remain undisturbed. However, unlike the Mute Swan, which gathers food with its beak on river or lake bottoms, the Greylag Goose forages not in water but on dry land, for it feeds on the green parts of plants and various seeds like domestic geese do. Geese are far more agile on dry land than swans and ducks because they have longer and relatively stronger legs. The Greylag Goose may fly several kilometres from its nesting site in search of food and thus its tracks may be seen in places where one would not expect to find them. Nevertheless, Greylag Goose tracks are found most often on the sandy shores of lakes and on the muddy bottoms of drained ponds. The species is mainly a winter visitor to the British Isles, but it nests in parts of north Scotland.

The track of the Greylag Goose is strikingly similar in shape to the Mute Swan's, but it is a third to a half shorter than the swan's. The middle toe is the longest — it measures 8.5 cm to 9.5 cm and is straight. The toes on either side of it curve in a faint arc from the hind pad towards the front but do not extend as far as the middle toe. The outer toe is 7.5 to 8.5 cm long, the inner about 1 cm less. All the forward-facing toes are connected by a broad web terminating at the tips immediately behind the short blunt claws. The hind toe is free and very short so that it impresses only as a small longish depression. The whole track of the Greylag Goose is 10 to 12 cm long (4), 8 to 10 cm wide and triangular in shape with rounded sides.

When walking the Greylag Goose turns the toes slightly inwards so that the right and left tracks are readily identified in the trail (2; 5), which has no appreciable width of stride. The middle and hind toes of the right foot (if the hind toe shows) point to the left and the toes of the left foot point to the right, towards the median line of the trail. The length of stride ranges between 10 and 20 cm increasing slightly at a running gait.

Great numbers of Greylag Goose tracks may be found on muddy and sandy shores during the autumn migration (3) when hundreds and thousands of individuals converge on favourite, regularly visited spots. Because the Greylag Goose is a relatively large and heavy bird (adult birds weigh 3 to 4 kg) its tracks show well even in drying mud (3); in thinner, softer mud its toes sink to a depth of 2 cm even though they are webbed (5). The Greylag Goose is one of several species of goose found in Europe but the other geese are smaller and their tracks are somewhat shorter and narrower.

Of the waterfowl it is the ducks that leave the greatest number of tracks on the muddy and sandy shores of still and flowing waters. However, it is almost impossible to distinguish the species making the tracks.

Duck tracks look very much like the tracks of swans and geese but are much smaller. Moreover, the toe prints are much more slender, the claws are relatively longer in proportion to the toes and show more clearly in the track. Despite the difficulties of identifying the individual species duck tracks can be divided into two groups according to the length of the separate toes.

Dabbling, non-diving ducks, which include the Mallard (*Anas platyrhynchos*), Gadwall (*A. strepera*), Shoveler (*A. clypeata*), Teal (*A. crecca*) and Garganey (*A. querquedula*), have the three forward-facing toes connected by a broad web and the fourth, hind toe, free (3a). The middle toe is the longest — that of the Mallard is 5 to 6 cm long. The outer toe measures 4.5 to 6 cm, the inner toe is a bit shorter. Both the inner and outer toes are faintly curved whereas the middle toe is nearly straight (4).

In diving ducks, which include the Pochard (*Aythya ferina*) (1), Ferruginous Duck (*A. nyroca*), Tufted Duck (*A. fuligula*) and Goldeneye (*Bucephala clangula*), it is the outer toe that is the longest (3b) or else it is the same length as the middle toe. Furthermore, the short hind toe has a leathery lobe which is absent on the hind toe of non-diving ducks. In a clearly defined track such a toe makes a broad print whereas the hind toe of non-diving ducks makes a short narrow groove. The middle toe of the Pochard is slightly curved and is 5 to 6 cm long, the outer toe is conspicuously curved and 6 to 7 cm long. The track of the Mallard is 7.5 to 8 cm long and 6.5 to 7 cm wide but even though the Mallard is heavier than the Pochard the Pochard's webbing, toes and whole track are slightly larger.

In soft ground, such as a fine layer of mud, the whole of a duck's track, including the webbing and hind toe, shows. On harder ground the hind toe print is sometimes completely absent (2) and then the track of small duck species, such as the Teal and Garganey, can readily be mistaken for the track of a gull.

Unlike geese, ducks are relatively awkward on land. Their legs are relatively short and located at the very rear of the body (see Plate 62), particularly in diving ducks, and this is what causes their waddling gait. This is reflected in the trail, which is wavy (4); the stride is only 10 to 15 cm long and the middle toes point strongly inwards towards the median line of the trail.

Bird Tracks

Plate 62

There are certain distinctive features that make it possible to distinguish between the tracks of diving and non-diving ducks. If you encounter a group of ducks marching along a muddy shore and making tracks there, it will be possible from a distance to tell by their posture whether they are diving or non-diving ducks, even though you will not be able to identify the species.

A typical representative of non-diving or dabbling ducks is the Mallard (*Anas platyrhynchos*) (la) and of the diving ducks the Pochard (*Aythya ferina*) (1b). On land you can see the typical posture and the location of the legs. In non-diving ducks the legs are located almost in the middle of the body, which is held at a slightly upward angle or nearly level, parallel to the ground (la). The legs of diving ducks are located at the very rear of the body, which is thus held almost upright (1b) and diving ducks stand as well as walk with bodies erect.

There are also marked differences between the two in water. Non-diving ducks float high in the water with about a third of the body submerged, the tail is always held above the water and the breast rises from the water at a slight angle (1c). Diving ducks float deep down in the water with practically half the body submerged, the body lies flat on the surface, and the tail rests on the water and drags along the surface (1d).

Non-diving ducks usually visit fields and meadows to forage for food and if they do hunt or gather food in water they rarely dive to the bottom. As a rule they dip only the bill and neck below the surface with the hind of the body pointing skyward — this is called upending (1e). Diving ducks, on the other hand, dive underwater to the very bottom where they search about with their bills for food (1f), remaining submerged for several tens of seconds before surfacing far from the spot where they submerged.

Lastly there is also a difference in the manner in which the two types of ducks take to the air from the water's surface. Non-diving ducks can fly straight up from the water (1g) whereas diving ducks must run several metres over the surface before taking-off (1h).

The trail of diving ducks is the typical duck trail (Plate 61) with tracks turned inwards towards the median line of the trail, but the prints of the outer toes are longer than the prints of the middle toes and are more curved (2a; 3). In the track of non-diving ducks it is the middle toe that is the longest and the hind toe is impressed less heavily than in the track of diving ducks (2b). Gull tracks, in comparison, are only three-toed (2c) (see Plate 63) and much smaller than duck tracks.

Bird Tracks Plate 63

The tracks of gulls are usually found on the seashore and offshore on islands but they may also be encountered far inland alongside still and flowing waters and in winter in snow, often even in bustling cities. For example, the Black-headed Gull (*Larus ridibundus*) (1) is a common inhabitant of ponds, lakes, marshes and bogs. It nests in colonies, often with hundreds of nests crowded in a small area, in muddy sections of ponds which are practically inaccessible. Gull tracks may be found not only near the nests but often quite far from water. Large flocks of the Black-headed Gull, for instance, follow in the wake of farm machines as they plough or till the ground gathering animal food that has been turned up and leave their tracks on the ground. What gulls find most attractive, however, are ponds that have been drained during the fishing-out season. Then huge flocks converge on the exposed mud of the bottom where they run rapidly to and fro gathering worms and young fish fry stranded in the puddles. At such a time the bottoms of ponds are covered with gull tracks (3).

Gull tracks greatly resemble goose and duck tracks in shape. Gulls have three forward-facing toes connected by a web up to the base of the claws. The hind toe, which is set high up on the leg, is small; the middle and outer toes are 3 to 3.5 cm long. The track is small, the toes are slender and the claws show. Because the hind toe is set high up and is rudimentary it shows only when the gull walks in soft mud. As a rule the gull's track is three-toed (3). The picture (2) shows various examples of gull tracks. At the top the gull was walking in drying mud and only the front toes and claws show. At bottom left the bird stepped into softer mud making two tracks in which the webbing shows and next to these is a perfect print showing all four toes and webbing.

The tracks of the Black-headed Gull resemble those of the Teal (*Anas crecca*) and Garganey (*A. querquedula*), which are only about 1 cm longer. It is possible to distinguish between them by the prints of the hind toes (the hind toe of ducks usually shows in the track whereas the hind toe of gulls does so only rarely) and by the position of the tracks in the trail. Whereas the tracks of ducks are turned inwards towards the median line of the trail when walking (4b), gull tracks are more or less parallel to the median line (4a). Gulls move by walking or running and the tracks are placed close together — there is no appreciable distance between them.

156

Bird Tracks

Plate 64

Gamebirds can be divided according to their habitat into two groups: inhabitants of open country with scattered woods and copses, such as the Pheasant (*Phasianus colchicus*), Partridge (*Perdix perdix*) and Quail (*Coturnix coturnix*) (this group also includes the Rock Partridge [*Alectoris graeca*] and Red-legged Partridge [*A. rufa*] which are found on bush-covered rocky slopes); and inhabitants of woodland, scrub, moorland and tundra, such as the Capercaillie (*Tetrao urogallus*), Black Grouse (*Lyrurus tetrix*), Hazel Hen (*Tetrastes bonasia*) and Ptarmigan (*Lagopus mutus*). All are birds that spend most of their life on the ground. Here they forage for food, build their nests and rear their offspring; only a few roost in trees or obtain plant food there.

a

The largest woodland gamebird is the Capercaillie (1). The cock is much bigger than the hen and also much more brightly coloured than the rufous-brown hen. The large feet of both have relatively long, strong toes with equally strong, blunt claws, which are used to scrape food from the ground. Capercaillie tracks are most often found in snow in winter. In recent years these birds have been declining rapidly in number and so their tracks are encountered only in deep and undisturbed forests. In the British Isles, the Capercaillie is found in pinewoods in eastern Scotland.

Grouse tracks differ markedly from those made by pheasants. The tarsus of the Capercaillie is covered with hair which extends down as far as the toes and this hairy covering becomes much thicker in winter (3). The toes of the Capercaillie are distinctive in that they are edged with a horny fringe that resembles a fine comb (3), a feature found in no other bird. This fringe, which also shows in a clearly defined track, greatly enlarges the area covered by the foot and prevents the bird from sinking into deep snow — it acts like a snowshoe. The Capercaillie, however, does not move about only on the ground. It roosts in trees at night, nips the buds and needles of conifers, and even performs its courting display on bare, horizontal branches. The long, fringed toes (and relatively long hind toe) allow the bird to retain a firm grip on branches and prevent slipping on an icy surface. In summer the fringe is shed and is replaced by a new one in autumn.

b

The Capercaillie cock's track is 8 to 12 cm long and 7 to 11 cm wide. The prints of the outer toes are spread wide, forming an angle of almost 180°. The hind toe, which is 2.5 to 3 cm long, is also heavily impressed as a rule. The middle toe is 6 to 7 cm long and up to 1.5 cm thick at the base. In wet snow the claws and large pad at the base of the toes also show (2a). The hen's track is similar in shape but about two-thirds the size (2b).

When the Capercaillie walks at a fast pace there is a distance of 20 to 30 cm between the tracks (6a) and grooves are made in the snow by the drag of the claws (4). The cock begins his courtship display before daylight perched on a bare horizontal branch. When dawn breaks he flies down to the ground and continues his antics. Then the tracks in the snow are crowded close together (5) with grooves on either side made by the lowered wing quills. In the trail the middle and hind toes point inwards towards the median line of the trail (6a, b).

6

①

②

a

b

③

④

⑤

Even though partridges have dwindled greatly in number in Europe during the past decades these birds can still be found in relatively large numbers in fields, meadows and on slopes with a light cover of vegetation. Occasionally groups of partridges are seen in open places in mountainous districts at heights of up to 1,000 metres, but they are most common in lowland country, chiefly on arable land.

The Partridge (*Perdix perdix*) (1), the most widespread European partridge, spends most of its time on the ground, resorting to rapid, direct flight only when danger threatens or to cover short distances. That is why its tracks may be found on field paths and in mud after a rainfall but best of all on snow in winter (see Plate 66). The track has the characteristic shape of all gamebird tracks. It shows three forward-facing, relatively strong toes ending in long, blunt claws adapted for scraping. The hind toe is much shorter and often all that shows in the track is the claw in the form of an elongate depression pointing inwards towards the median line of the trail. The outer toes form an angle of 90° but can spread out much more widely (4). A clearly defined print, in, for example, drying clay soil (2) or wet snow, also shows the prints of the pads on the underside of the toe segments as well as the pad located at the base of the four toes. The entire track is 4 to 5 cm long and the same in width. The middle toe is about 0.5 cm wide at the base and up to 3.5 to 4 cm long. The outer toe is 2.5 to 3 cm long and slightly narrower at the base than the middle toe. The inner toe is about 0.5 cm shorter than the outer toe. The hind toe impresses up to 0.5 to 1 cm behind the pad at the base of the toes.

When the Partridge walks there is no appreciable distance between the tracks made by the separate feet — often it is less than the length of the track (4). The trail is usually wavy or zig-zag, depending on where the Partridge was foraging for food. When walking at a faster pace or when running there is a distance of 10 to 15 cm between the tracks and the middle toe usually impresses parallel to the median line of the track; the hind toe, however, is turned inwards towards the median line. In deep snow the trail consists of deep hollows placed regularly behind each other and connected by shallow grooves made by the drag of the toes. In deep snow it is also possible to see where a Partridge took off and where it landed (3). The picture shows the trail of a Partridge taking off in flight: the bird was walking in the snow, then it jumped up, landed about 10 cm farther on, impressed its belly in the snow and at the same time also left marks made by the first wing beats. Then it stepped down lightly with the right foot and became airborne after striking the snow several times more with the wing quills.

①

②

③

Bird Tracks

Plate 66

In winter Partridge (*Perdix perdix*) flocks (1) often converge in places where there is a good supply of food. Then the snow is marked with their lengthy trails (4) which reveal what a hard life they have at this time of year. The food the Partridge feeds on is often buried deep under the snow and the birds must dig their way to it quite laboriously. Often the holes they dig are so deep that the birds completely disappear from sight. When the snow is light and dry it poses no problem, but when it is frozen on top and forms a hard cover several centimetres thick then the birds have a rough time of it. They cannot pierce the icy crust to get at the food beneath and if it is not broken through by Man they all starve and perish.

When the Partridge discovers a field where grain or some other farm crop is germinating beneath the snow several coveys of birds converge on the spot and the snow is then covered by a dense network of Partridge trails ending in holes dug in the snow (2). Often there are also well-treaded pathways marked by the birds' droppings. The holes, scraped out to the ground, are not very deep and measure about 20 to 30 cm in diameter. Because the birds always remain together in coveys in winter there are always many such holes in one spot and it is sometimes possible to deduce how many individuals were in the flock by the number of trails linking the separate holes. Often, however, the holes are so densely clustered and interlaced by so many tracks that one can determine the size of the flock only at the spot where the birds took to the air.

When the Partridge finds sufficient food beneath the snow cover it remains in the hole until it has gathered up all the food. It scrapes away the snow so thoroughly that the ground shows at the bottom of the hole (3). When doing so the Partridge swallows small grains of sand or small stones which aid in grinding hard and dry plant seeds in the gizzard.

Besides these holes one may also find resting places in which the Partridge passed the night. The Partridge never roosts in trees for its toes are not sufficiently adapted for the purpose. Instead it finds a sheltered spot where many of them crowd tightly together and sleep huddled on the ground. In winter the birds dig into the snow, often letting themselves be snowed under at night, and when they leave their shelter in the morning they always leave behind quite large heaps of droppings as mementoes of their stay.

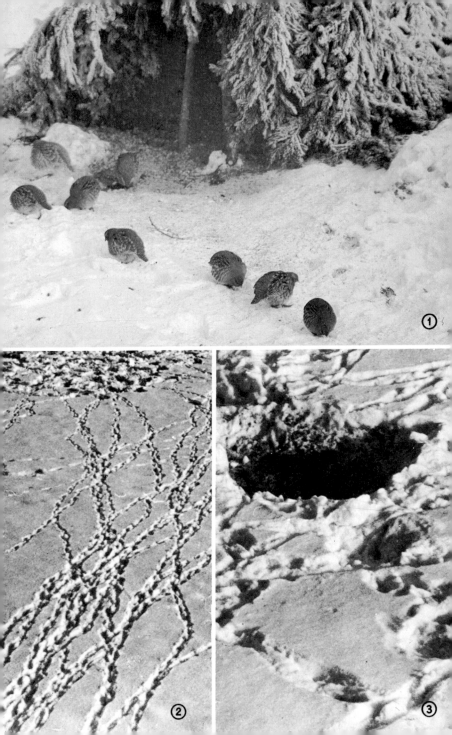

Unlike the Partridge the Pheasant (*Phasianus colchicus*) is found in both open spaces and woodlands throughout Europe. It is now found living wild in most parts of the British Isles, but originally it was an introduced bird. The natural populations are continually reinforced by birds bred for sport (see Plate 68). It is fond of warm lowland districts where fields and meadows are interspersed with small open woods, it also likes shoreline reed beds and is particularly partial to sunny, shrubby slopes. It is also often found in deciduous and mixed woods; it also likes shoreline reed beds and is particularly partial to heights above 700 metres. The male (cock) (1) is coloured a bright golden brown and during the courting period the red fleshy lobes round the eyes become greatly enlarged and two feathery 'horns' appear on the top of the head. The hen is streaked brown, buff and grey. A distinctive feature of the Pheasant is the long, pointed tail.

The tarsus (the exposed part of the leg above the toes) is relatively thick. It is not feathered; instead it is covered in front (2) with horny plates that serve to protect it from possible injury. On the underside of the toes (3) there are cushion-like pads with a horny surface that is quite elastic, and at the base of the three forward-facing toes there is another large pad. The two outer toes are joined at the base to the middle toe by a short web which shows in a clearly defined track. The hind toe is set higher up than the front toes and the cock furthermore has a horny spur about 3 cm above the hind toe on the back of the tarsus (2; 3). The shape and size of this spur serve as an aid in determining the age of the cock. Whereas the strong and relatively long claws on all four toes usually show in the track, the spur does not impress, not even in deep snow. Hens do not have spurs.

The middle toe is 5 to 6 cm long and is the longest toe, the outer toe is 3.5 to 4 cm long, the inner toe only slightly shorter, and the hind toe, which points inwards, is 1 to 2 cm long. The entire track with all four toes is 6.5 to 9 cm long and about 8 cm wide. This great variation in the length of the track is influenced by the bird's sex. A large cock weighs 1.2 to 2 kg and has the longer track; the hen weighs about 0.9 kg. As a rule all four toes show in the track as do the claws (5) and in a thin layer of snow or soft mud also the pads on the underside of the toe segments (4).

The Pheasant (*Phasianus colchicus*) (1) has become the object of particular concern on the part of hunters and gamekeepers. In many countries it has been affected by the harmful side-effects of modern large-scale farming — as much, for instance, as the Partridge — and is rapidly decreasing in numbers. The Pheasant is thus increasingly being bred and raised under regulated conditions by gamekeepers. Several hens are kept in an aviary together with one cock (the Pheasant is a polygamous bird) and the eggs that are laid are removed and put in incubators until the young hatch. The chicks are then fed the required diet and at the age of eight to ten weeks are released in the wild. Many of these artificially raised birds are killed during the autumn shoots but some survive till the following year when they breed and rear their offspring just as successfully as the natural Pheasant population.

The Pheasant is not noted for sustained flight but it can cover short distances with great speed. However, as it spends most of its time on the ground it can also run very rapidly. When a Pheasant is shot and wounded only slightly in the wing, so that it falls to the ground, it flees by running so rapidly that it is impossible to catch up with the bird. It can run hundreds of metres at this pace and unless there is a hunting dog on hand it usually disappears in a well-concealed shelter. At this fast gait the cock makes such long strides that the distance between the individual tracks may be as much as 50 cm.

In normal circumstances, when walking at a slow pace, the distance between the individual tracks is relatively small — at times approximately 10 cm (3), at other times twice to three times the length of the track (4). Both pictures show a trail made by a Pheasant in melting snow and both show how tracks can be distorted by the sun. No details whatsoever can be seen in the tracks, the edges of the toe prints are blurred and the whole track is increased in size.

When taking off and when landing, particularly in deep snow, the separate wing quills also show in the trail. The tail of the cock reaches a length of 40 to 50 cm and when the bird lands impresses in a thin layer of snow as a fan, the shape of which depends on how wide the tail was spread when the Pheasant landed (2). The hen's tail is 20 to 30 cm long and so it is possible to determine by the length of the print on the ground whether the track was made by a male or female Pheasant.

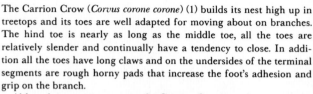

Bird Tracks

Plate 69

The Carrion Crow (*Corvus corone corone*) (1) builds its nest high up in treetops and its toes are well adapted for moving about on branches. The hind toe is nearly as long as the middle toe, all the toes are relatively slender and continually have a tendency to close. In addition all the toes have long claws and on the undersides of the terminal segments are rough horny pads that increase the foot's adhesion and grip on the branch.

Although it nests in treetops the Carrion Crow's tracks may also be found on the ground. The Carrion Crow is fond of visiting the edges of ponds, lakes and rivers as well as fields where it forages for animal food. In winter it even visits the neighbourhood of buildings and its tracks may be found on snow, particularly round waste heaps. It is found throughout Britain, but is not present in Ireland.

In a well-defined track three toes face forwards and may form a very acute angle. Strongly impressed are the pads on the undersides of the individual toe segments; the pads on the terminal segments and the claws impress most heavily because of the toes' constant tendency to close. The hind toe is terminated by a claw that is strongly curved and is the longest of the four claws. The middle section of the claws shows only faintly in the track but the tips of the claws dig deeply into the ground. At the base of the four toes there is an irregular pad (3).

The middle toe is about 4 cm long, the hind toe is only slightly shorter, and the outer toe measures about 3 cm. The track without the claw prints is approximately 7 to 8 cm long and about 3.5 cm wide, measured with the claws it is some 2 to 3 cm longer.

The distance between the tracks of a walking Carrion Crow is only a few centimetres, the width of stride is negligible and the front part of the track is turned inwards towards the median line of the trail (5a). In deeper snow quite long grooves are made by the claws (2). The Carrion Crow also moves by hopping, in which case the tracks are located side by side and the distance between them — the length of stride — is 30 to 50 cm.

The Wood Pigeon (*Columba palumbus*) (4) is also a tree bird with feet adapted for grasping branches like the Carrion Crow's. It is found everywhere in Britain in copses and low ground cover as well as in larger woodlands. It visits fields and meadows in search of food, chiefly newly sown fields where it gathers the seeds and that is where one is most likely to find its tracks. The tracks may also be found quite often beside water where the Wood Pigeon comes to drink.

Evident in the Wood Pigeon's track are the relatively strong toes and not very long, blunt claws. The whole track is about 6 cm long and about 5 cm wide. The middle toe, with a length of about 4 cm, is the longest toe; the outer toe is 3 cm long and the hind toe 2 to 2.5 cm long. When walking there is no appreciable distance between the tracks, they are close behind each other and the toe prints are turned inwards towards the median line of the trail (5b).

Bird Tracks

The Coot (*Fulica atra*) (1) is one of the commonest birds of lowland lakes and reservoirs in Europe, and is found throughout the British Isles. It is coloured black except for the beak and a narrow horny patch on the forehead, which are white. Its size is comparable to that of a small duck, it nests in reeds and shoreline vegetation and forages for food in water. It is a good swimmer and is equally adept at diving. The Coot is a migratory bird but in mild winters many do not leave their nesting grounds. Then their characteristic tracks may be found on snow; in summer look on muddy sections of the shore.

The Coot's feet are adapted for swimming and diving in a manner quite different from that of waterfowl and gulls. Unlike the latter the web of the Coot's foot is not complete; each of the three front toes is fringed separately by relatively wide leathery lobes. The hind toe is free and is not fringed. A similar adaptation is found in grebes, although their toes are edged with an entire, undivided fringe and furthermore their tracks are rarely encountered because grebes practically never leave the water.

The Coot's track (2) shows the prints of relatively slender toes ending in long claws. The hind toe is turned slightly towards the inner toe. Also strongly impressed in the track is the lobed fringe on each of the three forward-facing toes. The lobes on the inner side of the middle toe are slightly larger and broader than those on the outer side. Thus, the right track has larger lobes on the left side of the middle toe and the left track has them on the right side of that toe.

The whole track is about 12 cm long and 10 cm wide, which means that it covers a large area so that the Coot can move without difficulty even on very soft ground. The largest, middle toe is about 8 cm long, the outer toe about 7 cm. When the Coot is walking (5) there is no appreciable distance between the tracks, they are close behind each other and sometimes one even partially covers the other.

Another common wader is the Lapwing (*Vanellus vanellus*) (4) which also nests beside lakes and reservoirs. However, it may be encountered just as often in arable fields some distance from water. It is found throughout the British Isles. It arrives in its breeding grounds in early spring and in autumn departs again for warmer regions. Hence its tracks can be found only during the months in between — on muddy and sandy shores, in wet fields and on the exposed bottoms of drained ponds. There the Lapwing patters about pulling various small animals from the ground with its tweezer-like beak.

Like other waders the Lapwing's tracks are three-toed — the hind toe does not show because it is stunted and situated high up on the leg (3). The long, slender, narrow toes are terminated by narrow claws and at the base of the toes there is a prominent pad. The outer toe is connected at the base to the middle toe by a narrow web, but this does not usually show in the track. The whole track with widely spread toes is 3.5 to 4 cm long and slightly wider than that. In the trail the tracks are located close behind each other with the toes always pointing inwards towards the median line of the trail. When running the stride may be up to 15 cm long.

① ② ③ ④

Bird Tracks

Plate 71

Owls are superbly adapted for their nocturnal mode of life. By day they rest on the branches of trees or in cavities, setting out to hunt as twilight falls. The retina of their large eyes contains large numbers of nerve cells that enable the bird to see at night even with the minimum of light. The light perception capacity of an owl's eye is much greater than ours; it can perceive light where we cannot. Not even owls, however, can see in total darkness. The owls' second important sense that enables them to hunt at night is hearing. An owl can locate a sound to an accuracy of 1 degree, which means that an owl perching 20 metres from a gnawing fieldmouse can locate its position within a segment of about 35 cm. At a distance of 10 metres it can pounce with almost absolute accuracy because the victim's position will have narrowed down to a segment of 17 cm. And this is such a small distance that an owl is certain to seize its prey with its claws.

Small owls, such as Tengmalm's Owl (*Aegolius funereus*) (1), a rare visitor to Britain from the Continent, feed on small birds, voles, mice and commonly even large insects; large owls can down a mole, squirrel or hare; and the Eagle Owl (*Bubo bubo*), the largest European owl but rarely seen in Britain, can even down a hare, pheasant or fawn. Owls usually perch in an elevated spot waiting for prey and then swoop down on their victim in noiseless flight. They rarely move about on the ground and that is why their tracks are found only in winter when they surprise their prey in snow. Even then they leave only a few single prints bordered by marks made by the broad wings.

Owl tracks are distinctive in that they cannot be mistaken for the tracks of any other bird. The feet are feathered down to the toes, which are relatively long and terminated by long, sharp, curved claws. Two of the toes point forwards and two backwards. The reversible outer toe is turned back towards the hind toe, the inner and middle toes face forwards. All are relatively strong and the pads on the undersides of the toes, which are covered with tiny bumps as if they were coated with sand, impress strongly in the track. This rough surface provides a firm grip on branches and also serves to maintain a secure hold on prey. The prints made by the inner and middle toes resemble a very narrow letter V (2); the outer toe is turned towards the hind toe and points outwards from the track. All four claws are strongly impressed, particularly their sharp tips which dig deep into the ground.

There is not much difference in shape between the tracks of the species of European owl. The track of the Tawny Owl (*Strix aluco*) (3a) is only slightly shorter and less robust than that of the Ural Owl (*Strix uralensis*) (3b), but it is only in eastern Europe that the two could be compared on the ground. In an owl's trail the tracks are placed close behind each other and the outer toes usually point outwards and away from the median line of the trail (4).

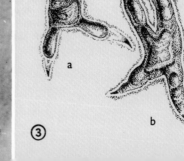

The similar structure of the bill and feet as well as the striking similarity in the manner of hunting and selection of food were responsible for the opinion that owls and birds of prey or raptors are closely related. Even today many people think of owls as nocturnal raptors. In fact, however, the two groups belong to completely different bird orders, and the only thing they have in common is their similar way of life.

A typical characteristic of the raptors is the strong, high, often massive bill. The sharp downcurved edges of the upper mandible overlap the lower mandible (see Plate 92). Unlike most other birds, however, raptors use the beak only to tear and divide up the flesh of their victims into smaller pieces— it is never used to seize prey. For this purpose the raptors use their long-toed, clawed foot. All raptors have four toes; the hind toe is turned backwards and the other three point forwards. Only the Osprey (*Pandion haliaetus*), which specializes in hunting fish, has a reversible toe. However, unlike owls, in which the fourth, outer toe turns towards the hind toe, in the Osprey it is the second, inner toe that is reversible. The undersides of the strong and relatively long toes are covered with horny pads (4a, b) that serve to maintain a secure hold on live prey. The Osprey's toe pads are furthermore covered with short stiff spikes that prevent the fish from slipping from its grasp. Raptors that hunt live prey — the Goshawk (*Accipiter gentilis*) (4b), eagles (4a) and falcons (1) — have large and strongly hooked talons, the ones on the first and second toes being generally stronger. With the aid of these specially adapted toes raptors seize and at the same time kill their prey. Vultures which feed mainly on carrion, have fairly short, blunt talons.

The tracks of raptors are encountered only by chance. Raptors rarely walk on the ground and when they do they take only a few steps. This is quite understandable, for their feet are not adapted for walking; the long curved talons in particular are a great hindrance. But the tracks can be found in winter on snow close by some dead animal. The Buzzard (*Buteo buteo*) is attracted to such a spot for the carcass provides the bird with an easy meal. Buzzard tracks are approximately 8 cm long with grooves made by the long claws in the snow extending from the tips of the toes. Very occasionally on the Continent one may also find the track of the White-tailed or Sea Eagle (*Haliaeetus albicilla*) (2), one of the largest birds of prey, beside carrion. Strongly impressed in the track, which may be more than 15 cm long (3), are the pads on the undersides of the toes, the hind pad and the claws. The size of the White-tailed Eagle's track is clearly evident when compared with the track of a Brown Hare, shown in the upper left-hand corner of the picture.

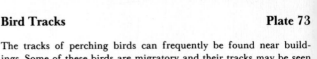

The tracks of perching birds can frequently be found near buildings. Some of these birds are migratory and their tracks may be seen only in summer; others are resident birds or transient migrants (dispersive birds) and the prints of their feet can be encountered throughout the year. In view of the size of these small feathered creatures the tracks they make are small and so much alike that it is very difficult, often almost impossible, to identify them. In all instances the tracks show the prints of three slender toes forming a sharp angle at the base and ending in short or long claws. The hind toe is usually the same length or longer than the middle toe and in some species, for instance wagtails, has a strikingly long slender claw.

Some perching birds move by walking in which case the feet are put down alternately with the toe prints of the right and left foot located a short distance apart (4) and pointing inwards towards the median line of the trail. Others move by making short or long hops. The trail of a Blackbird (*Turdus merula*) (3) hopping in deep snow is distinctive in that the tracks are in pairs and placed close together side by side. Each foot impresses only as a longish groove without visible toe prints, the bird's belly is also partially impressed and at each hop the toes make a shallow groove in the snow. At a slower pace the distance between the double tracks is about 20 cm; at a faster pace, when the Blackbird helps itself out also with the wings, it may be as much as 70 cm. When it lands in the snow the Blackbird often strikes it with the wings and then these show on either side of the track in the form of two large fan-shaped prints.

The greatest number of tracks made by these birds are to be found on snow — everywhere in the backyard or garden are prints made by sparrows, the Chaffinch, Greenfinch and other species that seek food around buildings. In summer perching birds visit the edges of ponds and streams to drink and often to forage for food in the mud, and leave traces of their stay.

In the woods in winter one may come across the tracks of the Jay (*Garrulus glandarius*) (1); these are about 5 cm long and 2 cm wide. The Jay moves on the ground either by hopping (with each hop it covers a distance of 20 to 50 cm) or by walking, in which case one foot is placed directly ahead of the other. The picture (2) shows the print of practically the whole body of a Jay which surprised a vole ploughing through the snow (the deep groove at the bottom), seized it and made off with it.

In terms of diet — the type of food it eats — the Brown Hare (*Lepus europaeus*) (1) is definitely a vegetarian, or herbivore, feeding on soft, green plant parts during the growing season and in the autumn nibbling at the above-ground parts of tubers and fleshy roots (see Plate 85). It does not dig up roots from the ground. With the onset of autumn there is a change in the Brown Hare's diet — it nibbles mainly buds, young annual shoots and bark.

Its teeth are specially adapted for browsing hard foods. There are two large, curved incisor teeth in the upper jaw and two in the lower jaw. These are set close together and have open roots so that they never stop growing and the ends are continuously worn down by gnawing hard food. Since the incisors are covered with hard enamel on the front, but only with a thin layer on the back, the back is worn more strongly that the front and the teeth acquire a chisel shape. Behind the two large incisors in the upper jaw are two more very small incisors (2) but these are not used in nibbling. The Rabbit (*Oryctolagus cuniculus*) has the same type of chisel-shaped incisors as the Brown Hare, and so do all rodents. Unlike hares and the Rabbit, however, rodents do not have the two rudimentary teeth behind the upper incisors.

In winter the Brown Hare usually ignores dry grass. What it seems to like best is bark, especially bark with a high concentration of water such as that of young deciduous trees and shrubs. Piles of branches of pruned fruit trees will be visited by hares until they are completely stripped of bark (3).

Each of the two upper incisors has a small notch in the middle of the cutting surface. As a result the teeth marks on the bark consist of a strip left by the gap between the incisors and two strips left by the notch in each, thus making it look as if the bark had been nibbled by a mammal with four upper incisors (4). The Brown Hare also feeds on slender branches, biting them from the trunk with its incisors so neatly that the smooth, slanting cut looks as if it had been made with a knife (5).

② ③

a

b

Meal Remains of Herbivorous Animals Plate 75

The largest European rodent, the Beaver (*Castor fiber*) (1), is found mostly in flood-plain woodlands traversed by brooks or streams. The Beaver lives in family groups or small colonies consisting of several families. If a pair of beavers finds a river or stream bank that is high enough they dig a burrow there beginning with an underwater entrance. The burrow extends upwards into the bank above water level and terminates in a spherical chamber. If the banks are too low and not suited for digging burrows the Beaver erects huge lodges in shallow water made of twigs and mud — these may be up to 1.5 metre high and more than 2 metres wide at the base and inside are one or two chambers with entrances that are also under water.

The building of beaver lodges goes hand in hand with their manner of feeding, the building material being the remains of the Beaver's feasts. During the growing season the Beaver eats a wide variety of juicy plants growing in the water or on the shore and partly also the bark of trees. In the second half of the year, however, it feeds mostly on bark and that is also its sole food in winter. The Beaver is not satisfied with merely nibbling bark as do other rodents and hares, but even cuts down trees 40 to 50 cm thick. As a rule it begins gnawing about 50 cm above the ground, biting out chips of various lengths with its large, reddish-orange, chisel-shaped incisors. The grooves made by the incisors are up to 8 mm wide (2; 3). Felling a tree is not an easy task — to remove 1 kg of wood the Beaver must cut 100 to 150 chips and clamp the incisors together approximately a thousand times. At the spot where the Beaver was at work there are always various bits and pieces of severed branches and trunks and all bear marks of the animal's teeth.

When the Beaver selects a sapling it begins gnawing it on one side, continuing to do so until the sapling breaks and falls to the ground. The stump is half gnawed and half broken off (4a). Stronger trees are gnawed all the way around giving rise to the characteristic feeding damage which looks like an hour-glass placed on its side or two cones touching at the apex (4b). The Beaver continually gnaws the trunk from the outside towards the centre and the tree then falls to the side where the Beaver worked hardest. The animal then gnaws off the branches, cuts them into smaller pieces and either eats the bark off on the spot or carries the branches to some place beside the burrow or lodge. The stripped branches are then used to strengthen its abode.

④

The Northern Water Vole (*Arvicola terrestris*) is a robust, brown-coloured rodent about the size of a small Brown Rat. It lives chiefly in shoreline vegetation, orchards, woods and fields. In banks it digs a system of underground burrows. However, it may also occur farther from water in woods or orchards where, like the Mole, it excavates long tunnels leading to supplies of food; often it also thrusts up small heaps of earth resembling molehills.

During the growth period the Water Vole feeds on juicy green plants above ground as well as on various rootlets, bulbs and tubers it comes across when digging its underground tunnels. In late summer and autumn it gathers a supply of roots and tubers which it stores in the subterranean corridors it has made. It does not hibernate, but feeds on its stored food supplies and continues its damaging activity underground. It not only gnaws the bark from roots but regularly severs them. Thin roots are severed with a single bite, stronger roots are marked with deep grooves 3.5 to 5 mm wide made by the incisors (2b). As a rule the Water Vole severs all the roots of a tree (2a) so that it can be pulled up readily from the ground or is readily uprooted by the wind. In this manner the Water Vole can destroy even trees more than 25 cm thick. It is particularly fond of deciduous trees (it causes great damage in orchards) but conifers are also eaten. It may gnaw the above-ground parts of trees, but because it cannot climb the bark is damaged only at the base, up to 20 cm above the ground. The trunk is gnawed round its periphery down to the wood and on the ground one may find twisted bits of bark left uneaten by the Water Vole.

The bark of trees is a favourite food of many other rodents including the Bank Vole (*Clethrionomys glareolus*) (1), commonly found in woodlands throughout Europe. It is about the same size as the Field Vole (*Microtus agrestis*) and a conspicuous characteristic is the rufous-red colour of the back. Like the Field Vole and Common Vole (*M. arvalis*) (see Plates 33 and 85) it periodically reaches plague numbers and then woods are flooded with the creatures. In such years the feeding damage they cause is encountered at every step. Unlike the Water Vole the Bank Vole is a good climber and so its feeding damage must be looked for quite high up. Usually it climbs up to a whorl of branches where it makes itself comfortable and strips the trunk and branches to all sides (4a). It exhibits a preference for coniferous trees with soft bark but also strips deciduous trees and shrubs so thoroughly that the whiteness of the exposed wood gleams from afar (3). Rougher bark shows distinct grooves made by the incisors — these are 1.5 to 2 mm wide and clustered close together (4b). Often scattered on the ground beneath the tree are fragments of rough bark, which the Bank Vole does not eat.

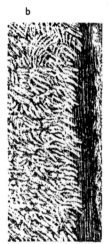

④

Meal Remains of Herbivorous Animals

Plate 77

In large spreading woods and game reserves one occasionally comes across trees with the bark partially scraped off. These may be single trees or groups of trees whose exposed wood (often large expanses) gleams palely from afar. This damage may be found on deciduous as well as coniferous trees and looks as if the bark had been removed with a sharp knife or scraper (2). All such scrape marks are feeding damage caused by hoofed animals. This type of damage is called barking or stripping and it often occurs on a wide scale, particularly where gamekeepers keep high numbers of Red Deer (*Cervus elaphus*), (1), Fallow Deer (*Dama dama*) or Mouflon (*Ovis musimon*). This is quite a problem for foresters because even mature, fully grown trees are damaged by barking and to date no satisfactory method has been found to protect forest stands and so prevent such damage. Trees are protected by mechanical means, such as fencing, as well as by chemicals, which are spread on the bark and are intended to deter animals by their unpleasant odour. Biological methods — the putting out of substitute food for the game — have also been used. But so far results have not been very satisfactory.

There are two main types of barking: summer barking and winter barking. In the first instance bark is stripped from trees not only during the summer but throughout the growing season when sap flows through the bark to branches and leaves and when the bark does not adhere as firmly to the wood as in winter. An animal first bites a hole in the bark at head level, grasps the loosened bark firmly with its teeth and with a sharp jerk peels off a long strip. The wound is smooth; the ragged edges remain hanging on the trees only where the bark was stripped from the trunk. With the onset of the resting or dormant period sap ceases to flow through the tree's conducting system and the bark adheres so firmly to the wood that it cannot be peeled off. This is when winter barking takes place; a better term for it is perhaps winter browsing, or nibbling, for the bark is actually nibbled only in small pieces and there are always distinct tooth marks made by the animal. Sometimes the browsing damage is sparse; at other times it is dense and covers a large area (4). Both standing trees as well as felled trees are subject to barking and browsing.

Red Deer damage young deciduous and coniferous trees also by nibbling at terminal buds and shoots. The growth of trees damaged in this way is then stunted and they have an irregular shrub-like shape (3).

Meal Remains of Herbivorous Animals   Plate 78

a

b

c

(5)

To understand the manner in which deer (1), cattle, sheep and goats damage trees and seedlings by barking and browsing it is necessary to take a closer look at their teeth and the position of them.

The Red Deer (*Cervus elaphus*) has six cheek teeth (three molars and three premolars) in each half of the row in both the upper and lower jaw. There are no incisor teeth at all in the front part of the upper jaw. In their place there is only a toughened pad that serves to hold food. The lower jaw is equipped with four pairs of incisor-like biting teeth and when the jaws are closed they press tightly against the hardened surface of the upper jaw (2a). These teeth have sharp chisel-shaped edges and are slightly concave on the inner side. Largest and broadest are the two middle incisors (3) which have the major share in biting food. Altogether there are three incisors in each half row of the lower jaw and pressed tightly behind them is a single canine. Canines are present in the upper jaw in Red Deer and only rarely in other deer and are located approximately midway between the tip of the jaw and the back teeth. They are never used in chewing food. The canines are not shown in the figure (2a).

When a Red Deer wishes to peel off a piece of bark it opens its jaws wide, curls back its lips, presses the hardened pad at the front of its upper jaw against the tree for support and pierces the bark with the incisors of its lower jaw (2b). After loosening the bark from the tree it presses the lower jaw against the upper jaw and then with a sharp jerk of the head tears off a large piece of bark. The strip of bark is then propelled into the mouth cavity where it is ground by the back teeth.

In winter browsing the procedure is only slightly different. Because the bark cannot be loosened in strips the animal nibbles only small pieces. The Red Deer places its upper and lower jaws on the tree in the same way as when barking but removes only short strips of bark by repeatedly opening and closing its lower jaw. In this case it leaves marks made by the incisors — two grooves placed side by side, each more than 0.5 cm wide (4).

The young shoots of trees and shrubs are often browsed by plant-eating mammals and which animal caused the damage can be determined by the manner in which the twigs are clipped. When a Brown Hare (*Lepus europaeus*) or Rabbit (*Oryctolagus cuniculus*) clips a twig with its incisors it leaves a smooth, slanting cut (5a). Because deer, cattle, sheep and goats have no incisors in the upper jaw they can bite a twig only halfway with the lower incisors (5b) and then they tear the remainder off leaving a ragged edge. If they bite the twig off with the back teeth then the whole end of the remaining twig is ragged (5c).

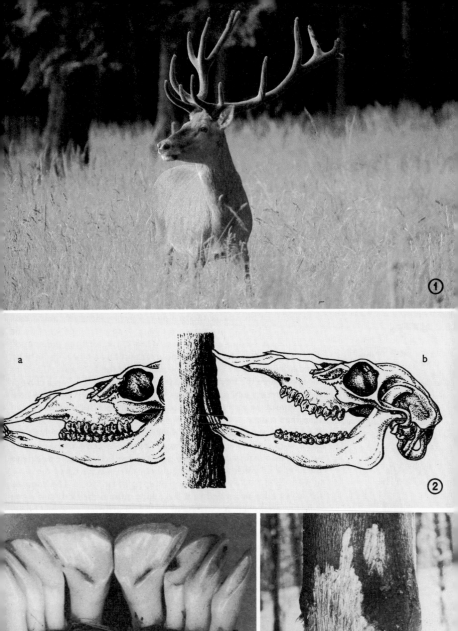

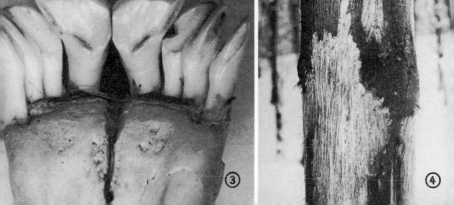

Meal Remains of Herbivorous Animals

Plate 79

In the trunks of trees you can sometimes find cavities, which may be circular, longish-oval, rectangular with rounded corners (3), square or irregular in shape (2). Some are several metres above the ground, others only a few centimetres above the roots. The edges are only haphazardly smoothed with small splinters often sticking out here and there (2). On the ground beneath there is a small or larger pile of wood chips and splinters (3). These holes are the work of woodpeckers, but they are not entrances to nesting cavities. On closer inspection you will find that they are only several centimetres deep and cone-shaped whereas the entrance hole of a nesting cavity is nearly circular, smooth, and always high up.

They are holes made by woodpeckers to get at the larvae beneath the bark and in the wood. The larvae of various beetles are regular items in the diet of the Black Woodpecker (*Dryocopus martius*), Green Woodpecker (*Picus viridis*), Grey-headed Woodpecker (*P. canus*) and Great Spotted Woodpecker (*Picoides major*) (1), all of which climb on the trunks of trees and extract insects from narrow cracks in the bark with their chisel-like beak. (Of these, only the Green Woodpecker and Great Spotted Woodpecker are found in the British Isles.) Every now and then they strike the tree more sharply and listen to its resonance. In all probability they are thus able to determine whether or not larvae are feeding on the wood. When it discovers the presence of a larva in this way the woodpecker begins drilling a hole with its beak. The blows are made with such precision that the hole always ends at the spot where the larva is located (4a). If the opening is large enough the woodpecker extracts the larva with its beak. However, if the hole is too conical so that the woodpecker cannot open its beak inside the hole, then it uses its specially adapted tongue to bring out the larva. At the base of and supporting the tongue is the hyoid bone, which extends at the rear into two prolonged horns to which are attached the muscles that manipulate the tongue. Woodpeckers are able to extend the tongue as much as several centimetres beyond the tip of the beak, in the case of the Green Woodpecker up to 10 cm (4b, c). The horns of the hyoid bone are coiled in a large loop around the skull and come together, are joined, at the base of the bill or are even anchored inside the upper bill (4d). A woodpecker's tongue is coated with a gluey substance and is equipped at the tip with small recurved barbs like a harpoon. When the bird drills its way to the larva it extends the tongue, hooks the prey and pulls it into its bill with the aid of the hyoid muscles.

a

b

c

(4)

Woodpeckers are able to find and exterminate insect pests of forest trees much quicker than we can. All larvae living in wood injure trees to some extent and often cause extensive damage. From time to time they reach plague numbers and the damage to trees is of catastrophic proportions; for example, bark beetles can destroy hundreds of hectares of forest. In the face of such infestations birds are naturally helpless and often even Man is unable to exterminate the pests with insecticides. Nevertheless birds (mainly woodpeckers) do keep the numbers of woodland pests within bounds.

Woodpeckers seek insects concealed beneath the bark of healthy as well as dying trees. When they come across a dead tree with loosened bark they readily chop off even large plates of bark with their beaks and these can then be found on the ground at the base of the tree along with the chips from their drilling (1). The birds extract larvae from peeled-off bark as well as from wood. If the bark is still firmly attached to the wood and cannot be peeled off in plates then the woodpeckers tear it into thick strips of varied lengths (2) as they try to get at the larvae. Healthy trees, where the bark cannot be separated from the wood at all, are marked with smaller or larger holes (3) drilled by the birds' beaks.

The larvae of bark beetles bore tunnels in the inner bark (phloem) of the tree, at the ends of which they pupate before emerging as adult beetles. The shape and arrangement of these tunnels are so distinctive for each species of bark beetle that they serve as a sure means of identification. Let us look at a few of these woodland pests. The Spruce Bark Beetle (*Ips typographus*) bores 6- to 12-cm-long perpendicular main galleries in the inner bark of spruce trees. Branching from these main galleries are the lateral tunnels made by the larvae which are broadened at the end to form a chamber where the larva pupates (4a). The tunnels made by the larvae of the Lesser Pine Shoot Beetle (*Myelophilus minor*) are quite different and are found in the inner bark of pine trees. The pattern of the main galleries, which are 3 to 10 cm long, resembles a bird in flight and the branch tunnels made by the larvae are only about 5 mm long (4b). Fir trees are attacked by the Fir Bark Beetle (*Pityocteines curvidens*), which excavates several main galleries at right angles to the main axis of the tree. These resemble the letter I or H laid flat. The lateral tunnels made by the larvae are relatively short (4c).

(4)

The ripening seeds of spruce, pine and fir trees are a welcome treat for many mammals as well as birds. They contain large amounts of nourishing and energy-rich oils and fats and are thus a favourite food particularly in winter, when the amount of energy expended by the body is greatest. They are not only a favourite food of squirrels, wood mice and the Bank Vole, which can climb to the tops of trees for cones, but are equally popular with other rodents, though these must be content with whatever falls from a squirrel's grasp or is knocked from the tree by the wind. An expert at extracting seeds from cones is the Crossbill (*Loxia curvirostra*), a resident in Scotland and a summer visitor to other parts of Britain; woodpeckers and nuthatches also extract oily seeds from cones. Each of these consumers has its own special manner of getting at the seeds thereby leaving distinctive marks that serve as a means of identifying the culprit.

The Red Squirrel (*Sciurus vulgaris*) (1) gnaws off the cone from the branch, grasps it with the front paws and gnaws off the scales, starting at the base of the cone. Because its teeth are so strong it simply tears off the first scales which are not so firmly attached to the stem. However, the scales farther up the stem are attached firmly and these the squirrel partly gnaws and partly tears off to get at the two oily seeds at the base of each scale. What remains when the squirrel finishes is the gnawed stem of the cone usually with a few, entire, ungnawed scales at the tip but otherwise covered with tattered bits of scales so that it looks hairy or bristly (2; 3a). The scales as well as gnawed cones are cast to the ground by the squirrel and there they can be found scattered over a large area.

The Bank Vole (*Clethrionomys glareolus*) and Yellow-necked Mouse (*Apodemus flavicollis*) cannot tear the scales out and so they must gnaw them off at the base to get at the seeds. As a rule they carry the cone to some hiding place and hence the scales and stems of the cones remain in a single pile. A spruce cone fed on by these rodents is left with several scales at the tip, otherwise the stem is gnawed smooth and rounded at the base where it was attached to the tree (3b).

The Crossbill neither tears out nor clips off scales but merely splits the scales lengthwise, loosens them slightly and extracts the seeds from beneath (3c) with its bill, which has crossed tips and is specially adapted for the purpose. Woodpeckers jab their flattened bill between the scales to get at the seeds. A spruce cone fed on by woodpeckers looks cracked and has a messy appearance (3d) (see also Plate 82). Pine cones fed on by a Red Squirrel (4a), Wood Mouse (*Apodemus sylvaticus*) (4b), Crossbill (4c) and Great Spotted Woodpecker (*Dendrocopus major*) (4d) bear similar marks.

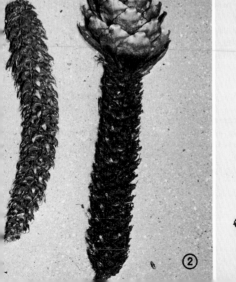

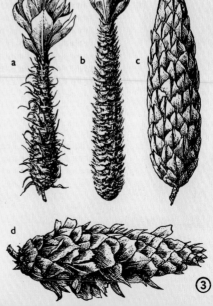

Meal Remains of Herbivorous Animals Plate 82

Pine tree cones from which the seeds have been extracted bear typical signs on the basis of which it is usually possible to identify the animal that made them, but sometimes it is rather difficult. It is impossible to tell whether a cone has been gnawed by a Bank Vole or a Yellow-necked Mouse and likewise difficult to distinguish between a cone fed on by a Red Squirrel and one fed on by a Yellow-necked Mouse, for a squirrel may feed like a mouse, leaving the stem of the cone smooth instead of rough.

Identifying cones fed on by woodpeckers, however, poses no great problem. Cones are eaten in winter chiefly by the Great Spotted Woodpecker (*Dendrocopus major*) and the remains of its feeding can always be found in coniferous woods. Such a cone always has a messy appearance, the scales are variously pulled back, pressed out, and partly broken (2). The hard cones of pine trees are often completely tattered.

The woodpecker must anchor the cone somehow so that it can chisel away at it. Best suited for this purpose is the cracked and deeply furrowed bark of old trees, for instance oaks or pine trees. The bird first clips the cone from the branch with its beak and carries it to the tree where it plans to eat it. There it first wedges the cone in some suitable crack with several blows of the beak so that the tip of the cone points towards the bird. In this position the woodpecker can best get its beak between the scales (3). When it has eaten the seeds from one half the woodpecker loosens the cone with its beak, turns it around and extracts the remaining seeds. The cones are wedged in high up above the ground or immediately above the roots of the tree.

Sometimes the bird puts each new cone in a different crack — when the bark is greatly furrowed, at other times it always puts them in the same crack, throwing out the old cone and replacing it with a new one. Beneath such a woodpecker's 'forge' one may find a whole pile of pecked cones and usually always one or two more still wedged in a crack in the bark (1) for the Great Spotted Woodpecker never discards a pecked-over cone until it brings a new one. That is why one so often sees cones wedged in bark. When the bird plucks a fresh cone from a tree it immediately flies with it to its 'forge', perches beneath the old cone (4a) and leans away from the trunk. It then slides the new cone between its belly and the tree (4b) almost all the way to its feet. Then it loosens the old cone with its beak, tosses it to the ground (4c), puts the new cone in the crevice (4d) and immediately sets to work. The blows of its beak are so rapid that it is finished with such a pine cone within a matter of minutes. When it cannot find a suitable crevice for its 'forge' it excavates one with its beak in no time.

④

194

① ② ③

The kernels of nuts and fruit stones are a favourite food of many mammals and birds. Each animal has a particular way of eating a nut and according to the marks on the nut it is possible to identify the animal or at least make a good guess as to its identity.

Voles and mice gnaw the shell of a hazelnut because they do not have the strength to crack it. As a rule they start gnawing at the base of the nut making a small hole with rapid movements of the lower jaw. Up to this point it is impossible to tell which animal made the hole for the teeth of small rodents are all approximately the same size and make similar grooves. However, as soon as the hole is big enough for the rodent to get its teeth inside then it is possible to tell whether the nut was chewed by a Yellow-necked Mouse or Bank Vole according to the teeth marks.

The Yellow-necked Mouse (*Apodemus flavicollis*) (1) has relatively long front legs and holds the nut at an angle between the paws quite far from the body (2a). Inserting the lower incisors into the hole it begins gnawing from the inside out that side of the shell that faces away from the body. It gnaws only with the lower incisors (the lower jaw is much more mobile); the upper incisors merely serve to hold the shell in place. When gnawing it continually turns the nut around and enlarges the hole. The edge of the hole is irregular, as if crumbled or broken off, the inner edge being slightly lower than the outer edge. On the outside of the shell, arranged in a fairly regular circle round the hole, are small marks made by the upper incisors (3a). In the case of smaller nuts and fruit stones the Yellow-necked Mouse is able to gnaw them also from the outside. The picture (4) shows an acorn (a), plum stone (b), dogwood stone (c) and hornbeam nut (d) eaten by a Yellow-necked Mouse.

The Bank Vole (*Clethrionomys glareolus*) eats a nut in a different way. Because it has short legs like all voles it holds the nut close to the body with the tip of the nut close to the hind feet (2b). After gnawing a hole in the shell it thrusts its whole nose and upper incisors inside and gnaws the shell from the outside in with the lower incisors, pressing the upper incisors against the inner wall of the shell. It thus leaves no teeth marks on the outside and the edge of the hole is neat, smooth and regular (3b).

As soon as rodents get at the kernel they bite off larger pieces which they pull out with the lower incisors. Then holding these with the paws they gnaw them into smaller bits. They hide in a clump of grass, under a tree root or under a shrub to eat and large quantities of shell remnants may be found in such a spot.

a

b

a

b

The diet of the Red Squirrel (*Sciurus vulgaris*) (1) and Grey Squirrel (*S. carolinensis*) consists primarily of ripening nuts. If there is plentiful harvest of hazelnuts the squirrel stores them, the same as other seeds, in various holes in the ground. It visits these places in winter when food is scarce. However, it often fails to locate all its hidden stores of food and when spring comes the seeds then sprout — the squirrel thus helps in spreading plants and contributes to the natural regeneration of the forest.

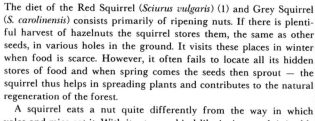

A squirrel eats a nut quite differently from the way in which voles and mice eat it. With its strong chisel-like incisor teeth it is able to split the shell in two. It usually starts by gnawing a small groove in the top of the shell at the pointed end. Holding the nut between its front paws it then readily bites off the tip with several movements of its lower jaw. Into the narrow slit the squirrel wedges the lower incisors, presses the upper incisors against the outer wall of the shell and with a prying movement separates the two halves of the shell (2). On the ground beneath the spot where the squirrel feasted one will then find a large quantity of cracked nut shells with short teeth marks on the top. Some cracked shells have many marks on the top, others only a few. Old, experienced squirrels know how to go about the task with the minimum of effort — only a few bites in just the right places and the shell is cracked. Young squirrels have a harder time of it. Often they start gnawing the nut on various sides, looking for the suture (the line of dehiscence) until they succeed in making a small hole through which they can get at the kernel. So shells eaten by old squirrels have only few teeth marks on them (3b), those eaten by young squirrels have a great many variously placed marks on the top (3a).

Birds crack open nuts and extract the kernel with their beaks. Even birds with slender bills such as the Great Tit (*Parus major*) know how to go about cracking a thick-walled shell. Walnuts, particularly thin-shelled varieties, present no problem. These are then marked with holes of various sizes with irregular broken edges (4). Tits eat nuts either on trees, where they do so while hanging from the nut by their feet, or on some solid object. They are fond of eating hazelnuts before they are ripe, leaving marks made by the blows of the bird's beak by the edge of the hole (5c). The Nuthatch (*Sitta europaea*) has a stronger beak and cracks the nut from the side after first wedging it into a crack in the bark of a tree (5d). Woodpeckers wedge a hazelnut into a crack in the bark with the top of the nut pointing out, then turn it so that the suture faces the beak and begin hammering at it with the beak. An insufficiently worked on, uncracked nut is marked with long scratches (5a); a cracked nut has a large, irregular hole (5b).

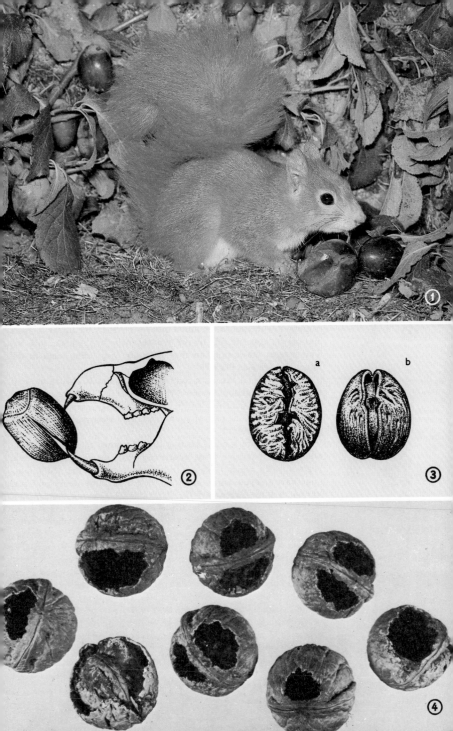

① ② ③

a b

④

Many mammals and birds find cultivated crops attractive to eat. They eat the green top parts (clover, sprouting grain), swollen underground roots and tubers (beets, potatoes), as well as ripening seeds (wheat, maize). The concentration of such plants in one field attracts large numbers of animals, which often cause great damage.

One of the most feared field pests on the Continent is the Orkney or Common Vole (*Microtus arvalis*) (1). In years when it reaches plague numbers this small rodent can cause damage running into millions of pounds. It often feeds on sugar-beet as well as mangel (a variety of beet used as food for cattle), eating the roots below ground. It starts by gnawing a small hole in the root which gradually becomes larger as it feeds (2). The top part of the swollen root and the leaves remain undamaged while below ground often all that remains is only a hollowed-out 'shell'. The Northern Water Vole (*Arvicola terrestris*) also eats beet roots below ground.

The Brown Hare (*Lepus europaeus*), on the other hand, leaves underground plant parts untouched because it does not dig the root out and eats only the top part of the root just beneath the leaves (3). Because the hare has a small sharp notch in each of the upper incisors this is also evident in the feeding damage. The soft pulp of the swollen root is marked with four longitudinal grooves made by the upper incisors and on the opposite side by two grooves made by the lower incisors. This creates the impression that there are four biting teeth in the upper jaw (see also Plate 74).

Beets are also a favourite food of hoofed animals, chiefly the Red Deer (*Cervus elaphus*). Like hares they eat only the parts above ground and their marks can be identified by the wide grooves made by the lower incisors. In the case of young beets Red Deer pull up the whole plant from the ground.

Small birds are fond of visiting fields of grain or ones sown with other crops that have tasty, nourishing seeds. As soon as the seeds begin to ripen, which is always in late summer when the young nestlings have fledged, fields are often visited by large flocks of birds. Various tits, the Greenfinch (*Carduelis chloris*), Linnet (*Carduelis cannabina*) and other birds find ripening poppy heads particularly to their liking. These are readily pierced with the birds' beaks and then it is no problem to extract the oily poppy seeds inside. The Linnet perches on top of the poppy head and breaks off the upper parts, leaving only the base attached to the stalk (4).

When grain begins to ripen and the kernels are still milky and tender whole flocks of the House Sparrow (*Passer domesticus*) and Tree Sparrow (*P. montanus*) converge on fields. They like the edges of fields outside villages, which is where they nest. They perch on the stalk below the spike of grain and then climb slowly upwards extracting the kernels from the bottom up as they proceed. Many stalks are broken during the process and seeds are cast to the ground. A wheat field visited by sparrows looks as if it had been hit by a hailstorm. The pictures show undamaged spikes of Foxtail Millet (5) and spikes of the same plant eaten by the House Sparrow (6).

⑤

⑥

①

②

③

④

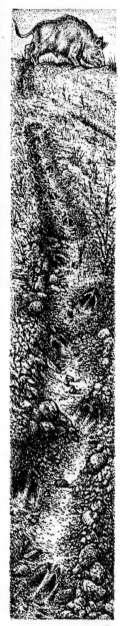

Meal Remains of Herbivorous Animals
Plate 86

The Wild Boar (*Sus scrofa*) (1) spends most of its time in deep woods where it can forage for food undisturbed. It is an omnivorous animal and so its diet embraces a wide range of foods. During the growing season it roams about eating various plant parts, berries and fungi. The time of greatest feasting, however, is in autumn when the ripe seeds of oaks, beeches and other deciduous trees fall to the ground. Ripe acorns, beechnuts and chestnuts prove so irresistible that the Wild Boar remains at the spot where these are found. The animal's presence is revealed by its tracks and droppings. The Wild Boar is also fond of animal food and will eat insects, slugs, the eggs of birds that nest on the ground, and carrion; occasionally it captures a young Brown Hare or Roe Deer.

The head of the Wild Boar is furnished with a long, cartilaginous snout which serves as an excellent tool for digging up food from the ground. With short movements of the head the animal digs into the ground with its snout and ploughs up large clumps of soil or turf looking for roots, tubers, bulbs, rhizomes, underground fungi and also worms, insect larvae and the nests of small rodents. Because there is always a larger number of individuals in a herd the traces of their digging are very conspicuous and extensive (4). Each individual in the herd selects a certain section of ground which it then proceeds to turn over and examine thoroughly. The herd thus leaves in its wake irregular circular or oval areas which are particularly clear and distinct in snow. The animals' tracks and droppings are naturally to be found there too (2).

The Wild Boar is extremely wary and does not go out in quest of food until late at night. It normally forages in woodlands, but it also looks for food in neighbouring fields and there, too, one may find traces of its digging (3). It finds fields particularly attractive during the growing season, especially those sown with oats and maize. When the grain ripens and the stalks are topped with spikes of tender, milky kernels the animals regularly converge on the field and hide in the grain even in daytime.

④

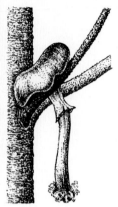

(4)

Fungi (mushrooms and toadstools) with their aromatic flavour are a popular food of many mammals, but they are never eaten by birds. Animals often feed on fungi that have an offensive taste or are poisonous by our standards.

Fungi are regularly eaten by deer. If the mushroom is not too big deer readily clamp it between their jaws and bite it off close to the ground with their lower incisors. All that remains in the ground is a tiny remnant of the stalk. If a Wild Boar (*Sus scrofa*) is nibbling a moderately large mushroom, it usually breaks off pieces of the cap in the process which it leaves lying unnoticed on the ground and goes off to nibble at other mushrooms.

Other mushroom-feeders include the Red Squirrel (*Sciurus vulgaris*), which carries smaller mushrooms into a tree. However, if the mushroom is too big for it to carry it sits on the ground and gnaws it from all sides. The feeding damage made by the Red Squirrel is readily identified by the marks made by the incisors — grooves about 4 to 5 mm wide. The Red Squirrel also stores mushrooms for future use. It either carries the mushroom in its teeth to the top of a tree where it wedges the cap in the fork of a branch, often directly beside the trunk of the tree, or it impales the mushroom on a broken twig. Mushrooms are thus preserved by drying (4). The Red Squirrel, however, has a poor memory and often cannot locate its store of mushrooms, which may then be found, completely dried, in the middle of winter.

You may come across mushrooms whose caps are marked with numerous tiny grooves packed close together. These are traces of nibbling by some small rodent. In woodlands it is usually the Bank Vole (*Clethrionomys glareolus*) (1) or Yellow-necked Mouse (*Apodemus flavicollis*). Boletus mushrooms attract rodents the most, perhaps because of their pronounced aroma. If the mushroom is rather big the Bank Vole or Yellow-necked Mouse jumps up and sits on the cap where it bites out thin strips of the flesh with its sharp incisors. Often the cap is so nibbled that the outer covering and hence the cap's original colour (2) have disappeared. The grooves made by the teeth are about 1.5 to 2 mm wide.

Mushrooms are also eaten by some slugs, but their feeding damage is quite different — whole areas are eaten, so that the mushroom has shallow depressions on it, and there are no teeth marks (3).

Meal Remains of Carnivorous Animals Plate 88

The Muskrat (*Ondatra zibethicus*) (1), being a rodent, eats plant food — rhizomes and the young shoots of aquatic plants, shoreline vegetation and fallen fruit, carrots and beets. This vegetarian diet is, however, augmented by ample portions of meat. Given the opportunity it hunts crayfish, plucking them out of their shell and devouring their tasty flesh. It is also fond of the tender meat of the bivalve mollusc *Anodonta cygnea* (the Swan Mussel), which it carries from the water to its feeding place, usually close to its burrow or in the shallows amidst reeds close to the runways leading to the Muskrat fortress. It slips its sharp incisors between the two halves of the shell and pries them open, breaking off bits from the edges in the process. It does not carry off the empty shells but leaves them where they fall and so often large quantities of these shells may be found at the Muskrat's feeding places (2).

Near water one may very occasionally also come across the remains of an Otter's repast. The Otter (*Lutra lutra*) is an excellent diver and swift and agile swimmer so that it can capture even rapidly swimming fish without much difficulty. Having caught its prey it carries it to a quiet spot on the shore, to a flat rock or to a rock in midstream, where it then eats it. As a rule it starts at the head (3), leaving only the tip of the tail or the largest bones when it has finished.

Land predators hunt vertebrates and generally drag their prey to some hiding place. That is why one rarely finds the remains of their meal. When, with luck, such feeding remains are discovered it is often difficult to identify the culprit, but tracks and droppings at the spot may provide clues. Many mammalian predators are so skilful that they are able to surprise even a bird. At the spot where the bird was caught or at the spot where it was eaten one may find scattered about large tail and wing feathers that have been bitten off and have their ends chewed and tattered (4a). The base of the quill remains embedded in the bird's skin. If a bird is captured by a raptor then its long feathers are pulled out by the roots and the shaft (rachis) is marked with distinct grooves made by the beak or else is partly broken in two (4b) (see also Plate 90).

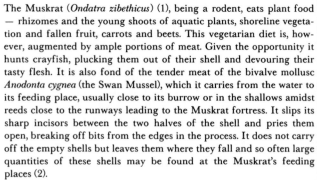

①

②

③

The eggs and the young of birds are a favourite food of many mammals and birds. The victims even include birds that nest in thickets and in the branches of trees, but the ones most affected are those that build their nests on the ground for they are open to attack by predators that cannot climb, such as the Fox and Badger.

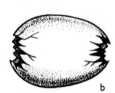

The Hedgehog (*Erinaceus europaeus*) (1) is a troublesome pest of Pheasant reserves. Setting out at dusk it ranges over the ground at a leisurely pace. When it comes across a bird's nest it puts even a sitting female bird to flight with its repeated attacks and begins eating the eggs on the spot. It starts by biting a large hole in the shell through which it sticks its tongue inside and licks up the contents of the egg. A nest that has been raided by a Hedgehog is readily identified because all that remains of the eggs are just shallow cups, the remainder of the shells being completely shattered, and the nest itself is splattered with their contents.

When carnivores raid a bird's nest they go about it in a different way. They do not eat the eggs in the nest but carry them in their mouths to some concealed spot where they either devour them or hide them in grass and leaves as a food supply for future use. The Fox (*Vulpes vulpes*) eats eggs by taking them into its mouth whole, crushing the shell and swallowing the contents. The Pine Marten (*Martes martes*) and Western Polecat (*Mustela putorius*) bite out a large, jagged opening roughly square in outline in the side of the egg and suck up the contents (3; 4c). The Stoat (*Mustela erminea*) and Weasel (*M. nivalis*) bite a hole in the top of the egg (particularly if it is a large egg such as a duck's or a Pheasant's) to get at the white and yolk inside (4b). It should be noted, however, that these characteristic signs may vary. The general rule is that egg shells damaged by carnivores are usually piled in one spot or close together. If we find a Partridge's or Pheasant's nest in which the two halves of the egg shells are one inside the other and the broken edges point inwards then it is a sure sign that the young nestlings hatched successfully.

Chief raiders of birds' nests on the ground are crows, specifically the Hooded Crow (*Corvus corone cornix*) (2), Carrion Crow (*C. corone corone*) and Magpie (*Pica pica*). During the nesting period they fly leisurely to and fro above field crops on the lookout for the nests of the Partridge, Pheasant and other birds. Sometimes they finish off the eggs on the spot (2), at other times they carry them to firmer ground (empty egg shells may be found in large quantities on paths, levees and railway embankments). They first make a small opening in the egg — either on the side (4a) or at one of the two ends — then insert the upper beak into the hole, raise the egg and drink the contents.

Meal Remains of Carnivorous Animals Plate 90

Raptors capture their prey in the air and on the ground. Falcons, for example the Peregrine (*Falco peregrinus*) and Hobby (*F. subbuteo*), hunt exclusively on the wing high up in the air and attack a victim on the ground only rarely. The Golden Eagle (*Aquila chrysaetos*) (3), one of the largest European raptors, hunts both in the air and on the ground. The Goshawk (*Accipiter gentilis*) (4) and Sparrowhawk (*A. nisus*) do not pursue their prey great distances but make the most of the element of surprise. They fly close above the ground or in the treetops where they readily catch up with and seize the unwitting victim. Their relatively short, broad wings allow them to manoeuvre very skilfully. Victims running on the ground or flying in the air are seized with the strong toes furnished with large hooked talons.

The talons of the Golden Eagle (5a) are several centimetres long and sharp as a dagger. Raptors have enormous strength in the toes so that the victim is speared through by the talons at the first contraction of the toes and quickly killed. The Osprey (*Pandion haliaetus*), which specializes in hunting fish, has, in addition, horny spines on the undersides of the toes (5b) which help maintain a secure hold on the slippery fish. The Buzzard (*Buteo buteo*) (1) is quite a large raptor but because its toes and talons are relatively short it specializes in hunting voles and mice, like the Kestrel (*Falco tinnunculus*). The Buzzard also feeds on all kinds of carrion (1) and when several individuals converge on a hare's carcass at the same time then fighting breaks out, with each bird defending its piece of flesh with widespread wings (2).

Raptors prepare their 'meal' thoroughly before eating. If the prey is a bird they first pull out the feathers (4), mainly the long, tough feathers from the tail and sometimes also from the wings. Unlike carnivores, which bite off several feathers at a time — for instance all the tail feathers — raptors pull out the single feathers by the roots leaving marks on the shaft (rachis) where it was clamped by the beak. At the spot where the raptor went about its task there is always a large pile of feathers which the wind usually scatters to all sides (4). It always pays to follow these scattered feathers for they will usually lead the tracker to the place of the raptor's feast.

When the raptor remains on the spot for a long time it also leaves its large, white and mushy droppings there. Carnivores also leave droppings beside their victims but these are usually dark, firm and cylindrical. Raptors pluck out the feathers or hair from their victims because they are unable to digest them. The Golden Eagle, when it captures a hare, first carefully plucks out the hair, at least from the spot where it intends to begin eating, and only then does it start eating the flesh (3). The many clumps of fur round the prey reveal that it was eaten by a raptor.

Meal Remains of Carnivorous Animals   Plate 91

When the prey is too large raptors usually eat it on the spot. Smaller prey, however, is carried to their favourite feeding places. The Sparrowhawk (*Accipiter nisus*) (2) always has several such places on its territory, usually the edges of woods, forest rides, clearings and glades. It need not always be the same place — the feathers of its separate victims may all be in one spot or scattered. If such feathers are found during the nesting period they also serve to indicate that the bird's nest may be close by. The Sparrowhawk generally nests in young, thick woods and single scattered feathers may reveal where the nest is. When the young nestlings are being fed some small remnant of the prey always falls to the ground below the nest.

The Goshawk (*A. gentilis*) (3) nests in tall trees. It does not have any special places where it regularly feeds. In a Goshawk's home range the remains of its prey are scattered haphazardly throughout the woods or in some covered spot. If the remains are those of a bird it is possible to identify the prey by the feathers, foot bones, beak or other parts of the skeleton. If the predator did not do a thorough job then it is not too difficult to determine the identity of its victim. In the picture (1) the black and white markings on the wings and the large white spot below the eye indicate that the Goshawk's victim was an adult male Goldeneye (*Bucephala clangula*). The task is more difficult when only a few feathers are found and these have no conspicuous, distinctive markings. If you wish to make a detailed study of the diet of raptors on the basis of their meal remains then the individual feathers and other remains should be put into a bag and the contents identified by comparison with a zoological collection.

It is not always possible to tell by the feathers found on the spot of the repast whether the prey was eaten by a Sparrowhawk or Goshawk. The kind of prey as well as its size, however, may serve as a sort of guideline. In the case of raptors the female is always larger than the male. The female Goshawk can capture birds as large as a pheasant, duck or Black Grouse; the smaller male can handle birds no larger than a partridge or pigeon. The Sparrowhawk is much smaller than the Goshawk, but the female captures prey the same size as that caught by the male Goshawk. The small male Sparrowhawk pursues birds smaller than or at most the same size as the Blackbird or Turtle Dove.

When raptors capture a bird they begin by eating the breast meat. When doing so it often happens that bits of the flat, thin keel of the breastbone are bitten out along with the meat by the sharp edges of the hooked beak (4a). These wedge-shaped notches with slightly jagged edges indicate that the predator was a bird of prey. The size of these notches sometimes also makes it possible to make a good guess at whether the feeding damage was caused by a raptor the size of an eagle (4b) or a Goshawk (4c).

212

Shrikes have a distinctive method of eating prey. They capture insects, mostly larger species, but many are also successful in capturing voles, mice or young birds. Shrikes are extraordinarily daring birds, just as aggressive and skilful as birds of prey.

Although they have nothing in common with raptors (they are perching or passerine birds) shrikes and birds of prey share a characteristic — the shape of the beak, which is adapted for capturing and eating similar food. The beak of raptors is relatively high with a downcurved upper mandible. In the Goshawk (*Accipiter gentilis*) the upper mandible is only slightly downcurved (4b), in other raptors it curves more strongly. Falcons, for example the Kestrel (*Falco tinnunculus*), Hobby (*F. subbuteo*) and Peregrine (*F. peregrinus*), have a horny 'tooth' in the upper bill (4a), which is believed to facilitate the tearing of flesh. The beak of shrikes is not as large nor as high as that of raptors, but it has a downcurved tip and a horny 'tooth' in the upper bill (4c).

When the Great Grey Shrike (*Lanius excubitor*) captures a vole (1), which it cannot eat right away, it stores it in a distinctive manner until some future time. Taking the vole in its beak it impales it on the sharp thorn of a wild rose or other thorny bush, returning now and then to tear bits of flesh from the animal. The related Red-backed Shrike (*L. collurio*) is fond of nesting in thorny shrubs and likewise impales its prey — captured insects — on thorns (2), sometimes even on barbed wire.

The Green Woodpecker (*Picus viridis*) extracts various larvae from the wood of trees (see Plate 79) but it, too, is one of the woodpeckers that is fond of eating ants in all stages of development. It often seeks out the nests of tree ants and stages a regular chase in the tunnelled corridors. Extending its long tongue into the ants' tunnels and chambers it catches ants, their eggs, larvae and pupae on its sticky surface. A Green Woodpecker found perching in grass and striking the ground with its beak is usually trying to get at the nest of ground ants. It also regularly visits the large anthills of woodland ants where it first stirs them up with its beak and then captures them with its sticky tongue. It excavates deep tunnels in anthills (3), capturing and eating not only the ants but also the larvae of various beetles that inhabit these nests along with the ants.

Droppings

Plate 93

Although animal droppings are not an attractive item they reveal the presence of animals of which we are otherwise unaware. On hard stony ground, as in mountainous areas, it is almost impossible to find hoof tracks or other footprints and only droppings tell us what animals may be found there. From an analysis of droppings we can determine to some degree the type of food that was eaten and sometimes the sex and even the condition of the animal.

a

In fields, meadows and woodlands the droppings of the Brown Hare (*Lepus europaeus*) are frequently encountered. These are readily identified by their rounded shape and by the fact that they are scattered all over the countryside. The greatest number is always found by a food supply. Brown Hare droppings are brown in colour, 12 to 18 mm in diameter and slightly flattened; they look as if they had been kneaded from cigarette tobacco (1; 5a). The remains of plant food can clearly be seen in the droppings. In winter when the Brown Hare eats dry food the droppings are a lighter brown and rather dry; in summer the juicy plant food the animal eats makes the droppings softer and often also darker.

b

The droppings of the Rabbit (*Oryctolagus cuniculus*) (2; 5b) look very much like those of the Brown Hare but are smaller, more regularly spherical and never more than 10 mm in diameter — they usually average 7 to 8 mm in diameter. They are also slightly darker than hare droppings. Moreover Rabbit droppings are found only in the middle of a Rabbit colony or in its immediate vicinity because the animals do not roam farther afield. They have regular latrines near the colony and in time there are great quantities of droppings in such places. The Brown Hare never adopts regular latrines.

c

Droppings of the Red Deer (*Cervus elaphus*) are usually found in places where the deer go to graze, at rutting grounds and on the runways leading to their food supply. In winter the runways trodden out in the snow are often covered with a continuous layer of their droppings. Red Deer droppings indicate the sex of the animal. Males have cylindrical droppings, pointed at one end and usually flattened at the other; they slightly resemble a cartridge in shape (4; 5c). In females they are elliptical in shape and slightly pointed or rounded at the ends (3; 5d). Red Deer droppings are dark and shiny when fresh; those of adult individuals are 20 to 25 mm long and 13 to 18 mm thick. In summer they are softer and stick together in clumps or may be almost of a mushy consistency.

d

(5)

Droppings

Plate 94

Because the diet of plant-eaters (herbivores) is not very nourishing the animal must consume large quantities of food daily and several time a day. The compound stomach of the Red Deer (*Cervus elaphus*), fo example, has a capacity of as much as 40 litres of mushy food. This allows the Red Deer to eat more than 24 kg of green fodder daily ir summer. Plant matter, which consists largely of cellulose, is not easily digested and so is first coarsely ground before being subjected to chemical action.

The actual decomposition of the plant matter, and hence its digestibility, is the result of the action of numerous bacteria and ciliate protozoans, which help break up the cellulose. At the same time they themselves become part of the herbivore's diet thus providing the animal with the required proteins. Nevertheless the amount of food the animal cannot digest is very great and that is why the droppings of herbivores, particularly ruminants, are so commonly found in the wild. Because of the similarity in diet and manner of processing the food the droppings of most ruminants are very much alike in shape and colour. The droppings of larger animals are naturally bigger; the size of the droppings is also determined to some extent by the animal's age.

a

The droppings of the Fallow Deer (*Dama dama*) greatly resemble those of the Red Deer in shape and colour (2). However, they are slightly smaller, roughly 10 to 15 mm long and 8 to 12 mm wide (5b). They are coloured black and fresh droppings are covered with a shiny membrane. The droppings are tightly clustered and pass out through the anal opening in a sausage-like group. However, this usually breaks up into separate droppings as soon as it falls to the ground.

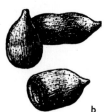

b

The droppings of the Roe Deer (*Capreolus capreolus*) are oval in shape (longish-cylindrical or longish-ovoid), 10 to 16 mm long and 7 to 10 mm wide (5c). Sometimes they are nearly spherical with a small point at the end. They are coloured black or brown; fresh droppings are shiny. In summer they contain more water, are soft and are stuck together so firmly that they remain together in a heap even when they fall to the ground. In winter (4) they are not as moist and the individual droppings separate more readily. The greatest quantities of Roe Deer droppings are found where the animals have been grazing and on the runways along which they travel. As hoofed animals often defecate when walking these runways are always covered with their dung.

c

(5)

The droppings of the Wild Boar (*Sus scrofa*) differ in shape and size from those of ruminants. They are in sausage-like or irregularly shaped lumps up to 7 cm thick and approximately 10 cm long (5a). They are black in colour (1) but turn grey after a time and the lumps break up into separate droppings (3).

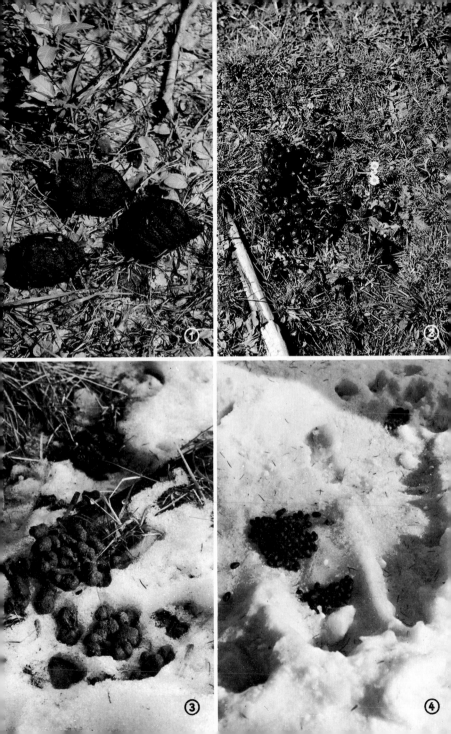

Animal food is much more nourishing than plant food and that is why meat-eating mammals do not need to eat as often or nearly as much as plant-eaters. Add to this the fact that most of the food is digested leaving few remains, then it is clear that the droppings of carnivores are encountered less often than herbivore droppings. However, because carnivores use droppings to mark out their territory and leave them in obvious places such as rocks, stumps and open stretches of forest, their droppings can be found here and there.

Droppings of the Fox (*Vulpes vulpes*) are coloured black to grey (1) and are cylindrical in shape with a long sharp point at one end (5a), about 5 to 10 cm long and 2 to 2.5 cm in diameter. Older droppings turn grey, often almost white and are slightly reminiscent of owl pellets because they contain bits of feathers, fur or bones. In late summer one may come across Red Fox droppings that are coloured blue or blackish indicating that the animal fed on blueberries or raspberries. In autumn when rowanberries turn ripe and fall to the ground their partly digested remains are regularly found in Fox droppings (4).

The droppings of members of the Mustelidae are usually almost black in colour. Yellowish droppings indicate a diet of eggs; blue and red droppings indicate that the animal fed on woodland berries. The droppings of the Pine Marten (*Martes martes*) and Beech Marten (*M. foina*) have a foul-smelling odour, are 8 to 10 cm long, about 1.5 cm in diameter, spirally twisted and terminate in a long point at one end (2). The droppings of the Western Polecat (*Mustela putorius*) are slightly smaller and sometimes difficult to distinguish from those of martens. They are twisted like a rope, 6 to 8 cm long and about 12 mm in diameter. The droppings of the Stoat (*Mustela erminea*) and Weasel (*M. nivalis*) are usually 3 to 4 cm long and no more than 1 cm in diameter as a rule (5c). The droppings of the Badger (*Meles meles*) resemble those of the Fox. They are cylindrical, 6 to 8 cm long and about 2 cm in diameter (3). They tend to break up and usually have a long point at one end (5b). Often found in Badger droppings are undigested remains, such as bones, hairs, hard parts of insects, fruit and berries. The Badger has the Rabbit's habit of using regular latrines. With its front claws it digs a shallow hole in the ground in which it deposits the droppings. The hole is not covered over but is used a number of times. Such a latrine serves as a sign that there may be an occupied Badger's burrow nearby because the Badger digs its latrines close to the entrance to its home.

Similar longish droppings are deposited by the Hedgehog (*Erinaceus europaeus*). These are deposited at random, most often on field and woodland paths. They are about 3 to 4 cm long and about 1 cm in diameter, shiny black in colour, cylindrical and pointed at one end and contain the chitinous remains of insects.

Droppings

The droppings of meat-eating birds — raptors, herons, cormo
storks, gulls, terns and owls — are very thin, almost watery, an
found on the ground and on trees in the form of large white spla
As a rule bird droppings are found beneath their roosting p
on trees or on rocks. Trees in which herons and cormorants per
roost regularly appear to be spattered with lime and their leave
completely burned by the droppings.

The droppings of plant-eating birds are much firmer an
shaped like variously contoured cylinders or heaps. As in plant-e
mammals the droppings of plant-eating birds are often encoun
because plant-eaters must feed often and in large quantities
because much of the plant food is indigestible.

In fields and meadows near water one will find the droppin
the Greylag Goose (*Anser anser*) (1). This goose feeds mainly by l
off the leaves of plants and this also gives its droppings their ch
teristic greenish colour (3). They are cylindrical, 4 to 8 cm long
about 1 cm in diameter and usually capped at one end with v
mushy urine. Places where the geese moult and shed their fea
also contain many large heaps of droppings left by the geese d
their lengthy stay in that spot.

The droppings of the Black Grouse (*Lyrurus tetrix*) (2) are fou
woods, but mainly on moors and in heather. As a rule there is al
a larger quantity in one spot, probably the Black Grouse's re
place. The droppings are brownish yellow in colour and contai
remains of buds from trees or the skins of woodland fruits. The
cylindrical, 2 to 4 cm long, about 8 mm in diameter and sli
curved. Under some bushes in deep woods one may come across a
quantity of cylindrical droppings 5 to 8 cm long and about 1 c
diameter (4a). These are the droppings of the Capercaillie (*1
urogallus*), the largest of the woodland gamebirds. Its winter (
pings consist solely of the remains of conifer needles and are colc
yellowish green; the summer droppings also contain the remai
woodland fruits. Such droppings indicate that this was the Cape
lie's feeding or roosting place.

The droppings of the Pheasant (*Phasianus colchicus*) are often f
in heaps under trees where the Pheasant roosts as well as sing
fields and woodlands. They are about 2 cm long, approxim
0.5 cm in diameter, and are often irregularly twisted (4b). As a rule
dropping is capped with white urine at the end. Partridge (*F
perdix*) droppings are found in fields and in larger quantities a
bird's resting place; they are only slightly smaller than Pheasant d
pings (4c). The droppings of the Green Woodpecker (*Picus viridis*
cylindrical, about 3 cm long and 6 mm in diameter. They are pa
with the remains of insects and covered with a fine whitish n
brane.

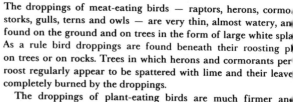

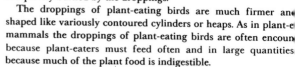

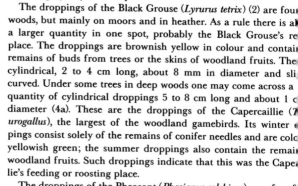

①

②

③

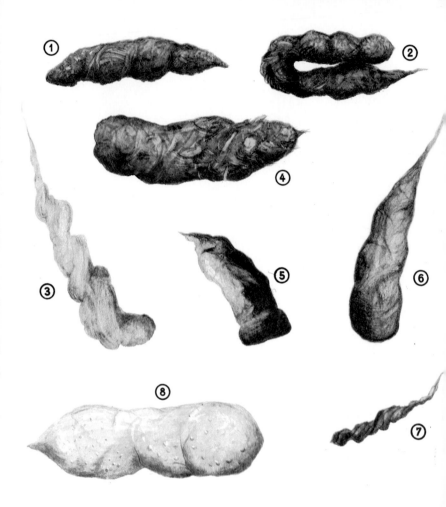

▲

Droppings   Plate 97   **Pellets**   **Plate 9**

1, Hedgehog (*Erinaceus europaeus*)
2, Marten (*Martes* sp.)
3, Polecat (*Putorius* sp.)
4, Badger (*Meles meles*)
5, Cat (*Felis* sp.)
6, Fox (*Vulpes vulpes*)
7, Weasel (*Mustela nivalis*)
8, Lynx (*Lynx lynx*)

1, Stork (*Ciconia* sp.)
2, Heron (*Ardea* sp.)
3, Rook (*Corvus frugilegus*)
4, Barn Owl (*Tyto alba*)
5, Buzzard (*Buteo buteo*)
6, Kestrel (*Falco tinnunculus*)
7, Tawny Owl (*Strix aluco*)
8, Black-headed Gull (*Larus ridibundus*)
9, Long-eared Owl (*Asio otus*)
10, Little Owl (*Athene noctua*)
11, Eagle Owl (*Bubo bubo*)

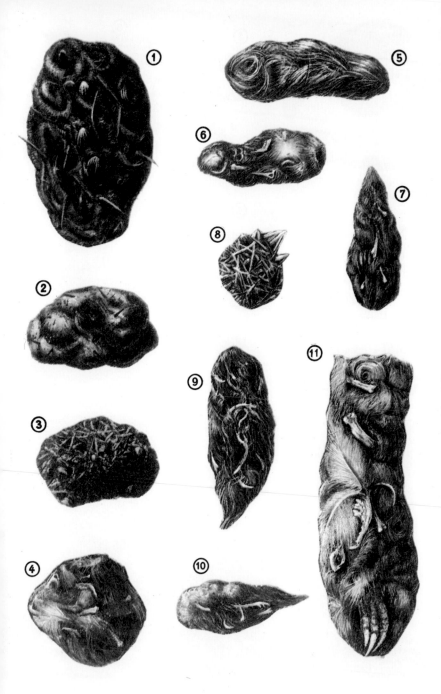

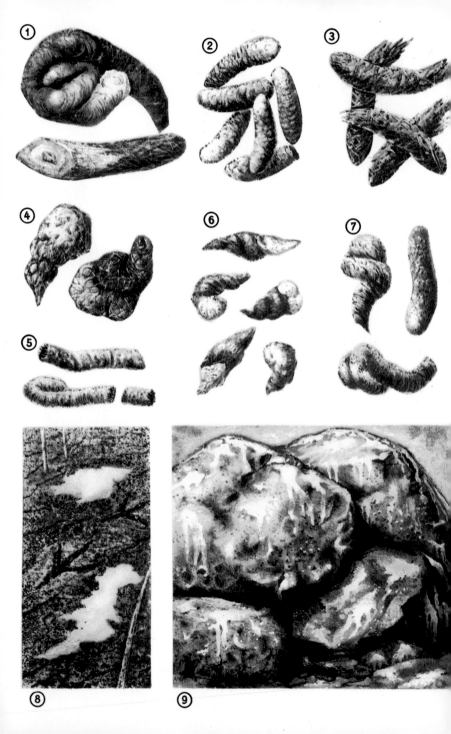

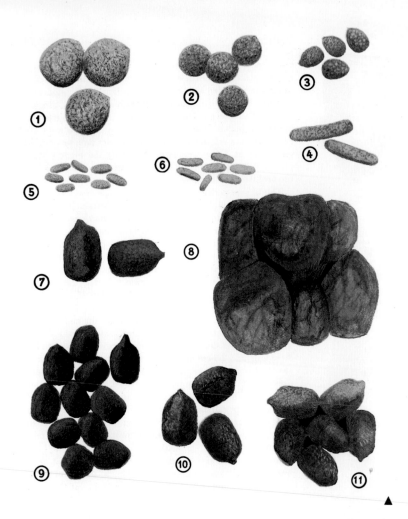

Droppings

Plate 99

1, Greylag Goose (*Anser anser*)
2, Black Grouse (*Lyrurus tetrix*)
3, Capercaillie (*Tetrao urogallus*)
4, Cross between Capercaillie and
   Black Grouse
5, Green Woodpecker (*Picus viridis*)
6, Partridge (*Perdix perdix*)
7, Pheasant (*Phasianus colchicus*)
8, Grey Heron (*Ardea cinerea*)
9, Buzzard (*Buteo buteo*)

Droppings

Plate 100

1, Brown Hare (*Lepus europaeus*)
2, Rabbit (*Oryctolagus cuniculus*)
3, Red Squirrel (*Sciurus vulgaris*)
4, Muskrat (*Ondatra zibethicus*)
5, House Mouse (*Mus musculus*)
6, Vole (*Microtus* sp.)
7, Fallow Deer (*Dama dama*)
8, Wild Boar (*Sus scrofa*)
9, Roe Deer (*Capreolus capreolus*)
10, Red Deer (*Cervus elaphus*)
    — winter droppings
11, Red Deer — summer droppings

Owls and birds of prey regurgitate food they cannot digest through their beaks in the form of pellets. Hairs, feathers, bones, claws and beaks are moulded into cylindrical pellets in the stomach and then coughed up out of the beak. Although other birds cough up pellets too, for example gulls, nightjars, storks, herons, kingfishers and bee-eaters, the pellets of owls and raptors are the ones most often found. First, they are relatively large and compact and, second, they are re-gurgitated at places regularly visited by the birds — their resting places. The shape and size of the pellets vary according to the size of the bird (see also Plate 92).

The largest pellets are those of the Eagle Owl (*Bubo bubo*) (1), but these are unlikely to be encountered in Britain. They are sometimes more than 10 cm long and up to 4 cm in diameter, grey in colour and even have large bones protruding from the mass. The varied diet of the Eagle Owl can be seen from a partly disintegrated pellet (2). The pellets of the Barn Owl (*Tyto alba*) are coated with a black mucilagi-nous layer that gives them a glossy sheen. They are large, plump and rounded at the ends, sometimes even spherical, between 3 and 8 cm long and about 3 cm in diameter. The pellets of the Long-eared Owl (*Asio otus*) are about the same length but much thinner (no more than 2.5 cm in diameter), are usually pointed at the ends and pale grey in colour. The pellets of the Tawny Owl (*Strix aluco*) resemble those of the Long-eared Owl, particularly in terms of colour. They are 4 to 8 cm long and 2.5 cm in diameter (5) but rounded at the ends. In them are well-preserved remains of bones, even whole skulls of their prey (4). Of all the commonly seen owls in Britain the pellets of the Little Owl (*Athene noctua*) are the smallest. Because the Little Owl captures large numbers of insects its pellets contain remains of insect wings and the wing cases of beetles (elytra). They are 4 to 5 cm long, strik-ingly narrow, approximately 1.5 cm in diameter, and often pointed at the ends.

Raptors can digest bones far better than owls and so their pellets usually contain only the fur and feathers of their prey. Buzzard (*Buteo buteo*) pellets are about 7 cm long and about 3 cm in diameter and look as if they are composed of tiny bits of grey felt compacted together (3).

Bird pellets are found in widely diverse places. The following gives a brief idea of where to look for them in Britain. In villages you may find the pellets of the Barn Owl, Little Owl and Kestrel (*Falco tinnun-culus*) on church steeples, in the attics of old houses and in similar places. Thin woods, old gardens, orchards and parks are the places to look for the pellets of the Tawny Owl and Little Owl. The Long-eared Owl, Sparrowhawk (*Accipiter nisus*), Goshawk (*A. gentilis*) and Hobby (*Falco subbuteo*) leave large heaps of pellets in woods, in the margins of woods and in thicker stands, but in Britain it is rare to see them. Buzzard and Kestrel pellets are often scattered in fields, at the base of trees, telegraph poles and boundary stones. On cliffs you will often find Kestrel pellets and occasionally — on the Continent only — those of the Eagle Owl.

⑤

Analyses of bird pellets have made it possible to determine in detail the diet of all the commonest owls and have proved how important these birds are to us in that they capture and feed on harmful voles and mice. The Tawny Owl (*Strix aluco*) daily eats at least three small rodents or the equivalent amount of other food. It is easy to reckon how many rodents it destroys in a year and what a great service it performs for us when the damage caused, for example by one Orkney or Common Vole (*Microtus arvalis*), is estimated at 2.5 kg ruined grain per year.

By studying owl pellets it is possible to get at least a rough idea of what food owls eat. It is not necessary to go into any details — knowledge of the skull characters of the various mammalian orders will suffice for identification. The skulls and skeletons of mammals are also found in open country and the animal can be identified by the arrangement and size of the teeth and the size of the skull. For more detailed study you should refer to specialized literature on the subject or compare your material with zoological collections.

Dental formulae:

Hedgehog

$$\frac{3.1.3.3.}{2.1.2.3.} \quad \text{(36 teeth)}$$

The Hedgehog (*Erinaceus europaeus*) (1) is an insect-eater and its prolonged snout indicates that the skull will also be very slender and elongated. The skull may be found, for instance, in the pellets of the Eagle Owl (*Bubo bubo*), which is well able to deal with the Hedgehog's defensive strategy (the animal coils up into a ball when attacked or alarmed thus presenting its long, sharp protective spines). The skull of the Hedgehog is 53.8 mm to 64.2 mm long, 32 mm to 39 mm wide and has a set of 36 sharp-edged pointed teeth (2).

Pygmy Shrew

$$\frac{3.1.3.3.}{2.0.1.3.} \quad \text{(32 teeth)}$$

Shrews are small insectivores with tiny, elongated skulls furnished with a large number of teeth. Their skulls are rarely found in pellets, probably because shrews produce a secretion with a foul, penetrating smell and perhaps also taste that deters owls. When we find a dead and bloody shrew in a forest it was most probably killed by an owl or carnivore but was left lying there because of its unpleasant odour. The Pygmy Shrew (*Sorex minutus*) (3) weighs about 3.5 grams and is about 5 cm long without the tail. Its skull is 14.4 to 16.9 mm long, 7 to 8 mm wide and has a set of 32 small sharp teeth with tips coloured brownish red (4).

Mole

$$\frac{3.1.4.3.}{3.1.4.3.} \quad \text{(44 teeth)}$$

The elongated skull of the Mole (*Talpa europaea*) (5) may be found in the pellets of the Eagle Owl, the Tawny Owl and the Long-eared Owl (*Asio otus*). It is 31.6 to 38.5 mm long, 11 to 13 mm wide and has a set of 44 sharp teeth (6). Prominent features are the long canines, particularly those in the upper jaw, and the sharp-edged back molars.

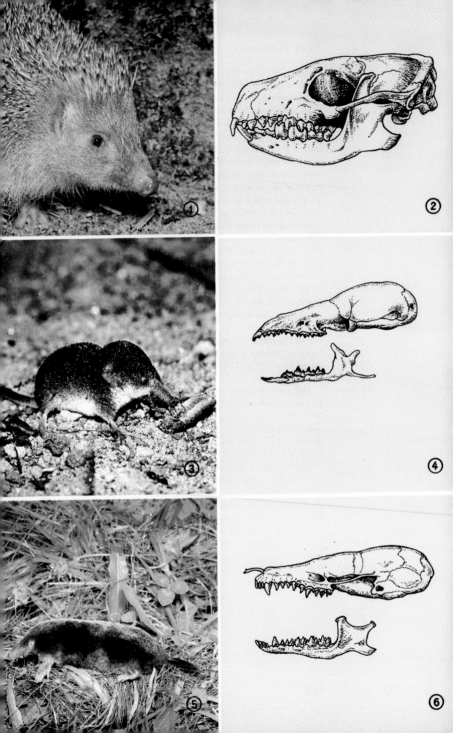

Carnivores differ from the other mammalian orders in many ways, chief of these being the distinctively shaped front part of the head with powerful jaws. The hinging of the jaws makes it possible to open them very wide, to an extent found in few other mammals. The jaws are furnished with strong, powerful teeth adapted for seizing, killing and tearing prey. Particularly striking are the large, sharp-pointed and slightly curved canines and the so-called carnassial teeth — the last premolars (anterior cheek teeth) of the upper jaw and the first molars (posterior cheek teeth) of the lower jaw specialized for slicing or shearing rather than tearing. When eating the animal always holds a large piece of flesh in the corners of the mouth as if it were biting it with the back teeth. In fact, however, it is pushing the food on to the crowns of the carnassial teeth and slicing it by clamping its jaws shut. Carnivores have enormous strength in their jaws and are able to shear even strong bones. The size of the carnassial teeth and the arrangement of the whole set of teeth are adaptations to the type of food the animal eats and the manner in which it is obtained.

Dental formulae:

Fox, Wolf, Dog, Jackal

$$\frac{3.1.4.2.}{3.1.4.3.} \quad \text{(42 teeth)}$$

Domestic Cat, Wild Cat

$$\frac{3.1.3.1.}{3.1.2.1.} \quad \text{(30 teeth)}$$

Lynx

$$\frac{3.1.2.(3).1.}{3.1.2.1.}$$
(28 [30] teeth)

The Fox (*Vulpes vulpes*) (1) is a canine (a carnivore of the dog family). The jaws are greatly elongated and a prominent feature are the long, curved, sabre-like canines, those in the upper jaw being longer than the ones in the lower jaw (2). When the jaws are closed the tips of the upper canines protrude below the lower jaw. The carnassial tooth in the upper jaw is strikingly large. The whole skull is long and tapered — 126 to 154 mm long and 71 to 87 mm wide — and it has a set of 42 teeth.

Felines (carnivores of the cat family) have a round head and the jaw is not as markedly elongated as in the dog family. The skull of the Wild Cat (*Felis silvestris silvestris*) (3) is almost hemispherical in shape and a prominent feature of the relatively short jaws are the long upper canines. The skull is 80 to 101 mm long, 63 to 80 mm wide and it has a set of 30 teeth. The skull of the Wild Cat is not usually found in open country because this cat is a relatively rare species, but it is very similar to the Domestic Cat's skull and has the same number of teeth. It often happens that a Domestic Cat (*Felis catus*) escapes into the woods where it turns wild, multiplies and frequently acquires the striped coloration of the Wild Cat. Some of these cats attain the same dimensions as the Wild Cat and so may readily be mistaken for the latter. The shape of the tail, however, will serve as an aid in identifying the animal. The tail of the Wild Cat is very thick and rounded at the end (4a) whereas the tail of the Domestic Cat (even if it has turned wild) is more slender and slightly pointed at the tip (4b).

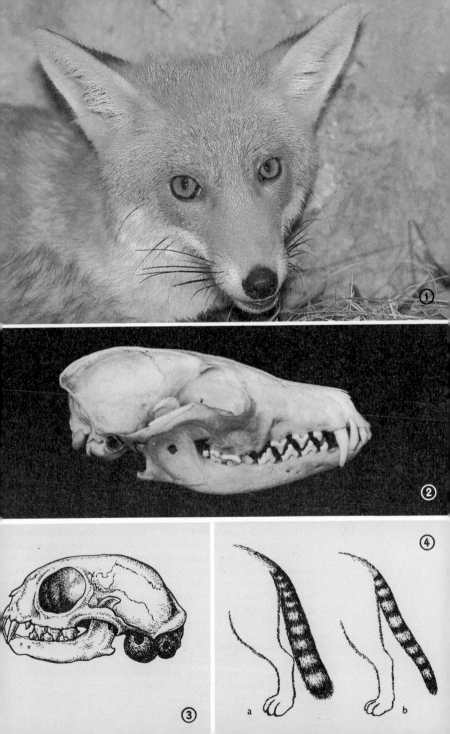

①

②

③

④

a   b

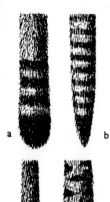

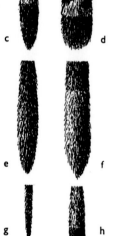

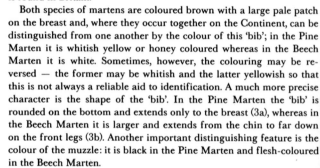

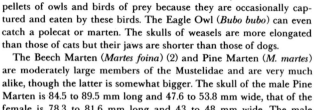

The skulls of members of the Mustelidae, mainly those of the Stoat (*Mustela erminea*) (1) and Weasel (*M. nivalis*), may be found in the pellets of owls and birds of prey because they are occasionally captured and eaten by these birds. The Eagle Owl (*Bubo bubo*) can even catch a polecat or marten. The skulls of weasels are more elongated than those of cats but their jaws are shorter than those of dogs.

The Beech Marten (*Martes foina*) (2) and Pine Marten (*M. martes*) are moderately large members of the Mustelidae and are very much alike, though the latter is somewhat bigger. The skull of the male Pine Marten is 84.5 to 89.5 mm long and 47.6 to 53.8 mm wide, that of the female is 78.3 to 81.6 mm long and 43 to 48 mm wide. The male Beech Marten's skull is 79 to 85 mm long and 48.6 to 55.0 mm wide and the female's is 75.9 to 80.0 mm long and 44.8 to 50.0 mm wide. Martens have a set of 38 teeth. Remember that only the Pine Marten is found in Britain.

Both species of martens are coloured brown with a large pale patch on the breast and, where they occur together on the Continent, can be distinguished from one another by the colour of this 'bib'; in the Pine Marten it is whitish yellow or honey coloured whereas in the Beech Marten it is white. Sometimes, however, the colouring may be reversed — the former may be whitish and the latter yellowish so that this is not always a reliable aid to identification. A much more precise character is the shape of the 'bib'. In the Pine Marten the 'bib' is rounded on the bottom and extends only to the breast (3a), whereas in the Beech Marten it is larger and extends from the chin to far down on the front legs (3b). Another important distinguishing feature is the colour of the muzzle: it is black in the Pine Marten and flesh-coloured in the Beech Marten.

The skull of the Badger (*Meles meles*) (4) is elongated (5) and measures 114.2 to 137.6 mm long and 69.4 to 86.6 mm wide. It has a set of 38 teeth, of which the largest are the upper canines. The carnassials and all the cheek teeth do not have sharp cutting surfaces, which indicates that the Badger is more of an omnivore than a typical carnivore. The projections on the surface (cusps) of the premolars and molars are bluntly rounded thereby facilitating the chewing and crushing of plant food.

The skull of the Western Polecat (*Mustela putorius*) resembles that of martens in shape but is smaller. It is 58.2 to 71.8 mm long and 32.2 to 43.2 mm wide but the maximum measurements do not reach the minimum length and width of the skull of a female Beech or Pine Marten. The Polecat has 34 teeth. The smallest skulls are those of the Stoat and Weasel, the Stoat's skull being 41.6 to 58.8 mm long and 21.4 to 30.6 mm wide, and the Weasel's skull being 31.4 to 42.7 mm long and 15.1 to 25.0 mm wide. Both the Weasel and Stoat have 34 teeth.

The size, shape and colour of the tail will help you identify the various species of carnivores (6): Wild Cat (a), Domestic Cat (b), Steppe Polecat (not found in the British Isles) (c), Lynx (d), Western Polecat (e), Badger (f), Weasel (g), Stoat (h).

①

②　③

a　b

④　⑤

a

b

c

Bone Remains   Plate 105

Owl pellets often contain the remains of small rodents — the whit-
ened bones of the whole skeleton, damaged to a greater or lesser
degree, and often the complete skull. These serve as a reliable means
of determining what animals the owls feed on. Sometimes in owl
pellets you find the remains of rare species of rodents, which reveals
their presence in an area where they had remained undetected by the
usual observation methods.

The skulls of small rodents are all very much alike in shape and
size but can easily be identified by the number and shape of the teeth
and the length of the row of molars. Rodent skulls are distinguished
from other mammalian skulls by the prominent gnawing teeth, that is
the front chisel-shaped incisors — two in each jaw. These have open
roots and so they never stop growing. There is a large toothless gap
between the incisors and the flat-topped molars.

The House Mouse (*Mus musculus*) (5c), Wood Mouse (*Apodemus
sylvaticus*) (5d), Yellow-necked Mouse (*A. flavicollis*), Harvest Mouse
(*Micromys minutus*), Brown Rat (*Rattus norvegicus*) and other less common rodents all have three molars in both the upper and lower jaws
with cusps (projections) on the surface in an irregular pattern (2a).
Dormice have four upper and four lower molars, all with lateral
ridges on the surface (2c). The Orkney or Common Vole (*Microtus
arvalis*) (1; 5a), Field Vole (*M. agrestis*), Bank Vole (*Clethrionymus glareolus*) (5b), Northern Water Vole (*Arvicola terrestris*) and Muskrat (*Ondatra zibethicus*) have three upper and three lower molars with smooth
surfaces characterized by a pattern of alternating triangles (2b).

The Common Vole, one of the commonest of field rodents on the
Continent, has a skull 22.5 to 27.6 mm long and 12.8 to 15.4 mm wide.
It has a set of 16 teeth. The row of molars in both the upper and
lower jaws is 5.4 to 6.4 mm long. The Bank Vole's skull is 22.2 to
26.5 mm long and 12.4 to 15.5 mm wide. Like the Common Vole it
has 16 teeth. The row of molars in both upper and lower jaws is 4.4 to
6.2 mm long. The House Mouse has a transverse notch in the upper incisors (3a); its skull is 19.2 to 22.8 mm long and 10.4 to 12.4 mm
wide. The length of the row of molars is between 3.3 and 4.3 mm.
The incisors of the Wood Mouse are not notched (3b), but the
molars are cusped like those of the House Mouse; the row of molars is
3.2 to 4.4 mm long. The Wood Mouse's skull is 21.6 to 24.6 mm long
and 11.6 to 14.0 mm wide.

d

(5)

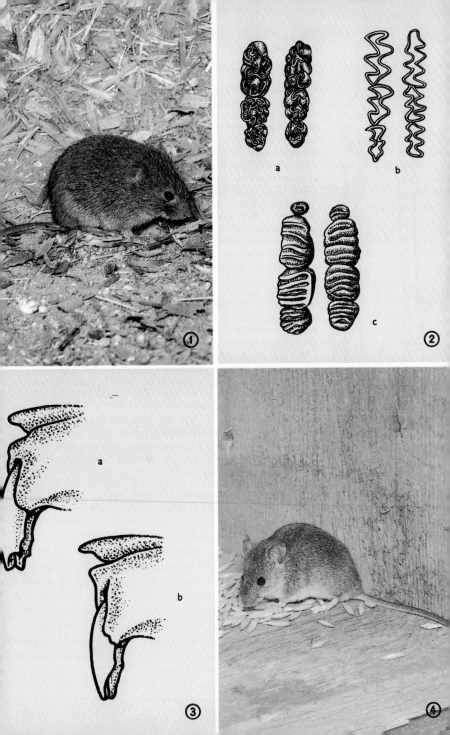

① ② ③ ④

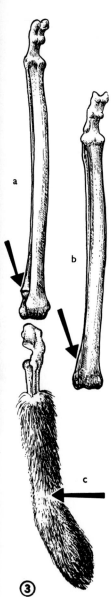

The Brown Hare (*Lepus europaeus*) (1) is hunted in autumn or winter when the young are almost fully grown. Neither the age nor the sex of hares can be determined without close examination of the captured or killed animal. There are several methods of estimating the age of hares but the following, which is quick and carried out with relative ease, is the most reliable.

Grasping the hare's front leg bend the foot as near to a right angle as possible and feel along the ulna on the outer side about 1 to 2 cm above the bend (3c). If there is a distinct knob on the bone (3a) then the hare is less than eight months old; if there is no knob and the bone feels smooth, then the animal is older (3b). When doing so take care not to mistake the carpal or wrist joint for the knob.

All long limb bones have, while they are growing, three sections: a long middle section of solid bone called the shaft or diaphysis and a short bone at either end of the shaft called the upper and lower epiphysis respectively. The three bony sections are connected by cartilage which enables the bone to lengthen. This cartilage forms a distinctive knob at the lower end of the ulna which gradually disappears as the animal ages. In young hares growth stops at about the age of one year when the epiphysal knob disappears (between the 8th and 12th months).

If a Brown Hare's skull is found in the wild it can be readily identified by the double incisors on each side of the upper jaw; the second is the smaller and lies behind the first. The Rabbit (*Oryctolagus cuniculus*) has incisors of the same sort but the skulls of the two animals can be distinguished by their size. The skull of an adult Brown Hare is 85.2 to 97.0 mm long and 45.2 to 52.0 mm wide; the row of molars is 17 to 22 mm long. The skull of the Rabbit is 68.2 to 75.0 mm long and 37.2 to 41.4 mm wide; the row of molars is 13.4 to 16.2 mm long. Both animals have a set of 28 teeth. On the Brown Hare's skull all the sutures are evident up to the age of six months (2a), the sutures on the occipital bone disappear between the age of six and eight months (2b), at the age of one year the sutures are very faint (2c) and in older hares the sutures are completely absent (2d).

a   b   c   d

If you are lucky enough to watch deer grazing from a pylon hide or some well-concealed spot then you can examine their tracks after the animals have finished their meal and left the spot. As has already been said it is possible to determine the sex and age of the animal, particularly Red Deer (*Cervus elaphus*), according to the shape and size of the tracks. Conversely, if you can estimate the age of an individual from its appearance, then that will help you understand the tracks.

The appearance of a Red Deer is determined by the shape of its head, the thickness and position of its neck and the stockiness of its body. In calves and young stags up to the age of five years the head is usually relatively small and narrow with seemingly long ears. The neck is slender, upright and seemingly long, and without a mane. The body is also slender, the belly does not hang, the back is nearly straight and the chest is not prominent. The antlers are relatively weak and short — at most a six- or eight-point head of sorts (2a). In stags of middle years (between six and eleven years of age) the head is still growing and increasing in size. The neck is thicker and more powerful, seemingly shorter and usually held less erect, and there is a mane. The body is larger and more thick-set and the weight is shifted more towards the front so that the chest becomes much broader and more powerful. The antlers are much more branched and quite long (1). In old mature stags, 12 or more years of age, the neck is thicker still and there is a prominent mane which makes the neck seem short; it is usually carried almost level with the ground. The withers (the highest part of the back between the shoulder blades) are prominent, the belly droops markedly and the centre of gravity is located in the huge chest. The antlers are spreading and greatly branched; however, in very old stags there may already be a reduction in the number of points or tines (2b).

The skeleton of a dead stag is rarely encountered but occasionally, particularly in late winter, one may come across the remains of a dead animal. The skull of a stag may be identified by the antlers or by the pedicels (two bony knobs on the skull on which the antlers grow). Hinds have neither pedicels nor antlers. The skull of Red Deer is 340 to 360 mm long and 140 to 150 mm wide; the row of molars is 105 to 135 mm long. There is a set of 34 teeth.

The age of a Red Deer can be reliably determined not by the antlers but by the amount of wear on the teeth. The molars of young individuals are little worn and have a sharp cutting (occlusal) surface — all are relatively high-crowned (2c). In Red Deer of middle years the occlusal surfaces are worn more or less flat and in old individuals the molars are worn down almost to the gums and the occlusal surfaces are greatly deformed (2d). The incisors and canines in the lower jaw also show an increasing amount of wear with increasing age. In young stags the incisors are high-crowned and wide (3a), in stags of middle years they are shorter (3b) and in old individuals they are practically worn down to the gums (3c).

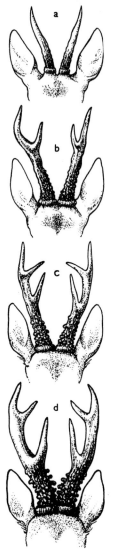

a

b

c

d

③

Determining the Sex and Age of Birds and Mammals

Plate 108

The principal characters for determining the age of Roe Deer (*Capreolus capreolus*) buck in the wild are body build, the manner of holding the head and neck, the onset of growth and time of fraying of the antlers and partly also the shape and size of the antlers.

A buck aged one or two years has a short, slender head with typical 'juvenile' features supported by a long slender neck. It carries the head high with neck upright (the younger the animal the higher it holds its head). The body is also slender and regularly cylindrical. It is this slenderness that makes the legs of young animals seem so very long (2a). The walking gait of young bucks is light, springy and elegant. In Roe Deer bucks of middle years the body is strong and thick-set and the head gradually becomes broader, larger, more angular and more muscular. The neck is likewise thicker and more powerful and hence seemingly shorter. At a walking gait, which is more leisurely than in young bucks, the head and neck are carried lower down.

Old bucks have a short, broad head with more powerful, bluntly wedge-shaped forehead. The neck is extraordinarily thick and hence seemingly shorter than in young bucks; when walking at a leisurely pace it is carried practically in line with the body. The head is bent close to the ground and moves rhythmically up and down when walking. The body is thick-set and the belly droops markedly (2b).

The Roe Deer buck (1) grows antlers, the doe does not. Old bucks cast their antlers in late October and during November, young bucks not till December or January. New antlers begin to grow shortly after the old ones have been cast. During the growth period the antlers are covered with a soft, furry skin known as velvet that supplies food through a network of blood vessels to the growing antlers and protects them. When the antlers are fully grown after about 90 days the velvet begins to strip and bushes — this is called cleaning or fraying. Old bucks clean their antlers about the beginning of April, bucks of middle years about mid-April and younger bucks not until the middle of May or even later.

If you find a Roe Deer skull with antlers then it is that of a buck. If there are no antlers but only pedicels on the skull then it is the skull of a buck that died at the end of the year. If the skull lacks pedicels then it is that of a doe. The Roe Deer skull is much shorter than a Red Deer's, being 172 to 207 mm long and 80 to 84 mm wide. The row of molars is between 53 and 68 mm long. Roe Deer have a set of 32 teeth, but occasionally there may also be canines in the upper jaw and then there are 34 teeth. The molars of young individuals are high-crowned and sharp-edged (2c), in old individuals they are worn down almost to the jaw bone (2d). The antlers of a yearling are normally no more than short, bare, simple spikes (3a), in two-year-olds they are forked (3b), in three- to four-year-olds they are a six-point head of sorts (3c) and in five- to seven-year-old bucks the six-point head is a large and good one (3d). This, however, is not a general rule. A few well-developed two-year-olds and even on the rare occasion a yearling may grow a six-point head.

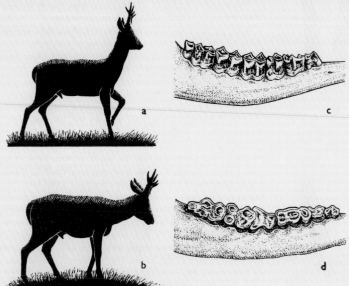

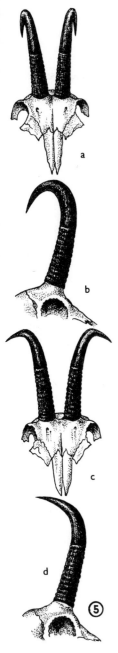

a

b

c

d

⑤

Determining the Sex and Age of Birds and Mammals

Plate 109

The largest family of hoofed even-toed ruminants, the bovids (cattle, sheep and goats), have paired horns instead of antlers. Both sexes usually grow horns, unlike most deer, the exception among deer being the female Reindeer (*Rangifer tarandus*), which also grows antlers.

Antlers and horns differ in several ways. Antlers are made of solid bone and grow from knobs (pedicels) on the frontal bone of the skull. The main shaft, or beam, forks and produces a varying number of short tines (points) or flattened extremities. Antlers are furthermore cast and regrown each year. They grow from the ends and so the oldest part is the section at the base, closest to the pedicels. Horns are hollow and are a modification of the outer layer of skin or epidermis, the same as hairs, claws and hoofs. They consist of a tough horny sheath on two long bony outgrowths on the frontal bone (4). They are variously curved and twisted but never forked. They remain on the animal's head throughout its lifetime, in other words they are not cast, and increase in length every year. They grow at the base and so the part closest to the skull is the most recent and the tips are the oldest.

The Mouflon or Wild Sheep (*Ovis musimon*) (1) is a common and widespread bovid on the Continent. The horns of the ram are long and spirally curled in a large arc round the head and are conspicuously grooved (3). Besides these regular ridges there are also more prominent annual rings that mark the year's growth of horn. The number of these rings makes it possible to determine with some accuracy the age of the captured or killed ram.

The continual growth of the horns also makes it possible to estimate the age of the Mouflon ram by the degree of curl. If we compare it with the hour hand on the face of a clock then the tip of the left horn in a year-old ram points to about one o'clock, in a two-year-old to three o'clock, and in a three-year-old and older rams it always shows two hours more than the actual age of the animal. This rule holds true till about the seventh year. After that the tip of the horn continually points to about nine o'clock (2). The horns of a female Mouflon are small and uncurled, or absent altogether. The Mouflon skull is 210 to 232 mm long and 94 to 106 mm wide; the row of molars is 63 to 75 mm long. There is a set of 32 teeth.

In the Chamois (*Rupicapra rupicapra*) both sexes have short hooked horns. Viewed from the side the horns of rams have downcurved tips (5b) whereas those of ewes point backwards (5d). Viewed from the front the horns of rams resemble a narrow capital letter V (5a) whereas those of ewes bend slightly outwards in the upper third (5c). This is not always the rule, however, and this feature is not reliable for identification purposes. In fact it is impossible to make a positive identification of the animal's sex at first glance. The yearly growth of horn is marked by deep annual rings, which are well defined particularly on the back surface of the horns. The number of ridges indicates the age of both rams and ewes. The skull of the Chamoix is 189 to 207 mm long and 82 to 90 mm wide; the row of molars is 52 to 61 mm long. There is a set of 32 teeth.

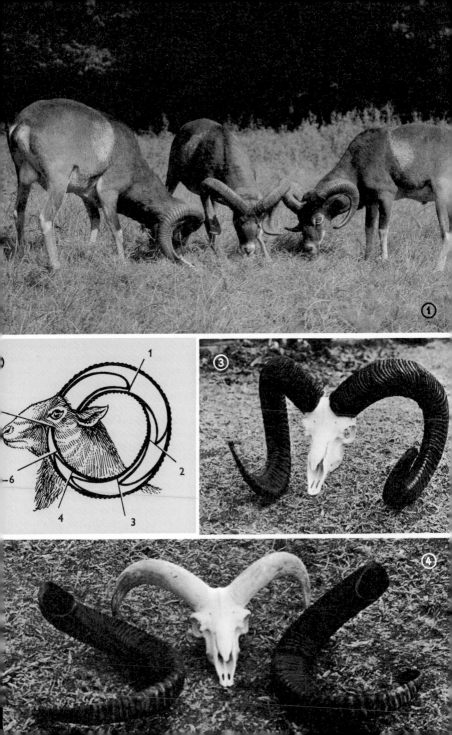

①

③

④

1

2

4   3

6

a
b
c
d ⑤

Determining the Sex and Age of Birds and Mammals

If you find meal remains (a bill or webbed toes) that definitely indicate that the victim of a raptor or carnivore was a duck, then you can try your hand at determining whether the duck was young or old. Given the opportunity you can use the same age determination method when buying a duck for cooking.

Ducks moult twice a year. In summer when the young are grown they shed all their feathers. This is called a complete moult and the new plumage that grows is called the non-breeding or eclipse plumage; at this time the coloration of the males resembles that of the females. In autumn there is another, partial moult, when the birds acquire their nuptial plumage, which they retain until the following complete moult. At this time the drakes are much more brightly coloured than the ducks, as can be seen in the picture of a Mallard (*Anas platyrhynchos*) (1). Newly hatched ducklings are covered with a fine coat of natal down which is replaced 14 to 26 days later by juvenile plumage. This resembles the female plumage of the duck and is retained until the autumn, sometimes until the beginning of the ensuing year, after which it is replaced by the adult nuptial plumage.

Whether a duck is less or more than a year old can be determined by the shape of the middle coverts — small contour feathers on the outer surface of the wing above the brightly coloured area (speculum). In juvenile plumage the middle coverts are relatively narrow and the vane or web terminates in a sharp point (5b, young drake; 5d, young duck). Because these feathers are not shed during the autumn moult they are retained in the adult plumage for the first winter. The middle coverts of ducks older than one year, on the other hand, are wider, the webs do not converge into a sharp point but are broadly rounded at the end or nearly square-tipped (5a, mature drake; 5c, mature duck).

The tail feathers are an indicator of age, but only for a limited period, until the partial moult in autumn. When the coat of natal down is being replaced by the juvenile plumage the tail feathers emerging through the skin push the old down feather out with the tip of the rachis (2a, b). At the tip of the new feather there is a V-shaped notch in which the tip of the shaft or rachis shows when the down feather falls (2c). After the autumn moult the tail feathers of all ducks are pointed (2d), without any notch. This is also true of geese. The tail feathers of a young Greylag Goose (*Anser anser*) (3, left) can be compared with the tail feathers of an adult goose (3, right). Besides the conspicuous notch at the tip there is also a great difference in the size and coloration of the tail feathers.

An adult Greylag Goose has a whitish belly with brown transverse markings and flesh-coloured feet. A young goose does not have the transverse markings on the belly, its feet are coloured grey and the goose itself is smaller (4).

246

①

②

c

a

b

d

③

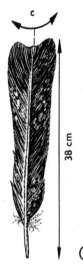

Determining the Sex and Age of Birds and Mammals

Plate 111

When hunting rare woodland gamebirds, such as the Black Grouse and Capercaillie, the hunter must observe certain rules and shoot only such birds as permitted by the local regulations. Hence he must be able to determine their age.

The Black Grouse (*Lyrurus tetrix*), as its name indicates, is coloured black. It weighs 1 to 2 kg. The hen is brownish rufous and weighs about half that amount. Black Grouse display on the ground (1). In spring the cocks arrive at the courting grounds before sunrise where they perform all sorts of antics, uttering hissing and burbling sounds all the time. There is always a number of cocks displaying together and these engage in 'jousts'. They attack one another with their beaks, but seldom fight seriously. The cocks also ruffle their feathers, droop their wings, spread their tail wide and run about with tiny steps like a toy powered by clockwork. It is the shape of the tail and the size of the tail feathers that help one to estimate the bird's age, though not with great accuracy.

The tail of the Black Grouse cock is composed of 18 feathers and the outer three (sometimes four) on either side are sickle-shaped and curved outwards. The hen's tail has a wedge-shaped notch at the end. The cock's sickle-shaped feathers lengthen and curl increasingly with advancing age and in the first year attain a length of 20 cm, while the whole tail measures 14 cm in length (2a). In the second year the sickle-shaped feathers are 22 cm long and the tail measures 13 cm in length (2b). In the third year the sickle-shaped feathers are 23 cm long and the tail only 12 cm because the feathers spread in width (2c). The sickle-shaped feathers are measured pulled out straight to their full length.

The largest woodland gamebird, the Capercaillie (*Tetrao urogallus*), begins its courtship display on the branch of a tall tree before dawn while it is still dark. When the sun rises it flies down to the ground where it continues its antics. Determining the age of a courting cock is just as difficult as for the Black Grouse, but the shape and size of the tail feathers provide clues. During the courtship display the cock spreads its tail wide, ruffles its feathers, raises its neck high and droops the wings. The widespread tail of a one-year-old cock embraces an angle of about 130 degrees (3a), the individual feathers are about 24 cm long and rounded at the tip (4a). A cock of middle years opens its tail up to 150 degrees (3b), the feathers are about 30 cm long, less rounded and more straight-tipped (4b). In four- to six-year-old cocks the tips of the feathers are usually straight. Old cocks have a very large 'fan' — their widespread tail may embrace an angle of as much as 180 degrees (3c), the individual feathers are about 40 cm long, up to 9 cm wide and faintly cut out in a half arc at the tip (4c).

248

14 cm

13 cm

12 cm

a   20 cm   b   22 cm   c   23 cm

②

a

130°

150°

180°

c

③

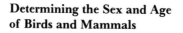

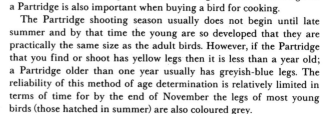

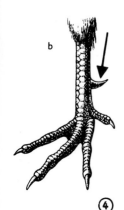

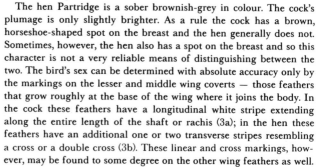

If you find the remains of a torn Partridge (*Perdix perdix*) (1) you can tell by examining them whether the victim was a cock or a hen and whether it was a young or old bird. Being able to tell the age of a Partridge is also important when buying a bird for cooking.

The Partridge shooting season usually does not begin until late summer and by that time the young are so developed that they are practically the same size as the adult birds. However, if the Partridge that you find or shoot has yellow legs then it is less than a year old; a Partridge older than one year usually has greyish-blue legs. The reliability of this method of age determination is relatively limited in terms of time for by the end of November the legs of most young birds (those hatched in summer) are also coloured grey.

The most reliable method of determining the age of a Partridge is by the shape and coloration of its primary feathers. If you come across the remnants of a Partridge with all the primaries the same colour and sharply pointed at the tip then it is a very young bird, less than a year old. If, however, the first two primaries are a different colour from the rest (lighter, more faded) and sharply pointed at the tip whereas the others are rounded (2a), then it is a bird hatched the preceding year and about 15 months old. If you find a wing with all the primaries the same colour and rounded at the tip (2b), including the first two, then the bird is about 27 months or older. However, it is never more than four years old because that is the maximum life-span of the Partridge in the wild.

The hen Partridge is a sober brownish-grey in colour. The cock's plumage is only slightly brighter. As a rule the cock has a brown, horseshoe-shaped spot on the breast and the hen generally does not. Sometimes, however, the hen also has a spot on the breast and so this character is not a very reliable means of distinguishing between the two. The bird's sex can be determined with absolute accuracy only by the markings on the lesser and middle wing coverts — those feathers that grow roughly at the base of the wing where it joins the body. In the cock these feathers have a longitudinal white stripe extending along the entire length of the shaft or rachis (3a); in the hen these feathers have an additional one or two transverse stripes resembling a cross or a double cross (3b). These linear and cross markings, however, may be found to some degree on the other wing feathers as well.

The age of a dead or captured male Pheasant (*Phasianus colchicus*) can be estimated by the shape and length of the spur growing on the back of the leg. If the spur is about 0.5 cm long and bluntly cone-shaped (4a) then the bird is usually an immature cock less than one year old. The spur of an old Pheasant is up to 10 mm long, curved and sharply pointed (4b).

Making Plaster Casts of Tracks

Learning to identify and interpret animal tracks requires years of training, patience and good powers of observation. The best way to remember a track is to draw it in your notebook. The drawing should either be the same size as the original or else reduced in scale. But your drawing will be almost useless unless you also record the dimensions of the track because the tracks of many animals are very similar in shape and one can easily be mistaken for another. If you are not good at drawing — and many people aren't — you will find it helpful to use a simple grid.

Begin by making a rectangular frame 15 × 20 cm of wire about 3 to 4 mm thick, soldering or welding the loose ends together. Mark off 1-cm spaces on the periphery and at each mark make a shallow notch about 1 mm deep with a triangular file. Then connect opposite notches with thin wire (soldering the ends fast) and when you have finished you will have a grid with openings that measure 1 × 1 cm. Strong thin string or nylon line can be used in place of wire. When you have done this draw one or more grids of the same size in your notebook and you are all set. Then when you find a track you want to draw place the grid over it and copy it, line for line, in the pencilled grid in your notebook. In this way you will have an exact copy of the track you found in the wild. This can then be retraced at home without the grid, shaded as required and filled in with any further details.

You can, if you want, take photographs of tracks instead of drawing them. Here, too, you must remember to record the actual size of the track if you wish to use the photograph for purposes of comparison. For this reason always place something such as a matchbox or other small object whose dimensions you know next to the track to show the scale of the print. If you want to photograph the tracks for their attractive arrangement and not for purposes of comparison or as documentary material, then there is no need to show the scale. This book is not intended to provide detailed instruction on how to take photographs. Every amateur photographer with a little experience knows how and if you are a novice you can find whatever information you need in special literature on the subject. You will soon learn that the best time to take pictures of tracks is in the morning or early evening when the sun is at an angle; this will throw a shadow on to the outline of the track and make it more visible. Instead of a good shaded picture of the track, however, the play of light and shade may produce a 'negative' picture in which the relation of light and shade of the original track is reversed. This happens when the photograph is taken at an unsuitable angle. The best pictures are those of tracks made in snow; those of tracks in wet snow or drying mud show the best details.

In addition to photographs and drawings you can keep a record of tracks by making casts of plaster of Paris or other similar material. This is a very attractive and interesting activity and the results have many advantages compared with drawing and photography. When making a plaster cast you obtain an exact replica of the track and there is no need to worry about measurements. Unlike a drawing or photograph which are flat a cast has the advantage of being three-dimensional and of showing all the dimensions of the track — the length, width and depth. Besides this you can have both a positive impression of the print, showing the track as it actually is, and a negative impression, showing how the underside of the foot is moulded. Last of all casts make a nice collection, either for specialized scientific purposes or for decoration in your home or garden.

The equipment for making plaster casts is relatively inexpensive and can easily be stowed in a small knapsack. You will need a small amount of plaster of Paris, a rubber or plastic bowl in which to mix the plaster powder with water, frames of stiff cardboard or thin metal sheet, water, a piece of soap, some vaseline, a flat brush 1 to 1.5 cm wide, an old knife, and some newspaper.

A collection of plaster casts requires a certain amount of storage space and so take this into account when deciding on the shape of the casts. A round or elliptical shape is unsuit-

Fig. 17 — Making plaster casts of tracks: a, placing the frame over the tracks; b, pouring plaster into the frame; c, removing the negative cast from the frame; d, fixing the negative cast in a frame to make a positive cast; e, joined blocks of the negative and positive cast; f, finished plaster cast of the track — negative cast on the left, positive cast on the right

able because such casts cannot be stored well, or rather they take up too much space. Much better and more economical are rectangular casts which can be stored like a set of building blocks. A tried and tested method are frames measuring 5 × 7.5 cm, 7.5 × 10 cm, 10 × 15 cm and 15 × 20 cm, which you prepare beforehand using a 5-cm-wide and 0.6-mm-thick metal strip. For the 5 × 7.5-cm frame cut two metal strips 7cm long and two strips 9.5 cm long. Measure off 1 cm from either end of each strip and with a pencil draw a line 2.5 cm long (half-way down) at right angles to the edge. Secure the strips in a vice and carefully cut along the marked line. The cut must be slightly wider than the thickness of the metal strip and its edges must be carefully filed. When these cuts have been made in all four strips the frame can easily be put together by fitting the slots in the separate strips into each other. The larger frames are prepared in the same way. You will need two of each, to give a total of ten frames of various sizes, which will suffice for making casts of large tracks or whole groups of small tracks as well as single small tracks. In place of metal the frames can be made of plastic or stiff cardboard. Paper frames are not suitable because they have a very short life. They are quickly soaked through and cannot be used a second time but must be discarded.

The track usually selected for casting is one with clearly defined details. However, it is also a good idea to make casts of tracks that do not show the whole outline of the foot or all the toes, so that you have a comparative series showing how the tracks of a particular animal differ under various conditions at a walking gait or how they differ when the animal is moving at different gaits (walking, trotting, galloping, jumping). If the ground immediately round the track and the track itself are covered with sand, dust or plant remains then these must be cleared away by blowing. Never try to pull out small twigs, plant stalks or tiny stones if they are firmly embedded in the track, for in so doing so the smooth side walls of the track are usually damaged and the print crumbles and is rendered worthless.

When you find a suitable track take out the strips of the frame of corresponding size and fit them together around the track so that it is located in the centre. Lightly push the frame into the ground and then lift it up again. This will leave the shallow impression of a rectangle in the ground. Deepen these grooves with a knife so that the frame slides in easily and when it is firmly embedded round the track tamp down the crumbled soil on the inside and the outside of the metal strips. If the slots in the metal strips are too wide and light shows through the chinks, then seal them by piling up some soil at the corners of the frame on the outside. Otherwise the plaster of Paris may ooze out through the slots.

The next step after the track has been thoroughly cleaned and the frame put firmly in place and sealed is to mix the plaster. Put the required amount of water into the rubber bowl (this you will have to estimate yourself; it is better to put in too much than too little) and dissolve the piece of soap in the water until it turns milky. You can use clear water but the soapy solution has its advantages. When clear water is used the plaster casts are heavy; the soap seems to make them lighter and less fragile. Into this soapy solution slowly add the plaster of Paris powder at one spot so that it becomes moist and sinks to the bottom. Continue adding the powder until it forms a small mound reaching to just below or slightly above the surface of the water. This serves as a rough estimate of the best proportion of powder and water to obtain the correct consistency. Then let the plaster stand for several minutes so that it becomes thoroughly moistened. Experienced casters say that plaster hardens best when it is stirred as little as possible and that is why it is left to 'ripen' a few minutes. After the 'ripening' period is up stir the mixture, remove any impurities and slowly pour the thin porridge into the frame. Do not pour it too rapidly or from too high above the track because then large bubbles form in the mixture or the plaster will not find its way into all the folds and depressions in the track. If the mixture forms a mound in the middle of the cast, level this with the finger by carefully spreading the mixture towards the edges of the frame.

Large casts are fragile and will break if handled carelessly. So when you cast a large track or groups of small tracks, use more plaster and pour it into a greater depth so that the cast will be sufficiently thick. In addition you can reinforce and strengthen the cast in the following way. Pour the plaster into the frame so as to cover the whole of the area to a depth of about 1 cm. Let it harden slightly and then place several pieces of wire of the required length crosswise on the surface or else a piece of thick wire mesh. If necessary you can also use dry pieces of healthy wood — twigs that are not too thick and have been stripped of their bark. Press this grid lightly into the thickening plaster and pour in some more plaster, enough to cover the whole grid completely, which means that the second layer of the mixture must again be about 1 cm thick. Casts produced by this method are more resistant to breakage, which is a great advantage when making positive impressions of the print.

After 15 to 30 minutes the plaster will be sufficiently hardened and the cast may be lifted with care. Hardening of the plaster is influenced by the ambient temperature — the mixture hardens more quickly in warm weather than in cool and damp weather. It is also influenced by the surface conditions — it hardens more quickly on dry, hard ground than on a damp medium. If you are casting on a soft surface, on hardening mud or sand, you can lift the cast and its frame without much difficulty. It separates readily from the substrate even with a thin layer of soil clinging to it. If you are casting on harder ground, for instance if you are casting an old, well-preserved track in dried mud, then you must take greater care when loosening the cast. Slip a sharp knife underneath the cast and move it back and forth to loosen it before lifting the cast. The cast generally has soil clinging to it, mainly in the hollows and grooves. This can be removed on the spot but when doing so take care not to damage the plaster which is not yet completely hard. It is better, however, to wrap the cast along with the adhering soil in a newspaper and clean it when you get home after the cast is completely dry and set hard. Then the dried soil can be removed with a soft brush or washed off under the tap. Before you leave the field clean the bowl by removing all the remnants of plaster clinging to the sides. If there is water nearby then the mixture, which is still semi-liquid, can easily be washed out. If you cannot do this let the plaster remaining in the bowl set hard and then break it loose by pressing the sides of the bowl.

This marks the end of your work in the field. The rest is done at home where it is much easier to do the job properly. When the cast has been thoroughly cleaned and it has dried and hardened, coat the negative cast with a thin layer of vaseline (so that when you make a positive impression the two blocks will not stick together). Spread the vaseline thoroughly over the whole surface and into all the folds and crevices. Where fingers cannot do the job use a fine brush. However, the layer must not be too thick because then the positive impression might be of a different shape. If you wish, you can also spread the vaseline on the sides of the cast.

Now place the same frame used to make the negative impression round the cast and seal all chinks with plasticine or putty. Then prepare a further amount of plaster in the same way as before and pour it slowly and carefully on to the negative cast in the frame. Pour in more plaster than before, because the positive impression needs to be a little thicker than the negative cast. In the places where the paw or hoof is deeply impressed the layer of plaster is much thinner than at the edges and the cast might break at these points. This applies chiefly to larger casts. Use a grid to strengthen the cast if you want to. When the plaster has set hard (best of all the following day) you can remove the frame. Even though vaseline was spread thoroughly over the surface the two blocks will still stick together quite firmly and cannot be separated with the hands alone. Here again the use of a knife will solve the problem. First of all carefully cut away the sides of the two blocks until you see the line separating the negative from the positive impression. (It is necessary to do so because when casting the positive impression the plaster sometimes runs into the loose spaces along the sides of the frame where it does not fit snugly and covers the dividing line). Then take a sharp knife and carefully insert the tip into the dividing line at intervals all around the periphery, trying to pry the two blocks apart by pressing lightly up and down as you proceed.

If the cast is small and the track not very deep then the blocks will come apart quite readily. In the case of large casts the process takes longer and requires greater care. When the two blocks are separated the positive cast will show a faithful replica of the original track found in the wild.

When you have finished casting all that remains is to give the cast a detailed cleaning and a few final touches. Every cast should be clearly labelled — best of all on the back of the positive cast. The label should include the name of the animal, the date and place of casting, the surroundings and type of surface on which the cast was made (sand, mud, forest ride, and so on), and particularly the gait at which the animal was moving (galloping, walking, hopping). When it is complete and ready to be stored you can spray the whole cast with clear varnish. This will not only give the plaster a firm coat but will also prevent the white plaster from rubbing off on garments and hands when the cast is handled. If, however, the slightly unnatural gloss is not to your liking you do not have to varnish the cast; you can paint it a soft brown, buff or ochre, best of all the colour that corresponds to the conditions of the place where the track was cast. You can add the paint directly to the plaster when making the positive impression.

The best way of storing your casts is in a box $22 \times 32 \times 5$ cm in which casts of various sizes may be fitted like building blocks. To make the collection neat and attractive the casts should all be of about the same height. Keep this in mind when casting the positive impression: every negative cast must be fitted in the frame so as to allow plaster to be poured in to a depth, say, of 4 cm. If you abide by this rule all the positive casts will be more or less at the same level and all the impressions of the prints will be at the same level as well.

As you become more experienced you will learn what mistakes you are making in casting and how to avoid them. Best for casting are tracks made in heavier, compact ground. Clay soil that is not too wet, contains no sand or small stones, and is beginning to harden gives the best tracks. If it does not rain tracks will remain a very long time in such a medium — sometimes for as long as two to four weeks — and will also retain their shape. However, even if you clean such a track thoroughly and it seems to be nice and smooth, the impression may still not be perfect. No matter what, particles of soil will adhere to the plaster and the surface of the negative cast will then be lumpy or porous. In time you will learn that the tracks for casting are ones that are not too deep, for then the negative and positive casts are readily separated from each other. If the track is a deep one and is impressed in the ground at a very steep angle, for example the impression made by the hoofs of a galloping Roe Deer in mud, then there are certain complications. The negative cast can be made with relative ease because the plaster will run even into the slanting holes and the soil can easily be washed off the hardened cast. The problems start, however, in making the positive cast when the point (surface) of contact between the two blocks (the positive and negative) is too sharply angled or curved making it extremely difficult to separate the blocks when the plaster has hardened. Sometimes it isn't possible at all — part of the negative cast breaks off and remains inside the positive impression. Then this remnant must be laboriously scraped out, often damaging the positive impression in the process. Sometimes the entire negative cast has to be broken. Therefore begin by casting tracks that are shallow and not too big and leave the more complicated tracks until later when you have more experience.

The task of finding tracks suitable for casting can be facilitated by preparing a space, a bit of ground for taking impressions — in other words a 'trap' of sorts. It is quite easy to do this. If you yourself are not well-enough acquainted with a local game or nature reserve to know where to look for the regular runways of animals or places where the animals are usually to be found, then ask the gamekeeper or warden. There are many such places in wildlife reserves but not every one is suitable for the purpose. Only clear spaces that are not exposed to direct sunlight and where the soil is of the required quality, that is neither sandy nor stony, are suitable for preparing a trap for prints. These are necessary requirements only if you want to make plaster casts of the tracks. If you just want to make a drawing or take photographs of the tracks then the 'trap' can also be on a sandy surface. Suitable spots can be found on forest rides, where the ground is shaded by the branches of the surrounding trees and in permanently wet places beside streams, rivers and reservoirs. There you can readily find a spot measuring several square metres. This must first be cleaned of all leaves, dry twigs and other objects. Then the soil should be loosened with a hoe, levelled with a rake and sprinkled with water until the surface is muddy. When the water has soaked in a bit you give it another sprinkling. The point is for the soil to be moist and yielding to a sufficient depth and for the water to level out, insofar as is possible, all the unevennesses of the surface. When the water has soaked in and the mud has hardened slightly the trap is ready to take the impression of any animal that crosses it. The trap can be further improved and made more efficient by adding bait. If you put sunflower seeds, grain, fruit, vegetables or some other kind of food at the edge of the prepared space you may be sure that the muddy surface of the trap will soon be covered with the prints of a wide variety of birds and mammals. If you make the ground ready in the evening the following morning it will bear the tracks of mammals that are active by night. Then you can set about casting, drawing or taking photographs. When the ground has been wiped clean of all the night-time tracks and made ready anew then it will soon bear the prints of animals that are active by day — mostly birds — and that are likewise attracted by the bait placed close by.

Measuring Tracks and Trails

If you do not want to keep a record by drawing, photographing or casting tracks then it is important to make a note of at least the basic measurements of the footprints you find. For this purpose always select perfect, well-preserved and undistorted tracks. Measuring tracks is quite simple. They can be divided into three groups and the following notes tell you how to go about measuring the prints in each.

For tracks made by mammals with paws we take two basic measurements — the length and the width of the track (Fig. 18). The length is measured by placing a ruler along the longitudinal axis and measuring the distance from the front edge of the pad of the longest toe to the back edge of the hind pad or wrist pad. The length of the track is always measured without the claws. The width of the track is measured at its widest point.

Hoof prints are measured in a similar manner (Fig. 19). The length is measured from the tip of the longest cleave to the back edge of the heel, the width is measured at the widest point of the track. The length of the heels (if these are clearly impressed) and also the spread or splay of the cleaves (the gap between their tips) are also measured.

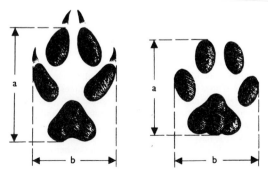

Fig. 18 — Measuring the tracks of mammals with paws (without the claws); a, length of the track; b, width of the track

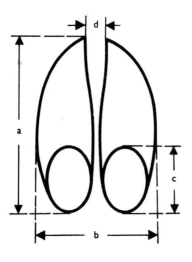

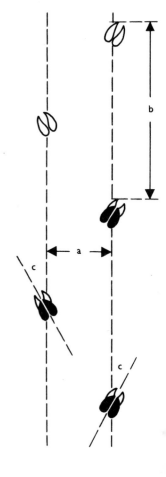

Fig. 19 — Measuring the tracks of mammals with hoofs: a, length of track; b, width of track; c, length of heel pad; d, distance between the tips of the cleaves

Fig. 20 — Measuring trails: a, width of stride; b, length of stride; c, splay or angle of spread

Bird tracks are measured in the same way. The length is measured from the front edge of the longest, in other words from the third toe to the back edge of the hind or first toe. Once again the claw prints are not included in the measurements. The width of the print is determined by the spread or distance between the second and fourth toes and is measured at the tips of the toes (without the claws).

The trail made by a moving animal consists of a series of double tracks arranged in parallel lines (Fig. 20). The space between these lines, or width of stride, is determined by the animal's size and the type of locomotion (gait). The length of stride is the distance between two consecutive placings of a particular limb and is measured from the front edge of one track to the front edge of the consecutive track. At a walking gait, when the hind feet are usually placed in the tracks made by the forefeet and the two overlap (they are in register), the length of stride is roughly the distance between one such registered track and the next. If we were to stretch a string connecting the midpoint of the tracks made by the feet on the right side of the body we would find that the prints of one animal may be in line with the string whereas those of another individual may turn slightly outwards, forming a smaller or larger angle with the median line of the trail. The degree of the angle of spread provides, for instance, information about the age and sex of the stalked animal.

For drawing tracks and in particular trails use graph paper. On it you can draw the track in its actual size (with the aid of the grid mentioned earlier in the text) and the trail to scale (for example 1 mm in the drawing is the equivalent of 1 cm). You can obtain all the basic measurements with the aid of a steel rule and then determine supplementary data, such as the angle of spread, when you return home.

Collecting Meal Remains

Meal remains can be photographed and sketched but they can also be collected, classified and displayed or stored. The items that make up such a collection of feeding damage and meal remains can only be plant and animal parts that do not decay. This limits the selection to hard objects that contain only a negligible amount of water.

Teeth marks and marks made by bird beaks will be found on trees and shrubs as well as on hard fruits and seeds. You can thus make a comparative collection of nuts, fruit stones, grain kernels, conifer cones, and the seeds of deciduous trees and shrubs that bear marks made by the teeth of voles, mice and squirrels or by the beaks of tits, nuthatches, woodpeckers, crossbills, finches, sparrows and many other birds. Meal remains of this kind are found in all sorts of places. However, you do not have to spend hours looking for meal remains. You can easily obtain them by placing food, say sunflower seeds, on a feeding tray and soon a whole flock of tits, nuthatches, greenfinches and other birds will converge upon the spot.

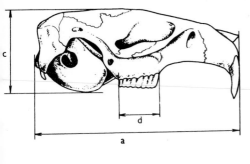

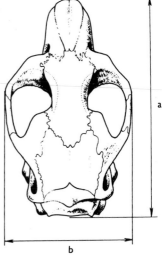

Fig. 21 — Measuring the skulls of rodents: a, length of skull; b, width of skull; c, height of skull; d, length of upper teeth

All will busily set to and if the feeding tray is on a windowsill then you can observe how each goes about cracking and opening the seeds. Afterwards you can take the cracked seeds inside and compare the different ways in which they were eaten by the various species of birds that visited the tray.

In the autumn gamekeepers thin the branches of fruit and other deciduous trees and put them in certain places in the game preserve for hares, rabbits and deer to nibble on. This, again, presents an excellent opportunity for the tracker-collector, for the stripped branches bear a great many marks made by the incisor teeth of the Brown Hare, Rabbit, Roe Deer or Red Deer. Your collection of the meal remains of plant eaters can also include annual shoots that bear the distinctive marks of having been severed by the teeth of a hare or a deer, as well as pieces of bark marked by the chiselling of a woodpecker's beak.

If you find a stripped branch that is still fresh, let it dry slowly and then cut out a small piece, one with the best teeth marks, label it and put it in a plastic bag. Nibbled or chewed seeds, nuts, fruit stones and cones are labelled and stored in the same manner.

The collector of meal remains of meat eaters has a more limited scope. Here you can collect only those body parts that are not subject to decay: feathers, fur, claws, beaks, horns, teeth and bones. However, on the basis of a few feathers, even an experienced ornithologist will often find it difficult to identify the bird that fell prey to a Sparrowhawk or Goshawk. The colours of the various parts of the Chaffinch's plumage may be familiar but when only a few scattered feathers are found it is difficult to identify them because the coloration of single feathers looks quite different from that of a whole group of such feathers packed closely together. A collection of bird feathers stored in a plastic bag to which newly found feathers of the same species are continually added in time becomes excellent comparative material for the purpose of identifying the victims of carnivores, raptors and owls. You can also add to the collection feathers that you pluck from individual birds you happen to find or capture. Similarly you can also establish a collection of the fur of various species of mammals and domestic animals.

Owl pellets are an excellent subject for collectors. If you are lucky to find a tree that is the regular roosting place of the Tawny Owl of Long-eared Owl then you do not have to worry about a supply of pellets for your collection. There is no need to feel any repugnance about handling them for they are devoid of all meat remains, do not rot and do not have a foul odour. Fresh pellets are slightly darker because they are still moist; old, dried pellets are a paler hue and lighter. When examining pellets dissect each pellet carefully with tweezers and take out all bones, skulls, beaks and claws. The felted portion of the pellet is composed of fur and feathers but generally these are no aid in identifying the prey. Much more reliable information can be obtained from bones and skulls which remain undamaged, that is unless they were broken by the owl when it seized or swallowed its victim. Skulls will give you the best idea of what and how much the owl eats. Owls swallow smaller prey whole so that in general each skull is the equivalent of a single captured victim. Even though you may not wish to go into detail and determine exactly the individual species of animals eaten by the owl, still, with the aid of the pictures in this book, you will be able to identify and distinguish between the skulls of insectivores, rodents and birds and thus determine what forms the mainstay of the owl's diet (Fig. 21). Bones found in pellets can easily be rid of any remnants of fur and washed with water to make them clean and white, so well are they 'processed' by the owl's stomach. Store the different bones in separate boxes or else fasten them with white thread on a black ground.

Suggestions for Further Reading

Bang, P. and Dalhstrom, P. *Collins Guide to Animal Tracks and Signs: The Tracks and Signs of British and European Mammals and Birds* Collins, London, 1974

Brink, F. H. van den *A Field Guide to the Mammals of Britain and Europe* Collins, London, 1977

Bruun, B. and Singer, A. *The Hamlyn Guide to Birds of Britain and Europe* Hamlyn, London, 1970

Černý, W. *A Field Guide in Colour to Birds* Octopus, London, 1975

Corbet, G. B. *Finding and Identifying Mammals in Britain* British Museum (Natural History), London, 1975

Corbet, G. B. and Ovenden, D. *The Mammals of Britain and Europe* Collins, London, 1980

Corbet, G. B. and Southern, H. N. (eds) *The Handbook of British Mammals,* Blackwell, Oxford, 1977

Fitter, R. S. R. and Richardson, R. A. *Collins Pocket Guide to Nests and Eggs* Collins, London, 1968

Harrison, C. *A Field Guide to the Nests, Eggs and Nestlings of British and European Birds with North Africa and the Middle East* Collins, London, 1975

Harrison Matthews, L. *British Mammals* Collins, London 1968

Heinzel, H., Fitter, R. and Parslow, J. *The Birds of Britain and Europe with North Africa and the Middle East* Collins, London, 1973

Hoeher, S. *The Pocket Encyclopaedia of Birds' Nests and Nesting Habits* Blandford, London, 1974

Lawrence, M. J. and Brown, R. W. *Mammals of Britain: Their Tracks, Trails and Signs* Blandford, London, 1973

Leutscher, A. *Tracks and Signs of British Wild Mammals* Cleaver-Hume, London, 1960

Leutscher, A. *Animal Tracks and Signs* Usborne Publishing Ltd., London, 1979

Peterson, P., Mountfort, G. and Hollom, P. A. D. *A Field Guide to the Birds of Britain and Europe* Collins, London, 1974

Stehli, G. and Brohmer, P. *The Young Specialist Looks at Animals: Mammals* Burke, London, 1965

Toman, J. and Felix, J. *A Field Guide in Colour to Plants and Animals* Octopus, London, 1974

Index of Common Names

Index of Scientific Names